Mary Lavin

Mary Lavin

Editor
Elke D'hoker

IRISH ACADEMIC PRESS

First published in 2013 by Irish Academic Press

8 Chapel Lane,
Sallins,
Co. Kildare,
Ireland

www.iap.ie

British Library Cataloguing in Publication Data
An entry can be found on request

ISBN 978 0 7165 3178 4 (cloth)
ISBN 978 0 7165 3181 4 (paper)
ISBN 978 0 7165 3182 1 (Ebook)

Library of Congress Cataloging-in-Publication Data
An entry can be found on request

Printed in Ireland by Sprint-print Ltd.

Contents

Acknowledgements

This book would not have been possible without the enthusiastic cooperation and excellent essays of all the contributors. It has been a pleasure working with them and I hope they will be pleased with the result. I am very grateful to the members of Mary Lavin's family, particularly Elizabeth Walsh Peavoy and Tadhg Peavoy, for granting permission to quote from her work. I would also like to thank James Ryan for his generous help and advice. My sincerest thanks go to Lisa Hyde from Irish Academic Press for her belief in this project and her continued support. I also wish to acknowledge the financial support of the Fund for Scientific Research, Flanders and of the Leuven Centre for Irish Studies. I dedicate this work to my four children, in the hope that they too will one day become avid readers of Lavin's fiction.

List of Contributors

Elke D'hoker is a lecturer in English and Irish literature at the University of Leuven, Belgium. She is the author of *Visions of Alterity: Representation in the Works of John Banville* (2004) and has co-edited *Unreliable Narration in the Twentieth-Century First-Person Novel* (2008) and *Irish Women Writers. New Critical Perspectives* (2011). She has published widely in the field of modern and contemporary fiction, with a specific focus on narrative theory, Irish studies and gender studies. Her current research project deals with the contribution of women writers to the genre of the short story in Ireland.

Anne Fogarty is Professor of James Joyce Studies at University College Dublin and Head of the UCD School of English, Drama and Film. She was editor of the *Irish University Review* 2002–2009 and is co-editor with Luca Crispi of the *Dublin James Joyce Journal*. She is co-editor with Timothy Martin of *Joyce on the Threshold* (2005); with Morris Beja of *Bloomsday 100: Essays on Ulysses*; (2009); and with Fran O'Rourke of *James Joyce: Multidisciplinary Perspectives* (2013). She has edited special issues of the *Irish University Review* on Spenser and Ireland, Lady Gregory, Eiléan Ní Chuilleanáin, and Benedict Kiely and has published widely on aspects of contemporary Irish fiction and poetry.

Derek Hand teaches in the English Department in St. Patrick's College, Drumcondra. He is interested in Irish writing in general and has published articles on W.B. Yeats, Elizabeth Bowen, Colum McCann, Molly Keane and on contemporary Irish fiction. He has lectured on Irish writing in the USA, Portugal, Sweden, Singapore and France. His book *John Banville: Exploring Fictions* was published in 2002. He edited a special edition of the *Irish University Review* on John Banville in 2006 and co-edited a special edition of the *Irish University Review* on Benedict Kiely in 2008. He was awarded an IRCHSS Government of Ireland Research Fellowship for 2008–2009. His *A History of the Irish Novel: 1665 to the present* was published in 2011. He is now working on a critical study of recent Irish fiction for Syracuse University Press tentatively entitled *The Celtic Tiger Irish Novel 1995–2010: modernity and mediocrity*.

Maurice Harmon is Emeritus Professor of Anglo-Irish Literature and Drama at University College Dublin, educated there and at Harvard University. Dr Harmon is an internationally known scholar, critic, literary historian, translator, editor, and poet. He has held a number of professorships in American institutions — the University of Notre Dame, the Ohio State University, the University of Washington, and others — and has been visiting professor at universities in Europe and in Japan. His many publications include *Seán O'Faoláin. A Life* (1994), *The Dolmen Press. A Celebration* (2001), *Selected Essays*, (2006), and *Thomas Kinsella*: *Designing for the Exact Needs* (2008). He edited, with introduction and notes, *No Author Better Served. The Correspondence between Samuel Beckett and Alan Schneider* (1998). His translation of the medieval Irish compendium of stories and poems, *Accalam na Senórach* has been published as *The Dialogue of the Ancients of Ireland* (2009). Dr Harmon is also a poet. Recent collections are *The Last Regatta* (2000), *The Doll with Two Backs* (2004), *The Mischievous Boy and other poems* (2008), *Love is not Enough. New and Selected Poems* (2010), and *Loose Connections* (2012).

Gráinne Hurley is a PhD student at University College Dublin where she is currently researching Mary Lavin's relationship with *The New Yorker* magazine as evidenced through their previously unexamined correspondence. Gráinne holds a BA in English, and Greek and Roman Civilisation, and an MA in Modern Drama from University College Dublin. She previously lectured in Renaissance literature in Dun Laoghaire Institute of Art, Design and Technology, and was an English literature tutor with UCD School of English, Drama and Film, and with UCD Adult Education Centre. Her other areas of interest include twentieth-century American Drama, Irish theatre and censorship, and *The New Yorker* fiction, with particular emphasis on the writings of Maeve Brennan.

Heather Ingman is Adjunct Professor in the School of English, Trinity College, Dublin where she specializes in women's writing, particularly modernist women's fiction and Irish women's writing. She has published extensively in both areas. Her publications include *Women's Fiction Between the Wars* (1998), *Twentieth-Century Fiction by Irish Women* (2007), *A History of the Irish Short Story* (2009) and 'Religion and the occult in women's modernism' in *The Cambridge Companion to Modernist Women Writers* edited by M. Linett (2010). Her study of Irish women's fiction will shortly be published by the Irish Academic Press.

Sinéad Mooney is a lecturer in English in the School of Humanities, National University of Ireland, Galway. Her research interests include modernism, particularly the work of Samuel Beckett, Irish literature and women's writing. Her most recent book, *A Tongue Not Mine: Beckett and Translation* (2011), won the American Conference for Irish Studies Robert Rhodes Prize. She is currently working on a book on Irish women's modernism.

Jeanette Shumaker is a professor of English at San Diego State University, Imperial Valley Campus, one mile from California's border with Mexico. Dr Shumaker publishes on Irish women writers, Victorian fiction, and Anglo-Jewish writers. In 1983, she completed a higher diploma in Anglo-Irish literature at Trinity College, Dublin. In 2009, she co-authored a book with William Baker on Leonard Merrick, a forgotten Edwardian Anglo-Jewish writer. She has published articles in such journals as the *New Hibernia Review, Estudios Irlandeses, College Literature, Studies in Short Fiction, Journal of the Short Story in English, English Literature in Transition, Dickens Studies Annual*, and *Women's Studies*.

Julie Anne Stevens is author of *The Irish Scene in Somerville and Ross* (2007) and co-editor with Helen Conrad O'Briain of *The Ghost Story from the Middle Ages to the Twentieth Century* (2010). Her essays and book chapters range across the work of writers and illustrators such as Edith Somerville and Martin Ross, Pamela Colman Smith, Percy French, Padraic Colum and Jack Yeats, Elizabeth Bowen, Elizabeth Enright, and Mary Lavin. She lectures on Irish writing, short fiction, and children's literature in St. Patrick's College, Drumcondra (Dublin City University), where she also directs the Masters in Children's Literature.

Giovanna Tallone, a graduate in Modern Languages from Università Cattolica del Sacro Cuore, Milan, holds a PhD in English Studies from the University of Florence. An EFL teacher, she is currently cooperating part-time with the Department of English at Università Cattolica, Milan. She has presented papers at several IASIL conferences and published articles and critical reviews on Mary Lavin, Éilís Ní Dhuibhne, Clare Boylan, Lady Augusta Gregory, Brian Friel, Dermot Bolger, James Stephens and Seamus Heaney. Her main research interests include Irish women writers, contemporary Irish drama, and the remakes of Old Irish legends.

Theresa Wray is a Postgraduate Research Student at Cardiff University. She has published in *The Politics of Irish Writing* (2010) and is currently in the final stages of her doctoral research on the short stories of Mary Lavin. She has been in involved in community education for many years, both as a lecturer and as an external examiner, working with A-level and mature students returning to education. She has contributed to research studies on IT access for Women and Information and Communication Technologies (1999) and the Action Research Project for Study Support Arrangements for Part-time General Education Students (2004). Her broader research interest lies in Irish women's writing of the mid-twentieth century, and feminist approaches to women's writing.

Foreword by Colm Toíbín

In 1972, when I came to Dublin, you could see Mary Lavin in Bewley's in Grafton Street, or in a cafe called the Country Shop, or in the National Library. She came a number of times to University College Dublin to read from her work and discuss it when I was a student there. She had an immense stately charm and warmth. She had a way of engaging anyone who spoke to her, but there was also something grand and serious about her. There was a light in her dark eyes, a warm way of focussing and concentrating as she spoke. She dressed in black, or dark colours.

I remember once after one of those readings asking her what she read, and she told me that she enjoyed literary criticism because it kept her mind engaged. In 1981, when her Selected Stories came out from Penguin, I went to her house in County Meath and interviewed her. The house was modern and beautiful, built on a bend in the river Boyne. The long living-room was on two levels and the walls were filled with paintings. Her talk was rambling and fascinating. She had a way of starting something and then letting it lead her elsewhere, but part of her mind never left the point to which she would eventually return. 'What was I saying?' she would say. But she would know what she was saying. She spoke like the mother in her story 'Happiness'. She told me that she often wrote a story in bed and then worked on many, many drafts.

And, when I asked her how would she decide to write one story if she had several in her mind, she told me that she had a contract with *The New Yorker*, but they only paid for the stories they used, and thus each time she began a new story, she chose to write the one they were least likely to take. And sometimes, she said, she was right and sometimes she was wrong. But she would not have written merely to please them.

Re-reading the stories now, it is clear that they include a sense of mystery and wisdom and a use of voice and tone which seems effortless and whose artistry might be easy to miss. Part of the power in her fiction comes from what has been left out. Mary Lavin was more interested in a character she had invented in all its strangeness and individuality than she was in the wider society; she was more interested in families than politics; she was more interested in the drama around the solitary figure than the drama around Irish history, or large questions of identity. It is the clarity of these interests and her refusal as an artist to be diverted from them that make her work seem now undated, make her stories have the still and severe presence of a painting by Morandi or William Scott.

Her stories chart the aura around small hidden dramas and provincial lives. She, from her own reading of Russian and French literature, knew that such limits had created a great tradition, the stories of Tolstoy or Turgenev, for example, or the best work of Flaubert.

Her work required a steely determination to follow the path of her characters and let society, or large questions of philosophy, look after themselves. This might have seemed easier than it was. In Mary Lavin's stories about solitude and widowhood, much is dispensed with. The stories are set in Ireland, but it is an Ireland normalised, as calm background, rather than an alarming Ireland. Mary Lavin thus could shine a more intense light on character, on consciousness, on motive in all its waywardness and ambiguity, on solitude, on need, on voice.

Often, we see the characters in Lavin's fiction in a time after love. Catholicism, like Ireland, is in the background. Lavin removes the props by which we might read her women simply; she refuses to allow us to come to know them by an easy set of signals or tensions. They live in a twilight time not of national life but of their own life; their desires are numerous and ambiguous and require a great deal of detail to describe. What happens must have the noise of delicacy and then a fierce or piercing after-effect.

When desires or fears come, they have an aura around them which is complex and uneasy. Lavin is not prepared to be simple about this, but she is capable of distracting the reader by a set of strategies which suggest simplicity of approach. Her system requires not only tact but a gentle irony.

In the poetics of solitude and loss, anything mentioned is a reflection of solitude and loss. Indeed, once the idea of solitude and loss has been established, then the less it is mentioned the more it will resonate, and the more carefully chosen details and images will throw glancing and refracting light on it. Her fictional ground can be deeply unstable. In the way she deals with personal loss and trauma, she is carrying, as a messenger might carry, some idea of a more public loss, and that she has found a private metaphor for it, thus moving her work to a level that is beyond the personal. But this is to make her fit into some idea we, or others, have that that is the job of writers to write their nation, and fiction as a way of finding strategies for that.

Mary Lavin read carefully enough in Jane Austen to know that nations change, but other things do not, and it is the job of the artists to care more about the other things. Thus instead of reading these stories of loss and trauma as metaphors for something that lived outside her stories, Mary Lavin's stories are best read as having taken all that in, the history of Irish loss, the idea of a public trauma in Ireland, and using it as a metaphor for something which she thought might endure – how strange loss is when it becomes personal, how sharp and unpredictable, and how interesting and wayward it is when reduced in this way, and how open and large it can become once trusted, as she in her art learned to trust it, if handled with all due attention and care, as she did when she worked. By having no further resonance beyond the personal, her stories can be more starkly dramatic, more powerful, more exact.

Mary Lavin has a particular skill in making the casual moment or the random detail pull in energy towards itself, remain true and modest but manage to send out signals. In her great story 'Happiness', the casual tone sets out to lull the reader into trusting the voice which is gentle, almost eccentric. And then the voice takes on an undertow which is unforgettable in its precision. It moves from the domestic to a set of images which are disturbing and original in their contours and their rhythms and the fresh truth they have to tell about fear and grief and death.

I remember Mary Lavin that day more than thirty years ago, the gaze as unflinching as the style in the story, the voice deep and strong, and an aura around her of what it meant to have faced things, to have come fearlessly on the page to create an image close to the image of the woman's head as she sank into death. The mother's head in the story 'Happiness' could equally have been Mary Lavin's words which 'sank so deep into the pillow it seemed that it would have been dented had it been a pillow of stone'.

Introduction

Elke D'hoker

In 2012, Ireland celebrated the centenary of Mary Lavin's birth with a variety of readings, lectures and events. These celebrations clearly testify to the wide and lasting appeal of Lavin's writing and to her status as one of Ireland's major writers. In an international context too, Mary Lavin is acclaimed as 'one of the finest short-story writers of the twentieth-century'[1] and her work continues to be read and studied, both in Ireland and abroad. This high regard follows on from the recognition and esteem which Mary Lavin received increasingly during her lifetime. Although her work had met with positive reviews from the start — her first collection of short stories, *Tales from Bective Bridge* (1942), won the James Tait Black Memorial Prize in 1943 — she received greater professional recognition in the 1970s, when she was given an honorary doctorate at UCD and was awarded the prestigious Gregory Medal. The stories she published in *The New Yorker* in the 1950s and 1960s also led to greater prominence in the US, where she was presented with the Ella Lyman Cabot Award of Harvard University in 1972 and the Irish-American Foundation Literary Award in 1979. As a public figure and a leading writer, Lavin served as a president of the Irish Academy of Letters and was elected Saoi by the members of Aosdána in 1992 for achieving 'singular and sustained distinction in literature'. Lavin's death in 1996 was front page news in *The Irish Times*, where she was hailed as 'one of modern Irish fiction's most subversive voices'.[2] An obituary in *The New York Times* praised Lavin as a writer 'whose short stories and novels about the conflicts in the hearts of her fellow Irish men and women transcended mere tales of life in Ireland'.[3]

Despite the honours Mary Lavin received and continues to receive, however, her work itself is now rather hard to come by. Of the nineteen short story collections she published during her lifetime, only two are still in print, having been reissued in the context of the centenary celebrations: *Happiness and Other Stories* (2011) and *Tales from Bective Bridge* (2012). Lavin's two novels, *The House in Clewe Street* (1945) and *Mary O'Grady* (1950) are also still available, but the three-volume collected edition of her short stories, which Constable published in the 1970s, can no longer be found.[4] Scholarly criticism of Lavin's work also seems to have lagged behind the wide public recognition she received during her lifetime.

One of the reasons for this may be that Lavin's short fiction does not easily fit the ideal of the modern Irish short story as it was developed by her contemporaries, Seán O'Faoláin and Frank O'Connor. Lavin lacks the political interests of these writers as well as their celebration of the romantic outsider or exile as the hero of the short story, and of 'loneliness' as 'the one subject a storyteller must write about'.[5] When O'Connor discusses Lavin's work in the final chapter of *The Lonely Voice*, he is clearly ill at ease: 'An Irishman, reading the stories of Mary Lavin, is actually more at a loss than a foreigner would be', he writes, and proceeds to vaguely identify a 'different set of values' which, he argues, 'make her more of a novelist in her stories than O'Flaherty, O'Faolain [*sic*], or Joyce'.[6] Whether her perspective and interests are more novelistic or not, they clearly did not fully square with the predominantly male tradition of the mid-twentieth-century Irish short story and this may account in part for her somewhat ex-centric position in Irish literary histories and criticism of the past 50 years.[7]

Following Lavin's growing literary fame in the 1970s, three important critical monographs were published in the US – by Zack Bowen (1975), Richard Peterson (1978) and A.A. Kelly (1980) – and *Irish University Review* devoted a special issue to her work in 1979. Since then, however, only a dozen scholarly articles have appeared, discussing various aspects of her work. In the 1990s, Lavin's work received some attention in the context of feminist criticism, by critics such as Ann Owens Weekes, Jeanette Shumaker and Patricia Meszaros. Still, Lavin did not benefit as much as other Irish women writers from feminist recovery projects, perhaps because, as Meszaros remarked, Lavin can hardly be called 'a feminist in the contemporary sense' and some of her views on motherhood or career women sit uneasily with contemporary feminists.[8]

Recently, however, there have been signs that things are changing. Some interesting new approaches to Lavin's work have appeared over the past few years and Heather Ingman reserves a central place for Lavin in her *A History of the Irish Short Story* (2009). The centenary celebrations referred to earlier can also be expected to generate renewed scholarly interest in her work. This collection of critical essays is both inspired by this new momentum and hopes to strengthen it, by bringing recent critical theories and new insights to bear on Lavin's work. The essays collected in this book address the main formal and thematic issues of Lavin's novels and short stories and highlight their stylistic innovations and fundamental humanist wisdom from a variety of angels. While the individual essays tend to focus on a specific selection of her writing, the book as a whole hopes to offer a comprehensive overview of her oeuvre, which spans almost half a century.

A person well-placed to review this oeuvre in its entirety is Maurice Harmon, a close friend of Mary Lavin, whose essay opens this collection. Harmon offers a perceptive introduction to Lavin's life and work, situating it in the larger Irish context and highlighting her main concerns: middle-class Irish life, love in all its varieties, the power of self-deception, and family struggles. Summing up her achievements as a writer, he concludes that 'Hers is a disturbingly honest vision, a portrayal of human nature which we cannot ignore and which we value for its psychological depth.' In a second overview essay, Heather Ingman breaks new ground in Lavin criticism by scrutinizing Lavin's representation of male characters. Drawing on recent work in masculinities studies, Ingman shows how Lavin's men often struggle with the positions of power and authority they are expected to embrace. Compared to other women writers, Ingman argues, Lavin's work is remarkable for its varied and understanding depiction of male characters: from workaholic professionals and authoritarian priests to sensitive, feminine men and caring fathers. 'By exposing contradictory ways of being male', Ingman concludes, Lavin's 'writing leaps over the feminist protests of the 1970s and 1980s to a postmodernist recognition of the fluidity of gender roles'.

In the third essay, Anne Fogarty casts an entirely new light on Lavin's debut collection, *Tales from Bective Bridge*. In a detailed analysis of the aesthetic and stylistic aims of the collection, she shows how Lavin continues the modernist aesthetic of disruption, ellipsis, indeterminacy and ambiguity in spite of a seeming adherence to conventional realism. In a perceptive, close reading of well-known stories such as 'Lilacs', 'Sarah', 'At Sallygap' and 'The Dead Soldier', Fogarty also brings out the radical, taboo-breaking nature of these stories and argues that they capture 'the flux, negation and savagery' central to Lavin's apprehension of the world. Lavin's early stories also form the topic of Giovanna Tallone's essay, which centres on three stories — 'Miss Holland', 'Fogger Halt' and 'The Becker Wives' — to highlight the theatrical dimension of Lavin's short fiction. Tracing theatrical elements in both the plot and the symbolism of these stories, she argues that they serve to bring out Lavin's acute psychological insight into the individual's struggle to take on socially expected roles or identities in a — mostly vain — attempt to belong.

'"Trying to Get the Words Right": Mary Lavin and *The New Yorker*' is the first of two essays to use previously unexplored archival sources to shed new light on Lavin's oeuvre. Gráinne Hurley draws on the extensive correspondence between

Lavin and her *New Yorker* editors to clarify Lavin's aesthetics and her writing practices. Sixteen of Lavin's stories were published in *The New Yorker* between 1958 and 1976, and from 1959 onwards she had a first-reading agreement with the magazine. Hurley shows how the publication of Lavin's stories sometimes involved a lengthy and laborious process of revision, in terms of both language and content. Some of these changes were retained by Lavin in the subsequent book publication of the stories, others were reversed again. Hurley also argues that *The New Yorker* has to be credited for inspiring Lavin to write again after the death of her husband and for significantly boosting Lavin's literary esteem, particularly in the US.

Lavin's relation with the US also forms the topic of Theresa Wray's essay, albeit in an entirely different form. In her essay, she examines the influence of Lavin's Irish-American background on her short fiction. Wray convincingly locates this influence in two groups of stories: stories of emigration and return, which highlight the differences between both countries and the inevitable sense of loss these moves entail, and stories of Big House life in Ireland. On his return to Ireland, Lavin's father was appointed estate manager of Bective House and this opened up a whole new world for Lavin. In her Big House stories, Wray argues, Lavin shows herself acutely sensitive to class distinctions and her outsider approach to Ascendancy life significantly transforms the Big House tradition.

Class distinctions also figure largely in Jeanette Shumaker's detailed analysis of two stories, 'The Small Bequest' and 'The Mock Auction', in which Lavin foregrounds the relationship between retainers and their employers. Drawing on René Girard's *Deceit, Desire and the Novel* (1965), Shumaker analyses the rivalry and snobbery which motivate Adeline's attitude to her faithful servant Emma, but which also implicate the first-person narrator of the story. Although similar class struggles can be observed in the second story, Shumaker shows its retainer protagonist to be more successful in negotiating changes. In depicting elderly spinsters as 'unlikely proto-feminist rebels', Shumaker argues, Lavin not only reverses traditional plot patterns but also affirms values of generosity and communalism.

Any critical study of Lavin's work, of course, cannot neglect her novels. While these novels have often been judged (and found wanting) in relation to Lavin's larger body of short fiction, Derek Hand breaks new ground by placing the novels within the tradition of the novel form in Ireland. In a perceptive reading of *The House in Clewe Street*, Hand demonstrates how Lavin appeals to several nineteenth-century novelistic forms — social critique, family story, *bildungsroman*

— and struggles to apply them to an Irish context, which is at once clearly localized — a fictionalized Athenry — and strangely ahistorical. In *Mary O'Grady*, Hand argues, Lavin more successfully confronts stereotypes of Irish life and culture, in particular the myths of motherhood and the home.

As an extended exploration of family life, the sequence of five stories about the Grimes family, which Lavin published in the fifties, continue some of the preoccupations of her novels. Yet, as I argue in 'Family and Community in Mary Lavin's Grimes Stories', the deliberate discontinuities and inconsistencies between these stories serve to highlight the different, sometimes contradictory, perspectives which Lavin brings to bear on the Grimes family. While offering different explanations for the family's disintegration, the stories all demonstrate the way individuals are enmeshed in a network of relations, whether on the level of family, community or society. Comparing Lavin's social vision with that discussed in Arensberg and Kimball's *Family and Community in Ireland* (1968), I contend that they are alike in locating personal responsibility and agency within rather than outside of these networks.

Two final essays focus on short stories from the last decades of Lavin's career. In the first of these, Julie Anne Stevens takes a closer look at 'The Yellow Beret', a story about a double murder in Dublin. She places the story in its larger cultural and social context, revealing echoes with E.A. Poe and other mystery stories, contemporary developments in art and aesthetics, and an actual murder case in Limerick some years previously. These influences, in turn, allow Stevens to reflect on Lavin's own aesthetics of the short story and her profound awareness of the double nature of reality. In the final essay, Sinéad Mooney discusses Lavin's so-called widow stories in terms of their representation of bereavement and mourning. Using psychoanalytic theories of Freud and Kristeva, she shows how Lavin's widow stories performatively enact the labour of mourning which also preoccupies their protagonists. Mooney perceptively demonstrates how the stories question Freud's claim that separation and transfer of desire successfully end the process of mourning. For Lavin, Mooney argues, 'all selves are, by definition, elegiac, defined by lost or impossible attachments' and this love — whether lost or impossible — has to be defended against the repressive forces that threaten to diminish it.

Taken together, the essays amply testify to the richness and variety of Mary Lavin's work, to its many guises, interests and influences. At the same time, the essays also identify some recurrent preoccupations in her work: love and its absence; loss or betrayal; the fraught relation between self and society; and the moral necessity of personal responsibility. The radical dimensions underlying Lavin's deceivingly conventional stories are also highlighted. Lavin's subversion of gendered stereotypes, her critique of Catholic hypocrisy and middle-class snobbery, and her undaunted staging of taboo subjects are revealed as central forces driving her work. Finally, several close readings clearly demonstrate the complexity and subtlety of Mary Lavin's art. The lucidity and power of her language, her compelling visual imagery and the absorbing detail of her descriptions are the product of a consummate artistic power combined with diligent hard work and tireless revision. In all, these essays fully justify Lavin's position as a major Irish writer and as one of the most important contributors to the short story in English. I hope, therefore, that this collection will inspire many readers and critics to continue to read her stories and to further explore their multiple meanings, contexts and concerns.

Endnotes

1   B. McKeon, 'An Arrow Still An Arrow in Flight: The Pleasures of Mary Lavin', *The Paris Review*, 12 June 2012. Online: http://www.theparisreview.org/blog/2012/06/12/an-arrow-in-flight-the-pleasures-of-mary-lavin/.

2   E. Battersby, 'Story Writer Mary Lavin dies at 83', *The Irish Times*, 26 March 1996, p.3.

3   J.F. Clarity, 'Mary Lavin, 83, Wove Tales of Irish Experience', *The New York Times*, 27 March 1996. Online: http://www.nytimes.com/1996/03/27/nyregion/mary-lavin-83-wove-tales-of-irish-experience.html.

4   For a detailed overview of the publication histories of Lavin's short stories, see Heinz Kosok's dateline in 'Mary Lavin: A Bibliography', *Irish University* Review, 9, 2 (Autumn 1979), pp.279–312.

5   F. O'Connor, *The Lonely Voice: A Study of the Short Story* (London: Macmillan, 1965), p.112.

6   Ibid., pp.203, 211.

7   In J. Kilroy's *The Irish Short Story. A Critical History* (Boston: Twayne, 1984), Lavin is discussed in a chapter with Elizabeth Bowen and other female writers, while Frank O'Connor and Seán O'Faoláin are given chapters of their own. Declan Kiberd similarly devotes only a few pages to Lavin in his monumental *Inventing Ireland: The Literature of the Modern Nation* (Cambridge: Harvard University Press, 1995; London: Jonathan Cape, 1995) and the situation is even worse in J.W. Wright's (ed.) recent two-volume *Companion to Irish Literature* (Malden, MA: Wiley-Blackwell, 2010), which mentions Lavin only briefly on two occasions. In Rüdiger Imhof's *A Short History of Irish Literature* (Stuttgart: Ernst Klett, 2002), she is not referred to at all.

8   P. Meszaros, 'Woman as Artist: The Fiction of Mary Lavin', *Critique: Studies in Modern Fiction*, 21, 1 (Fall 1982), p.39.

1 | Heartfelt Narratives: Mary Lavin's Life and Work

Maurice Harmon

One night in 1960 at a party in Dublin, Mary Lavin came up to me and said, 'I'm passionately interested in the short story'. She had heard that I was studying the work of Seán O'Faoláin and wanted to talk about his short stories. That was the beginning of a friendship that lasted until her death in 1996 and eventually included Michael Scott, her second husband. When I met her, she was already a well-known writer. Born in East Walpole, Massachusetts, in 1912, she returned to Ireland with her mother, Nora, in 1921 and went to live with her mother's people in Athenry, County Galway. There she was struck by the contrast between the life she had known in America and the more restricted life she experienced in a small western town in Ireland. The Mahons, her mother's people, were shopkeepers, middle class, Catholic and proud of their class superiority. Their snobbishness, as a source of unkindness and cruelty, permeates many of her stories, as does their inability to love unreservedly. They could be extreme in their hatreds, stubborn in their values, and foreshadowed the dominant class that would emerge in post-revolutionary Ireland. They also had a strong sense of sin that she had not known in America. She attributed her emergence as a writer in part to the shock of that encounter with a strange culture and to being an only child who had to invent imaginary companions.

Mary Lavin arrived just as the revolutionary period was coming to an end — the Anglo-Irish War had finished, the Civil War would last less than a year, and sporadic violence would decrease. She belonged, therefore, to a different generation of writers. Whereas Seán O'Faoláin and Frank O'Connor had been shaped by revolution, she was affected much less. Revolutionary activities and figures are present in their early fiction but, except for one short story, 'The Patriot Son' (1956)[1], and a few references in other stories, they are absent from her work. She did not experience the heady, idealistic nationalism that marked her predecessors. They knew disappointment when the movement for independence turned into civil war and an unattractive middle-class Ireland came into being. She was much less idealistic than they were and following the shock of her encounter with the mercenary family in Athenry, Lavin looked critically at Irish life from the beginning.

The new middle class, mainly peasant in origin, largely uncultivated and indifferent to artistic standards, created the kind of stifling and oppressive society against which writers and intellectuals struggled. It included a denial of liberal values and a form of protectionism directed not only at native industry but at ideas and cultural developments generated from abroad. The influence of the Catholic Church increased after the revolution. Mary Lavin found Irish Catholicism restrictive and more clericalist than what she had known in America. She hated the idea of Limbo. She had a natural independence, derived to some extent from living in America during her formative years, when she knew a less restrictive religion and educational system. Furthermore, she had an instinctive sympathy for outsiders. She was keenly aware of what happened when an aunt married against her family's wishes and, as a result, was excluded from her mother's will. This became the subject of 'The Will' (1944). She also saw the capacity of Irish people to engage in sharp verbal exchanges and these also appeared in that story. In her early collections, she explored the nature of the middle class, particularly in 'The Becker Wives' (1946), many stories about the Grimes family, and the novel *The House in Clewe Street* (1945). In Athenry, her eyes opened to the operation of greed, class distinction, and bitter speech.

O'Connor and O'Faoláin knew the unforgiving mindset of the Catholic Church, saw its effects on the lives of ordinary people and sympathized with the small-town intellectual. Lavin was similarly concerned but with a significant difference; whereas they rounded out the portrayal of the rebellious hero by putting him on the emigrant ship, she never needed that solution. Like Daniel Corkery in *The Threshold of Quiet* (1917), she portrayed lives of quiet desperation, men and women who stayed put.[2] The Catholic Church's control of the individual life was an inherent part of these psychological dramas. What she most resented was the way in which the Church kept people in ignorance, preferring passive obedience to the freedom that knowledge bestowed. Her anger is clearly channelled in 'Sunday Brings Sunday' (1944), where the growing attraction of a young couple for each other takes its natural course — but in sexual ignorance. Her deeper subject was not social but psychological. Affairs of the heart, emotional struggle, and the complexity of the individual temperament were her primary concerns.

Read chronologically, Lavin's stories absorb the emergence of a dominant, almost wholly Catholic, middle-class society in the decades after revolution that replicated what she had experienced in her mother's family. She lived through the period of the Second World War, economic stagnation, continuing emigration, and the social transformation that flowed from the economic programmes of the late 1950s and 1960s. The country then became more liberal and the power of the Catholic Church declined. Her later stories are less concerned with the social issues that marked her work up to the appearance of *Selected Stories* in 1959. In her final collection, *A Family Likeness* (1985), she returned to memories of her father, Tom Lavin, with whom she had a close relationship, memories of the Athenry family, and a portrayal of her mother, Nora, with whom she had a difficult relationship. In all situations, love or its absence, the complexities of the human heart, are the driving preoccupations. Revolution comes and goes, society changes, a church weakens, but love in its various manifestations is ever-present.

Mary Lavin's emergence as a writer was unexpected. When she entered University College Dublin in 1930, a few other students were known to be interested in becoming writers — the novelists Flann O'Brien and Mervyn Wall, the poets Brian Coffey and Dennis Devlin. Her emergence as a writer was almost accidental, the result of an impulse when she gave up writing her PhD thesis on Virginia Woolf and wrote 'Miss Holland', which was first published in *The Dublin Magazine* in 1939[3], and then in her first collection, *Tales from Bective Bridge* (1942). This collection identified her work with a particular place and was launched with an enthusiastic preface by her neighbour, Lord Dunsany. For her, the most significant event of her student years was meeting Michael Scott, an Australian seminarian and an exceedingly handsome and attractive man. They became friends but he went to Switzerland to continue his preparations to become a Jesuit, having been given permission by his superiors — cleverly, she thought — to write to her. It was the beginning of an extraordinary, intense, prolonged, and complicated romance. Its effect on her life and work was far-reaching. Above all, it forced her to reflect on a personal relationship between a man and a woman which was not consummated, enabled him to lead a sheltered existence, and required her to suppress sexual desire.

In 1942, Lavin married William Walsh. They went to live in Bective House, County Meath, and she became the mother of three children; Valdi, who was born in 1943, Elizabeth in 1945, and Caroline in 1953, all of whom she loved intensely. In 1947, they moved into the Abbey Farm which they had built. William died in 1954 and she was left exhausted and depressed. In the years that followed, she continued her career as a writer, obtained a *New Yorker* contract in 1958, received two Guggenheim Awards, in 1959 and 1961, and raised and educated her daughters to third level. A few years after William's death, she bought an old coach house in Lad Lane in Dublin and transformed it into a mews. It became a gathering place for writers; the established, like Frank O'Connor and Seán O'Faoláin; the aspiring, like Thomas Kilroy and Nuala O'Faolain; and her daughters' many friends. She divided her time between there and the farm. The Abbey Farm was set far back from the country road. Screened at the back by a wood, it looked towards the River Boyne that flowed around one side of the property towards the ruins of the twelfth century Bective Abbey and the arches of Bective Bridge, through which the river disappeared. It is a steady presence in her work, the setting for many stories. There she absorbed the rhythms of the countryside, knew local farmers and farm labourers, and listened to their slow speech in which little was said and, if said, was expressed indirectly. For country people, she said, there was more meaning to be got out of looks and glances than there were for people of the town.

Michael Scott continued to write, giving advice and support; he managed to get off occasionally to meet her and they went on holidays together with the children, sometimes to Italy. The relationship was close, the question of clerical celibacy never far away. She examined the issue of the unconsummated relationship in 'A Woman Friend' (1951) and particularly in 'A Memory' (1972). She once illustrated their closeness by telling of how they once met in New York, she travelling from Ireland by ship as she always did, he travelling from Australia by plane. As she arrived she was thinking about him and when she looked down at the pier, there he was! It was a remarkable proof of their closeness. They were married in 1969 after he was laicized and lived together until he died in 1990. His death was not part of their plan. Late one night when she was recuperating in a nursing home, I was sitting by her bedside and the phone rang. It was Michael. They talked for a few minutes, then she turned to me and with a stricken face said 'He says he won't be able to keep his promise.' Michael had been diagnosed with cancer. Years before he had promised to look after her to the end. Now it was his life that was coming to an end. She loved him very much, depended on him, valued his steadiness, admired his probity. For many years he combined his duties as a priest with his friendship for her, carried out his duties as educationalist and administrator, developed an interest in church architecture, but kept up his correspondence with the girl he had met at university. Love was at the heart of it but within restrictions. Lavin was morally upright but was forthright in her belief that clerical celibacy should be voluntary. When Bishop Eamonn Casey was shown to have fathered a son, she pointed triumphantly to his example as proof that clerical celibacy should not be imposed on priests.

Love in its varying manifestations is at the heart of Lavin's entire output in stories of romantic love, frustrated love, love that is self-deceiving, love remembered, and stories about its complications within families, which are central to the novel *Mary O'Grady* (1950). In 'The Will', a story of cruel rejection, Lavin finds her true subject, a psychic matching of writer and material from which many subsequent stories emerge. Here she focuses in a plain style on the bitter aspects of a middle-class family gathering on the death of their mother, their impoverished emotional response to their rejected sister Lally, whose capacity to love and forgive contrasts with their hardness of heart and mechanical expressions of sympathy. Lally never regretted her choice of husband even though it meant going against her mother's wishes and now, when her siblings suggest they each give a small portion of what was left to them in their mother's will in which she has been disinherited, she refuses. 'It would be in the interests of the family', her brother Matthew says, speaking snobbishly for all of them, 'if you were to give up keeping lodgers'.[4] Their mother never forgave her for that and they are similarly disposed. When her sister Nonny says that she does not see why she was so anxious to marry when it meant keeping lodgers, Lally's reply is exact: 'I was willing to keep lodgers because it meant I could marry him.'[5] She will not stay for even one night, nor accept the room they have booked, nor agree to the idea that she should run a hotel, with financial help from them, to improve her social position and save them from the disgrace of having a sister running a boarding house. At the height of the story, the wounding language that Lavin had heard in Athenry is echoed in the clashes between Lally and her family — it is intense, hurtful, shameless, exposing pettiness of spirit and jealousy of a love that has never dimmed in Lally's heart although she is worn down and cannot dress well. Scattered through the story are poignant images that evoked the girl she had been — the dress she wore for her first dance, the blue flowers she had pinned to her hat on the day she told her mother she was going to be married. She had run away to find the mystery of life, now she knows there is no mystery, anywhere: 'Life was just the same in the town, in the city, and in the twisty countryside. Life was just the same in the darkness and the light. It was the same for the spinster and for the draggled mother of a family. You were yourself always, no matter where you went or what you did.'[6] As she runs now to catch the train, she feels compelled to have a Mass said for her mother's soul and with her own money: 'Pictures of flames and screaming souls writhing on gridirons, rose before her mind …'.[7] She fears that because her mother died without forgiving her she will suffer in the next world and shares the harrowing of conscience that Lavin had seen in her aunts in Athenry.

Lally has a quality that most Lavin heroines enjoy — a great vitality and love of life — but their inexperience makes them vulnerable. The girl in 'An Akoulina of the Irish Midlands' (1954), who is full of positive energy, comes up against the obstacle of her Protestant lover's resistance to her decision to convert so that they can be married. He has no intention of marrying her. When she arrives sopping wet, he hurries her deeper into the wood; his sexual intentions do not need to be explained. For Lavin, the experience of love is inseparable from the love of life. In 'Asigh' (1959), she expresses a depth of appreciation — for life, natural growth, the love that should animate human existence, for a young girl's romance with a local farmer, together with great pity for the actions and culture that work against its realization. These later stories have a mature feel to them, are more relaxed in manner, more open in style. The writer sees into a number of characters — the young girl, her father, her older admirer, her brother, the human background and its values, and the countryside itself. The language of bargaining between her father and her admirer, Tod, over the price of hay is the language of matchmaking. She is well able to read its metaphors and her heart fills with joy. But her father's action puts an end to that story.

When she was still a girl, he struck her with a head collar whose buckle must have been poisoned because the blow caused an ulcer on her leg which never healed. In a farming community, a girl thus weakened could not do the heavy work required and so her admirer never concludes their romance. Instead of a home of her own with the man of her choice and a family, she is condemned to the long imprisonment and diminishment of life with her father whom she fears. The natural world is a metaphor for her life: 'Closed in by summer, the fields were deeper and lonelier than ever, and the laneway that led out to the road was narrowed by overhanging briars and the wild summer growth of bank and ditch.'[8] Her leg throbs with pain and she pities her brother's wasted years as a bachelor. Tod never marries and never forgives fate for depriving them of love. By the time he admits this, their youth has gone and she can only look at him with pity. Long ago she had condemned him for not knowing that love was enough and for thinking only of breeding. Now her mind is fixated on the possibility that her brother and his girl can marry and have children. But that hope is also doomed to disappointment. In the middle of the seasonal renewals of a lush countryside, she is isolated in disappointment and barrenness.

'Frail Vessel' (1955) embodies the notion of love as an unquenchable force. It is to some degree a continuation of the choice Lally has made in 'The Will' and once again the Grimes family is involved. When the mother dies, Bedelia and the shop boy Daniel go ahead with their marriage to keep the business going and to make a home for her sister Liddy, the youngest daughter. Liddy, however, is attracted to Alphonsus O'Brien. Bedelia scoffs at the idea of romance. Nothing more underlines the tepid nature of Bedelia's own romance than the explanation that all Daniel has to do is take his old alarm clock from his room on the back landing across to Bedelia's room. There was, she tells Liddy, nothing mushily romantic between herself and Daniel, to which Liddy merely smiles 'a little, dreamy, secretive smile'.[9] Through scenes of growing insight, the conflict between the sisters is worked out. Bedelia, pregnant, resents Liddy's romance and wants to humiliate O'Brien. After he and Liddy are married, he takes on an insurance agency to increase his income and embezzles money. When he has to leave town hurriedly because he has no means of paying it back, Bedelia will not advance Liddy the money needed to save him. Liddy stands by her man but with cold calculation Bedelia advances the money on condition that O'Brien leave town immediately without knowing that she will repay the money. The story reaches its poignant climax. O'Brien has gone, Bedelia has had her way and Liddy has to come back home. What Bedelia has not known is that Liddy too is pregnant. She has not told O'Brien, not wanting to add to his worries, but when Bedelia tells her cruelly that she probably will not see him again, she is not quashed; she has 'a radiance and glory' about her.[10] Now, Bedelia complains cuttingly, she and Daniel are 'saddled with rearing another man's brat!', but the jibe that she may never see O'Brien again is offset by the young girl's response: "'Even so!" Liddy whispered. "Even so!"'[11]

Lavin's preoccupation with the vagaries of the human heart includes love's enduring and transformative power. 'Frail Vessel' leaves the outcome to our imaginations. 'The Will' shows what became of Lally's romance. The deeply ironic 'A Happy Death' (1946) plunges into that later story, turning the world of the Grimes family upside down. The mood is bitter in this unrelenting exposé of a woman who is so determined to do what she wishes for her husband — to keep

him well-dressed and healthy, to deceive herself with the dream of happiness —
that she fails to see his actual state, his real needs, and the abysmal conditions in
which they live. The story is unified by Ella's single-minded, obsessive nature
and by a naturalistic style that drives through repetitive responses and opinions.
She is a monster in her resolve, 'tireless in her determination to achieve her end'[12],
the epitome of many wilful characters in Lavin's fiction. Ella is another of those
Lavin characters who refuse to face reality. She persuades herself — in this case
relentlessly over a long period — that her version of reality is true when in fact it
is not, when what she says, does, and plans is the opposite of what is staring her in
the face. Her ability to convince herself that what she thinks is true is extraordinary
and irrational. Yet the amazing thing is that we feel sympathy for her. Despite
her bizarre and contradictory behaviour, despite her cruelty and neglect of her
husband, we do not dismiss her as a crackpot. Although she and Robert began
life in the meadows of romance and looked ahead with love and hope, they have
ended in a miserable situation, running a boarding house, in dirt and grime, with
Robert seriously ill and unable to work. As Lavin notes with pitiless accuracy,
'irreparable bitterness had come into every word they said to each other'.[13] This
is not strictly true. Despite the abysmal conditions, they continue to remember
and to evoke the promise that once enveloped them and to the very end Robert
forgives her for all the harsh things she has said and done to him; to him she is
still beautiful. He has never ceased loving her: 'You always made me happy, just
by being near me. Just to look at you made my heart brighter. Always. Always.'[14]
This is another example of that self-deception already fully demonstrated in Ella,
extreme in both cases. The tension between that enduring vision and the ongoing
misery is painful but in the end the story descends into melodrama. Everything
is exaggerated, the language is heightened, Ella is monstrously dishonest and
horrendously irrational in her feverish planning. The notion of their intimacy
being indissoluble she finds abhorrent: 'two people never are one … they always
were, and always would be, two separate beings, ever at variance in their
innermost core, ever liable to react upon each other with unpredictable results'.[15]
The pity is that Ella is genuinely unable to comprehend how they have reached
the state in which they are: '"What happened?" she asked in a whisper. She truly
did not know.'[16]

The title of the story refers to the grotesque scene in which she is unable to
accept that Robert is dying, forces gifts upon him, surrounds him with religious
objects — an accumulation of crucifixes and blessed candles, holy water and holy
medals — and rushes about the city from church to church, lighting candles and

arranging for Masses to be said. She tries desperately to ensure his salvation by having a priest give him Extreme Unction. When a man in another bed, an atheist and blasphemer, makes a deathbed confession she immediately wants to bring about a similar outcome for her husband, even though as everyone tells her Robert has led a blameless life. The nun urges her to put her trust in God, whose ways are wonderful and who works in mysterious ways. The chaotic scene is charged with savage satire. Neither faces actuality. Ella urges Robert to say an Act of Contrition, repeats it for him, wants him to confess, to seek atonement for his sins, but all Robert can do is affirm the undying power of love. His Heaven is in the meadow where they walked as young lovers. He recalls her beauty and forgives her for the hurt she has caused him. He has loved her wilfulness, the very quality that has driven her like a lunatic through this story, but the term has a variety of meanings that include obstinate, self-willed, perverse, undisciplined, and wanton. Robert also is unable to face stark reality. At the end, he finds the serenity of death, a happy death, not by religious intervention but ironically by the power of love, a love that is a fiction. But Ella, blind to the end, cannot understand why God has not heard her prayers, has not 'vouchsafed to her husband the grace of a happy death'.[17]

Self-deception, Lavin believes, can only be avoided by rigorous honesty, as she said at the end of 'The Widow's Son' (1946): 'Perhaps all our actions have this double quality about them; this possibility of alternative, and that it is only by careful watching, and absolute sincerity, that we follow the path that is destined for us, and, no matter how tragic that may be, it is better than the tragedy we bring upon ourselves.'[18]

Bedelia's insistence that she wants to provide a home for Liddy is one example of self-pretence; another is the notion that the Conroy family in 'The Will' want to help Lally. 'The Long Ago' (1944) is a merciless study in self-deception. Hallie, who has been left by the man she wanted, imagines the past as a romantic place, as Robert does. She subscribes more and more to the notion that she and her two married friends, Ella and Dolly, can be as they were in the past. How they remember the past and how she remembers it are not the same. For them, it is a dreamy land which they will never enter again. Hallie has never left it. When the man she wanted married someone else, she forgave him, entered a false world in which she mourned him when he died, visits his grave and buys the plot beside his so that eventually they can be near each other. This behaviour turns reality on its head until in a shocking denouement Hallie virtually welcomes the death of Ella's husband because, as she tells the hysterical Ella, it means that the three friends can be together again as they were long ago. Her insensitive reaction alienates both old friends.

In the brilliantly inventive 'The Becker Wives', the four wives are dull, solid creatures, overweight, secure in their position, surrounded by possessions, breeding with bovine regularity, and almost indistinguishable from one another. But when their younger brother marries the slim, birdlike, imaginative Flora, she is critical of their tastes, punctures their respectability, and transforms their lives. She is an artist; she paints, writes poetry, acts, and entertains. Her pretence, when she first meets the Beckers, to be a photographer with a tripod who takes a picture of each of them, her pretence that she sees and cuddles a little green dragon, captivate the Beckers, who even cooperate with her in her enthralling enactments. She is able not only to imitate their external characteristics — a physical appearance, a walk, a way of speaking or sitting — but to see and to project herself into 'the very essence of another being'.[19] She mimics each of them, imagines their lives but then becomes what she imagines, loses her own identity and goes mad. She can even impersonate herself but, as Julia begins to notice more and more, the charade becomes unbalanced when she impersonates the pregnant Honoria in particular and refuses to answer to her own name. A narrative that begins in delight, brings entertainment, descends into tragedy, and Flora has to be taken away for treatment, her future uncertain. The air, colour and light that she has brought into the Becker lives vanish and they return to their stolid existences.

With satirical humour and verve, Lavin has brought several characters vividly alive, has written with enjoyment of the power of her central, distinctive character. Flora's difference is the kernel of the story. Lavin loved to impersonate her, to enact the dramatic occasion of her meeting with the family, going through the motions of being the photographer with tripod and screen. She would explain that Flora could not survive her creations. The irony was not lost on her; the artist brings characters to life, lives through them, but when she can no longer bring them into existence, her reason for existence ends. Lavin thought of the artist as a kind of Christ figure giving his life for others. The theme of artistic struggle is voiced again in 'Trastevere' (1971) about Vera Traske: 'When she's working she can't sleep and she can't eat and she gets upset over nothing.'[20] It is significant that Flora brings life but is herself destroyed, just as Clem in 'The New Gardener' (1962) creates but is the cause of death, or that Vera in 'Happiness' (1968), source of a cyclonic energy, takes refuge in gardening but suffers her final illness there. The closeness of creativity to destruction is an ongoing theme, the proximity of tragedy and comedy to each other. To find peace from her hectic life Vera goes to work in her garden and it is there she suffers an attack from which she quickly dies. Lavin also found solace in the garden; she once said that she'd love to write a column on gardening for the *Irish Farmers Journal*.

Literal and detailed, with lengthy descriptions of interiors and of the people who live in them, 'The Becker Wives' is written in naturalistic manner. Lavin's stories often depend on the depiction of a single narrator and interior monologue. They are focused through a limited perspective in which the character of the narrator determines the range and depth of the story. If the narrator is short of ideas, limited in feeling, and if she is too understated, then the story suffers. The closest analogy is found in *Dubliners* (1914), in stories about the individual, such as the ineffectual Eveline in the story of that title or the timid Chandler in 'A Little Cloud'. There the method is indirect, the sensibility revealed through self-questioning, hesitation, and irresolution, the story kept within a reasonable length, whereas in Lavin's work there is often an unnecessary amount of description and incident.

'A Single Lady' (1951) is a case in point. The scope is almost unlimited; the narrator is allowed to proceed at length, to be repetitive and is at the mercy of compulsive reactions. Isabel's inability to be decisive is realized over and over, with the result that the reader understands her psychological difficulties and limitations — they are clearly stated — and does not require the elaboration of incident and feeling that the story provides. That elaboration, however, is part of character creation. In the end, what Lavin's stories achieve is an extended dramatization, a prolonged and repetitive enactment of the movements of a woman's mind, the hesitations and half-choices, the reservations, the urgings, the blunt revelation of inadequacy that the story highlights.

In 'A Single Lady', Isabel cannot understand and cannot accept her father's distasteful relationship with the woman servant whom she can only refer to as 'the creature' and whom she always sees in degrading terms — slatternly, dirty, coarse and lower class, whereas her father is an educated, refined, and travelled man, a man of taste whom she has revered and obeyed without question. The issue is how should Isabel deal with the unexpected and disagreeable relationship? She is incapable of discussing it with him or of confronting the servant. Being a single lady, she does not understand the sexual force that is at work. Her ruse to tell a story that illustrates her perception of the situation fails because she has neither the courage nor the strength to bring it to its challenging conclusion. When the artist fails, the story is ineffective. By fudging the ending, Isabel dilutes the impact and has to retreat in defeat, leaving the woman and her father beside the fire while she goes back to her lonely room. Length is an issue in several stories. 'A Single Lady' is too long, so is 'The Little Prince' (1956), and so is 'Posy' (1947), which has material that is not relevant. 'A Happy Death' is stretched beyond its aesthetic boundary. Sometimes the will of the artist forces the imagination too hard.

Lavin's narrative methods are well established. One is the relentless flow that is closer to the tale than to the short story, and at times closer to the yarn. Sometimes grounded in the naturalistic mode, it occasionally slips into fairy tale. The relentless narrator is also the self-centred narrator, the focus of attention, controlling the audience, holding their interest. Lavin needed the scope of the extended narrative; many of her shorter stories fail to ignite. When she published 'The New Gardener', she was pleased to receive a complimentary letter from Seán O'Faoláin. It was the kind of short story he liked: it had brevity, compactness, little characterization, focused on one event, used implication to suggest meaning, and left much for the reader to discover. Clem, the gardener, has a green thumb, is gentle with growing things, including his children and in particular baby Pearl. He has that destructive quality found in many Lavin characters but the absence of a wife hardly registers, until detectives arrive and arrest him for murder. In retrospect, we detect various hints that her absence is not voluntary: there is also the mystery of the scar on Pearl's underarm and his talk about caring seems obsessive. The incident of the frog screeching in pain and Clem's blazing anger harks backward. His explanation that he only saw a cruel thing done once and that he could not stand it anticipates the ending. The detectives speak gently to him as though reluctant to take him into custody. The story is carefully handled, everything is relevant, at its heart the sad contrast between a man committed to life and loving, so capable in what he does, his hands so creative, but whose affirmation of loving protection drives him to murder. It is the old dichotomy in Lavin's perception of creativity and destruction.

The truth of the imagination, she used to say, is an absolute truth. Our conversations about the short story are summarized in 'Conversations with Mary Lavin' that appeared in my *Selected Essays* (2006). 'I write short stories', she said, 'because I believe in the form as a powerful medium for the discovery of truth; the short story aims at a particle of truth. I hope to convey something of what I have learned. I like its discipline, its combination of experience, imagination, and technique. It combines them, compresses them, telescopes them, working towards a solution.'[21]

She came to her full powers in the concluding collections — *In the Middle of the Fields* (1967), *Happiness* (1969), *A Memory* (1972), *The Shrine* (1977), and *A Family*

Likeness. Two subjects interest her — widowhood and family disagreement. She looks back at her family, her father, her aunts in Athenry, Michael Scott, and her mother, Nora, who died in 1969. The first widow story, 'In a Café' (1960), appeared six years after William Walsh died. The woman in the story can only remember fragments of what her husband Richard looked like, 'limned by love and anguish, before they vanished'.[22] If she could not remember him at will, she thinks, what use was it to have lived the past 'if behind us it fell away so sheer'; and she feels 'the noise of a nameless panic', her mind is 'a roaring furnace'.[23] She longs to see him whole, to possess him in memory. She lost her identity willingly in marriage; she has lost it doubly in widowhood. Meeting an artist in the café, she goes to the address he has given her, looks through the letter box, hears his voice, and thinks that all she could say to him was 'I'm lonely. Are you?' and knows that in this ridiculous act, it is Richard she seeks.[24] When she sees him whole, she knows she possesses him again.

Other stories in the collection — 'Bridal Sheets' (1959) and 'Loving Memory' (1960) — focus on widows but not with the control and depth of feeling that are present in later stories. In them, Lavin engages with the trauma that had caused her depression. In these widow stories, we witness a working out of suffering; by externalising pain, Lavin brings it under control and makes it more understandable. An identity that was under threat is recovered; doubt and self-questioning are replaced by reassurance. In 'Loving Memory', the widow indulges in excessive grieving. A similar excess occurs in 'Heart of Gold' (1964), where a widower marries again and expects the second wife to fit into his dead wife's shoes, thereby prolonging the first marriage. The insensitive and dominating relationship voices Lavin's fear of a relationship that would be diminishing.

The new quality of her work is apparent in the title story of *In the Middle of the Fields* which describes her home in Bective and serves as a metaphor for her stubborn, sensuous nature, and the loneliness of widowhood.

> Like a rock in the sea, she was islanded by fields, the heavy grass washing about the house, and the cattle wading in it as in water. Even their gentle stirrings were a loss when they moved away at evening to the shelter of the woods. A rainy day might strike a wet flash from a hay barn on the far side of the river — not even a habitation! And yet she was less lonely for him here in Meath than elsewhere. Anxieties by day, and cares, and at night vague, nameless fears — these were the stones across the mouth of the tomb. But who

understood that? ... What was it but another name for dry love and
barren longing?[25]

The story is sturdy in its account of business dealings between the widow, who
is never named, and Bartley Crossen, the farmer who has agreed, after some
haggling, to cut grass for her. Their exchanges reveal her strength of character,
shrewd business mind, and ability to stand up for herself. Behind their transaction
lies a warmth of feeling that arises from memories of Bartley's first wife who has
the kind of impetuous, loving nature present in all Lavin's portrayals of young
love. The memory of that first love and of Bridie, the young girl he married, rises
in Crossen's mind when he sees the widow with her hair hanging about her head.
Impulsively, he tries to kiss her, overcome by unexpected desire. His sheepish
apology causes her to forgive him at once; she knows it was the image of his young
love that came back to him. Between them also is the fact of bereavement. She has
lost Richard, feels alone, and burdened with his memory; Crossen has lost his
young wife. Although he seems to have forgotten her, the widow is not convinced
of that. For her, dry love and barren longing have not ceased. The contrast between
her and the lush grasslands does not have to be stated. She is the first of Lavin's
widows, whom she brings to life with compassion and full understanding of
what they are going through. She never deprives them of the sense of love found,
then lost, and never undervalues their struggle for independence from crippling,
entombing grief.

In 'The Cuckoo-Spit' (1964), the widow Vera Traske has the good sense to avoid
a relationship with a young man, although she finds him attractive. There is, she
thinks, a kind of peace at last when you face up to life's defeats. It is not that you
are better at being able to bear things, but that you get weaker and stop trying.
Now she thinks she could not bear anything, even happiness. What she has found
troubling is the way people changed Richard in their memories, diminished him,
made him into a man of marble, and altered her own perception of him. She has
been angry at him for being so perfect and so dead. At that point, as the young
man Fergus perceptively says, she had her husband back again — 'unchanged,
amused' at her anger.[26] More deeply, as she now realizes, she blamed Richard
for leaving a void that no one less than him could fill. She is drawn to Fergus,
likes talking with him, arranges to meet him in Dublin, and he is attracted to her.
Here too identity is at stake: she is trying to get back to being the woman she
was before she met Richard. But Fergus is not the answer and she firmly breaks
off the relationship. 'Happiness' is a more philosophical search for definition.

Here the widow Vera Traske has three daughters and a priest friend — Father Hugh. The narrator, the eldest daughter, tries to figure out what the happiness is that their mother keeps talking about. The truth of the story lies in its narrative method, the characterization of the widow, and the dramatic manner. Happiness is a faith, a belief in one's self, something affirmed through the telling. The widow in word and action embodies the invisible power of happiness, but for Father Hugh, happiness is inseparable from suffering. Her blazing energy engulfs the family; she is forceful, animated, determined, and vocal, consciously in pursuit of happiness. The widow Vera is not only another example of that positive force that animates the lives of lovers, she is closely related to the blind determination that fills the mind of the woman in 'A Happy Death' who has a similar obsessive and destructive energy. She is harrowed in the same way that the Lavin aunts in Athenry were. Such women have a force that is like a life force, but it consumes them, is impervious to logic and common sense, and is frustrating for those who have to deal with it.

> I don't think you realize the onslaughts that were made upon our happiness! The minute Robert died, they came down on me — cohorts of relatives, friends, even strangers, all draped in black, opening their arms like bats to let me pass into their company. 'Life is a vale of tears,' they said. 'You are privileged to find it out so young!' Ugh! After I staggered to my feet and began to take hold of life once more, they fell back defeated. And the first day I gave a laugh — pouff, they were blown out like candles. They weren't living in a real world at all; they belonged to a ghostly world where life was easy: all one had to do was sit and weep. It takes effort to push back the stone from the mouth of the tomb and walk out.[27]

Whatever it is, it baffles her daughters, who only see the enormous effort involved, the chaos of her life, her inability to bring order to her affairs. In this self-justifying story, Lavin writes a defence of her life and character. In her mind, Vera trusts in private conscience, is independent of clerical restrictions, and the movement in Father Hugh from detached friendship to an intimacy resembling a lover's is a kind of pastoral renewal, something that has been of deep concern to Lavin. It affects her portrayal of the inflexible, heartless priest in 'A Wet Day' (1944), of the skinflint Canon and demented curate in 'A Pure Accident' (1969), and her deeply felt condemnation of the idea of Limbo in 'The Lost Child' (1969), a haunting story of a miscarriage. Lavin admired the flexibility and subtlety of women's minds. In many stories, the shifting nature of their thoughts and feelings contrasts with the more rigid mental and emotional nature of men. The line of development in those stories is more often psychological than plot-centred and more often connected with women than with men. Lavin stands back from herself and looks objectively, with humour, understanding and integrity; she accepts the way she is. When Michael Scott decided to spend his life looking after her, it was partly to impose order on her affairs, to pay bills, deal with correspondence, reassure her in times of panic, and leave her free to write. Like Flora in 'The Becker Wives', Vera in 'Happiness' embodies a quality that she cannot give to others. Like a number of Lavin stories, particularly those about widows, she achieves a sophisticated angle of vision; she writes about herself, her family, and her relationship with a priest with an effective objectivity. The honesty with which she does so measures her integrity; the sensibility, personality, ideas and gestures are indistinguishable from their living models. The immediacy of the transference from reality to fiction, almost a fusion, gives the story a remarkable vividness and credibility. We are drawn into the fiction, become part of its developing psychological and spiritual drama. If Lavin is sometimes obsessive, she is so in the interests of truth. She places characters in testing situations then subjects them to merciless, exponential exposure.

'Trastevere' and 'Villa Violetta' (1972) continue these examinations of widowhood. Mrs Traske appears in both. The former is a study in relationships and in the nature of enduring, satisfying love, which Mrs Traske has protected by not making it public. The wife Della gives a different slant to the controlling or manipulative woman. Her husband Simon and his friend Paul are totally dependent on her; she gathers them close, while at the same time belittling her husband's abilities, his taste in food, the lack of children, and their dependence on her money. Her apparent strength is a magnet for people like her husband and his friend, but Mrs Traske notices that Della is tired. Like Flora, she is able to sustain life in others, not in herself. She needs to dominate them, to order them about, to belittle them, and in the process to draw strength from them, but the strain leads to her suicide. The contrast is between that dependent relationship and the affirmative relationship between Mrs Traske and her lover in which neither suffers diminishment. 'Villa Violetta' is an extended account of Vera's vain attempts to find a place in Florence to stay with her three daughters, a place where she can write. The entire region is bathed in warm sunshine, sentiment and sensuous appreciation. Vera is indecisive and impractical, but a priest comes to her aid and through his generous and thoughtful action she is given suitable accommodation, the girls are delighted, and a sick girl recovers.

The question of diminishment appears throughout *A Memory*. In 'Asigh', the young girl is cruelly thwarted, her brother cannot have a normal sexual relationship with the girl he loves, and their father terrifies the two children. In 'Trastevere', Della dominates but is herself damaged. In 'A Memory', the dependant man and the accommodating woman live in an unreal, cosseted relationship in which both are reduced. The story is in three parts. The first, written from the man's point, reveals his male chauvinist attitude to Myra and to women in general; in the second she rebels explosively against the cosy nest in which they meet and where she has provided dinner for him for years; in the third, he is driven to his death in the woods. In the first part, Lavin satirizes him for his feelings of male superiority; in steadily accumulating detail, he is exposed for what he is and his selfish acceptance of the secluded nest in which he and Myra have dinner. He is a reclusive scholar; private, fastidious, nervous, self-preserving, and inclined to misinterpret motives, including his own. He appreciates 'the uniquely undemanding quality of her feelings for him'.[28] The self-deception that he and Myra practice is anathema to Lavin. They both lack the rigorous honesty Lavin espoused. Failure to achieve it results in their unreal situation and to the kind of indecision shown by Isabel in 'The Single Lady'. James has had only one intense, natural relationship — with Emmy, his student, whom he selfishly ditched when he was awarded a Travelling Studentship. By chance, now married, she currently lives across the River Boyne from his cottage. In the first part of the story, Lavin intimates Myra's devotion to James in subtle ways. The narrative is relaxed, humorous and clinical. In the second part, Myra reminds him of the sacrifices she made for him through the years, 'So many, many years,' she whispers. It was, he thinks silently, only ten.'[29] She has, she thinks 'denatured' herself for James, deflected his feelings away from herself, and 'cemented him into his barren way of life'.[30] She is overcome by grief, thinks he might comfort her, but all she perceives is his coldness. It is as though she speaks for all the women in the world who have felt themselves thoughtlessly taken for granted by men. Their voices fill her ears. He determines to leave; she tries to stop him, thumps him, stands with her back to the door, and hears him asking what she hopes to gain by this 'performance' — 'This nailing of yourself to the door like a stoat!'[31] She flings herself onto the sofa face downward, screaming and kicking her feet in a caricature of the hysterical woman. The third part accompanies James as he leaves in bewilderment, assuming blame — even wrongly — trying in vain to understand what has happened. He catches a bus that passes near his cottage, gets off blindly at the wrong stop, blunders into a wood near where Emmy lives, and dies with his mouth pressed into wet leaves. In these endings, Lavin punishes both of them; the woman for indulging a foolish dream, the man for failing to marry the girl.

When we talked about this story, she said with impatient emphasis, 'He should have married the girl.' For that failure she drove him relentlessly and beyond sympathy into vague and confused thinking, in deep pain, delirium, and a self-pitying cry for Emmy, then for Myra: 'Both of them had failed him.'[32] A story that began with delicate perceptions has descended into melodrama. Lavin has allowed personal feeling to get in the way. The parallels with Lavin's own life are evident; the story is set in her mews in Lad Lane and in her cottage at Bective. Myra creates a false place with a celibate academic, and he, like Michael Scott, rejected her when they were students to continue his studies abroad. Lavin imagines herself as both the foolish, post-menopausal woman and the girl foolishly rejected. In real life, however, it was not easy to change from a state of supportive companionship to actual marriage; she stated that she had to have a double whiskey before she could bring herself to go up to bed.

In the title story of *A Family Likeness* (1985), Lavin is concerned with the 'squalls that no amount of tact, no amount of love could stop from blowing up out of a clear sky'.[33] Now a grandmother and conscious of failing strength, Ada tries to keep the peace when she walks with her daughter and granddaughter to the woods to collect primroses, or when she visits another daughter in the south, but inevitably the squalls of conflict and disagreement arise. The touch is light and distinctive but the honest revelation in these stories deals with the ability to hurt and wound, to voice sharp responses while at the same time feeling or remembering happier times. The inevitable, pitiful fact, as 'A Marriage' (1985) shows, is that the couple quarrel, belittle, have regrets, become calm, tender, or protective only to have those moods disturbed once again. Feelings of resentment, suspicion, irritation are forever ready to displace the opposite urge to avoid conflict, to give credit, to ignore hurt. The tension, both fruitful and creative, between these forces is always present. Lavin refuses to pretend that old age is considerate or wise. Throughout the entire span of her work her intelligence and imagination are deeply engaged with the human capacity to quarrel and the human inability to live by love and understanding, to overcome division, to control retaliation. The language of argument recurs like an identifying stain in story after story and is a measure of her greatness as a writer that she faces disagreement, deals with it at all stages of her career, does not shirk its troublesome and ugly presence. In these final stories, while some have the serenity one may associate with age, others deal with disagreeable emotional irruption.

If we try to measure Lavin's importance as a writer, we may do so in two ways. In one, we acknowledge the amount and variety of the work. Over a lifetime she has illustrated the complexities of human nature, its urge towards love and honesty, its lapses and failings. She has made us understand tensions within families, made us appreciate the intensity and appeal of love in individual lives, heartbreak and yearnings. We see people blindly thrashing about, sometimes driven by good intensions, sometimes immersed in self-deception. Hers is a disturbingly honest vision, a portrayal of human nature which we cannot ignore and which we value for its psychological depth. Towards the end of his life, Seán O'Faoláin read all the short stories of Guy de Maupassant and of Anton Chekhov. He came to the sobering conclusion that each would be remembered for a handful of stories. So it is with Lavin. We recognize the overall achievement, the prolonged engagement, the struggle, but ask if there are stories that will stand the test of time. Among those discussed in this all too short and selective essay are those that determine her lasting achievement.

Endnotes

1   Dating for all stories is for their first publication, and based on Heinz Kosok's dateline in 'Mary Lavin: A Bibliography', *Irish University Review*, 9, 2, (Autumn 1979), pp.279–312.

2   D. Corkery, *The Threshold of Quiet* (Dublin: Talbot Press, 1917).

3   M. Lavin, 'Miss Holland', *The Dublin Magazine*, 14 (April–June 1939), pp.30–62.

4   M. Lavin, 'The Will', in *Selected Stories* (New York: Macmillan, 1959), p.11.

5   Ibid., p.12.

6   Ibid., p.17.

7   Ibid.

8   M. Lavin, 'Asigh', in *A Memory and Other Stories* (London: Constable, 1972), p.67.

9   M. Lavin, 'Frail Vessel', in *The Patriot Son and Other Stories* (London: Michael Joseph, 1956), p.159.

10 Ibid., p.179.

11 Ibid., pp.179, 180.

12 M. Lavin, 'A Happy Death', in *The Becker Wives and Other Stories* (London: Michael

Joseph, 1946), p.178.

13 Ibid., p.133.

14 Ibid., p.181.

15 Ibid., pp.141–42.

16 Ibid., p.152.

17 Ibid., p.183.

18 M. Lavin, 'The Widow's Son', in *A Single Lady and Other Stories* (London: Michael Joseph, 1951), p.194.

19 M. Lavin, 'The Becker Wives', in *The Becker Wives*, p.59.

20 M. Lavin, 'Trastevere', in *A Memory*, p.57.

21 M. Harmon, *Selected Essays*, B. Brown (ed.) (Dublin & Portland, OR: Irish Academic Press, 2006), p.210.

22 M. Lavin, 'In a Café', in *The Great Wave and Other Stories* (London: Macmillan, 1961), p.53.

23 Ibid., pp.53, 54.

24 Ibid., p.68.

25 M. Lavin, 'In the Middle of the Fields', in *In the Middle of the Fields and Other Stories* (London: Constable, 1967), p.9.

26 M. Lavin, 'The Cuckoo-Spit', in *In the Middle of the Fields*, p.82.

27 M. Lavin, 'Happiness', in *Happiness and Other Stories* (London: Constable, 1969), p.24.

28 M. Lavin , 'A Memory', in *A Memory*, p.169.

29 Ibid., p.194.

30 Ibid., pp.195–6.

31 Ibid., p.199.

32 Ibid., p.223.

33 M. Lavin, 'A Family Likeness', in *A Family Likeness and Other Stories* (London: Constable, 1985), p.8.

2 | Masculinities in Mary Lavin's Short Stories

Heather Ingman

There has been a tendency in recent criticism to focus on the female characters in Mary Lavin's stories and particularly on the tensions in the mother-daughter relationships which feature so prominently in her work. In this chapter, I would like to re-examine the question of gender in her short stories by exploring her portrayal of male characters. Unlike some Irish women's fiction, particularly that written during the 1970s when feminism was getting off the ground in Ireland, Lavin's work displays sympathies that are divided equally between male and female characters with her male characters suffering as much as women from the restrictions of their environment, though often in a different way. For my analysis, I will be drawing on some of the extensive work done in masculinity studies since the 1990s while also taking into account the particular context of Irish masculinity.[1]

Unlike feminist theories which can be traced back at least to the eighteenth century and the writings of Mary Wollstonecraft, the study of masculinity is a relatively recent phenomenon, dating from the 1990s. Until then, too often the male was seen as the unproblematic norm against which the female was measured, but by the latter part of the twentieth century, masculinity had come to be regarded as a construct reflecting particular social and cultural values. In Michael Kimmel's words: 'Manhood is neither static nor timeless; it is historical. Manhood is not the manifestation of an inner essence; it is socially constructed.'[2] Under the influence of Judith Butler's analysis of gender as performative, there was a shift to the notion of masculinity as a series of fictions that are neither fixed nor stable. Masculinities were seen to be formed by a network of disciplinary codes and institutions, such as schools, the legal system, religion, art, and the media.[3]

Feminist psychoanalysts like Nancy Chodorow and Dorothy Dinnerstein who draw on object-relations theory in their work argue that gender is produced and maintained through cultural arrangements rather than anatomical ones, as in Freud. In Chodorow's analysis, gender is constructed through identifications and values learned within the (western) family. A son learns that dependency on his mother is a sign of weakness and lack of masculinity: 'Masculine gender training becomes much more rigid than feminine. A boy represses those qualities he takes to be feminine inside himself, and rejects and devalues women and whatever he takes to be feminine in the social world.'[4] The world of secondary socialization, of school, work, success and autonomy, comes to be viewed as superior and masculine in comparison with the maternal world of nurturance, with the result that connection and the blurring of boundaries between self and other must be denied or devalued. Mothers collude in this gender policing, Chodorow argues, by pushing their sons out into the world, while keeping their daughters close. In *The Rocking of the Cradle and the Ruling of the World* (1978), Dorothy Dinnerstein analyses exclusive child-rearing by women that makes mothers seem all-important in the eyes of the child, though in the wider society they may have little power.[5] Memories of powerlessness as a child produce young men with a psychological need to separate themselves from women and to deny the female in themselves for fear of being engulfed by the feminine. Masculinity becomes a constant process of proving oneself in the outside world, hence the masculine drive for power and domination and what Virginia Woolf called in 'A Room of One's Own': 'the instinct for possession, the rage for acquisition which drives them to desire other people's fields and goods perpetually; to make frontiers and flags; battleships and poison gas'.[6]

In this analysis, masculinity comes to be equated with sexual and physical assertiveness, competitiveness, aggression, and emotional control. As Michael Kaufman describes it: 'The acquisition of hegemonic (and most subordinate) masculinities is a process through which men come to suppress a range of emotions, needs and possibilities, such as nurturing, receptivity, empathy, and compassion, which are experienced as inconsistent with the power of manhood.'[7] In turn, this suppression of the emotions is what renders masculinity such a fragile construct, as Lynne Segal explains: 'Since all the linguistic codes, cultural imagery and social relations for representing the ideals of "manliness", or what is termed "normative masculinity", symbolize power, rationality, assertiveness, invulnerability, it is hardly surprising that men, individually, should exist in perpetual fear of being unmanned.'[8] It is my contention that Lavin's portraits of male characters in her short stories anticipate much of this theoretical writing on masculinity.

Masculinity is not of course constructed in a vacuum: men are pressurized into performing masculinity in particular ways in line with their culture's expectations. In Ireland, Irish masculinity was perceived as fragile and in peril due to the colonial stereotype of the Irish as effeminate and childish. To prove his masculinity after independence, the Irish male had to become assertive in the public sphere, police female sexuality and exclude homosexuals from inclusion in the Irish nation's definition of itself. All of this was reinforced by the Catholic Church's view of the man as head of the family and by a nationalism that positioned men as defenders of the Irish nation, with women as its biological and ideological reproducers guaranteeing the nation's purity. Fixed concepts of gender became institutionalized in Ireland's juridical structure and after 1922, women saw a gradual erosion of their political rights. In theory, the Irish male held a privileged position both in public life and as head of the family; however, as Michael Kaufman has pointed out, patriarchy does not just consist of men's power over women but also of 'hierarchies of power among different groups of men and between different masculinities'.[9]

These hierarchies of power are very much in evidence in Lavin's stories portraying small town Ireland dominated by the Catholic Church and a rigid class system. Hierarchies among the classes become all the more important to maintain since her shopkeepers and small farmers are aware that they are only one step away from the servant and labouring classes. The priests in the early stories are powerful because the institution to which they belong is powerful. Middle-class men like the Beckers are powerful because they have consolidated their position in society through their possessions, their stout, placid wives, and their children. By contrast, shopkeepers like Daniel Dogget in 'Posy' (1947) or Manny in 'At Sallygap' (1941) are not socially powerful. Yet in mid-century Ireland, plagued by widespread unemployment and emigration, men who had work felt that they were fortunate, even if that work involved soul-destroying routine. Work thus became an important definition of identity and social status. To work behind a counter, however filled with drudgery, meant that, like Daniel in 'Posy', you owed it to your family not to fall in love with a servant girl. There was a tendency, also like Daniel, to be obsequious to the few members of the professional classes encountered. When the man's work outside the home failed, as Robert's does in 'A Happy Death' (1946), the woman might take over the wage earning role; but when added to her all-important role within the home, underpinned by the Irish Constitution, this could lead to an imbalance of power in a family. While Irish men may have occupied the public space and positions of power, that does not mean, as an analysis of Mary Lavin's stories will show, that individual males always felt empowered.

There were two influences in her early life that may have led Lavin to pay particular attention to male characters in her work. One was her reading of Virginia Woolf on whom she had originally intended to write a PhD thesis. As she began her writing life, Lavin would have been familiar with Woolf's arguments in 'A Room of One's Own' (1929) and 'Three Guineas' (1938) that male superiority relies on positioning women as other and inferior and that male rage against women arises out of fear that their power will be usurped. Lavin's close relationship with her father, in contrast with her rather fraught relationship with her mother, must also have increased her understanding of masculinity. Lavin associated Tom with fun and uncomplicated love. Despite his own lack of education, he had a great respect for learning and was ambitious for his daughter.[10] He encouraged her in sport and generally promoted her sense of independence and self-worth. In *On Men*, Anthony Clare points to studies showing that a father's willingness to involve himself in a daughter's growing sense of her own potential is highly influential.[11] There is a sympathetic portrayal of Lavin's father in her short story, 'Tom' (1973), where he comes across as an affectionate man, comfortable with intimacy with his daughter, if not with his repressive wife. In 'Lemonade' (1961), an autobiographical account of Lavin's return to Ireland with her mother in 1921, lemonade becomes a symbol of the generous, uncalculating love associated with Maudie's father and later with the friendship that springs up, much to her mother's disapproval, between Maudie and the school's pariah, Sadie, the daughter of Mad Mary. In this, Maudie is shown as rejecting the petty social divisions that rule small town Ireland and that are upheld by her mother's family in favour of following her father's tolerant example.

In Lavin's work, fathers are shown mediating in the often fraught relations between mother and daughter. In 'The Nun's Mother' (1944), it is the husband and father, Mr Latimer, who has a healthy attitude towards the body whereas his wife, trained in convent school to dress and undress under her dressing gown, is unable to speak frankly to their daughter about the sexual pleasures of marriage. In 'A Cup of Tea' (1944), Sophy identifies with her intellectual father against her mother, whose life is centred round domesticity. The father here is not Tom but the situation is autobiographical in that Lavin's mother was often jealous of the close relationship between Mary and her father.

When set beside the sometimes stereotyped portrayal of men in later Irish women writers such as Edna O'Brien, the varieties of masculinity in Lavin's work are notable. Lavin is able to describe conventional middle-class men, like the Becker males and Lally's brothers in 'The Will' (1944), but she is also, in 'The Girders' (1944), able to enter into the consciousness of an Irish construction worker, accurately capturing the sights and sounds experienced by an exhausted city labourer. Male competitiveness and one-upmanship are portrayed in 'The Joy Ride' (1946), where fear of loss of face leads the domestic servants, Purdy and Crickem, into ever-greater feats of recklessness until their day of freedom ends in disaster. Lavin persuasively conveys the anxiety that hides behind masculine performance, and the role of alcohol and women in male competitiveness. Comparing Lavin with her predecessors in Irish women's writing — Somerville and Ross, Elizabeth Bowen and Kate O'Brien — highlights how unusual she was in entering the world of the male working class and reminds us that her models were not so much earlier Irish women writers as women writers from outside Ireland who focused on the working world, including Sarah Orne Jewett and George Eliot, authors Lavin cited as influences.

In 'Three Guineas', Woolf connects masculinity with militarism and there are portraits in Lavin's stories of men for whom masculinity means fighting, whether in the British Army, like Matty in 'The Dead Soldier' (1942), or for Irish independence like Sean Mongon in 'The Patriot Son' (1956). 'The Face of Hate' (1985), set in Belfast 1957, traces the making of a bigot. Like Jennifer Johnston's portrayal of the Catholic Logan family in Shadows on Our Skin (1977), Johnny's family in 'The Face of Hate' is divided between his elder brother Sheamus who, egged on by their father, belongs to the IRA, and his mother who has sympathy for Protestants as poor as themselves. Johnny is eventually provoked into an act of violence against Protestants, thus becoming part of that population in Northern Ireland for whom masculinity is identified with physical force.[12]

It is priests, however, rather than soldiers, who feature prominently in Lavin's work. Terence Brown has described the way in which, when they moved from rural life to the towns, the sons and daughters of small farmers brought with them the values they had been raised in, namely economic prudence, puritanical sexual mores and a nationalistic conservatism. They were encouraged in these values by a priesthood largely drawn from the same class, leading to a church, in Brown's words, 'dominated by the acquisitive prudery of farmer and shopkeeper.'[13] In Lavin's stories too, small farmers, shopkeepers and priests largely share the same values and attitudes. In the priests' case, however, their authority is bolstered by the powerful institution to which they belong and they use the authority invested in them by the Catholic Church and by its central place in Irish national life to police women's lives. 'Sunday Brings Sunday' (1944), contains early and outspoken criticism of the sexual repressions of Irish rural life that leave a young girl dangerously ignorant about her own body. The curate preaches against 'company-keeping' but this term is not precise enough for Mona who sees many young people around her keeping company without running into danger. Inevitably, without quite knowing how it has happened, Mona becomes pregnant. The implication of Lavin's story is that church and society are to blame for keeping a young girl in ignorance about her own body. In a later story, 'The Shrine' (1974), she depicts a Canon obsessed with controlling his female parishioners' sexuality. If their bodies escape his control and they become pregnant outside marriage, he quickly arranges to have them married off. Having learned to be ashamed of their bodies, these women in turn help the Canon marry off other young girls. Masculine ability to safeguard the purity of their women was a crucial aspect of Irish nationalism (it is a salient feature of Edna O'Brien's *Country Girls* trilogy) and in Lavin's work, priests are criticized when they share the prudery, the social ambition and the unloving attitudes of the society around them.

Lavin's early years in America allowed her to experience a different kind of Catholicism with the result that hers was a much looser mode of Catholicism than that of most Irish Catholics. She was less concerned with the rites and rituals and the folk aspects of Catholicism — the rosary beads, the shrines, holy pictures, statues, religious medals — in favour of going to the heart of spiritual life. Her stories reveal a dislike of religion where it means superstition and unthinking adherence to the church rather than a genuinely thought out faith, and she was in advance of her time in her concern about the power of celibacy to deform character. Unmediated by human affection, celibacy breeds the self-centredness of the priest in 'A Wet Day' (1944) and the mean-minded callousness of the Canon in 'A Pure Accident' (1969). In 'The Shrine', celibacy has gradually caused a vacuum in the life of the Canon, originally a loving and even a cultured man. This vacuum can only be filled by his devotion to the shrine and the thought of the money it will bring to the local community from tourists. Through the words of the Canon's niece, Lavin condemns a profession that cuts men off from human affections:

35

> Love, she thought sadly; it was love that was at the root of all the contradictions in him. He thought he had cut out all need for it from his body, and although for a time his natural feelings for her mother, and later for herself, had seemed to fill the vacancy, it was not enough. The vacuum had to be filled and he had filled it with devotion to the Shrine.[14]

In the end, the Canon is prepared to sacrifice even his niece's future to his ambitions for the shrine.

In one of Lavin's early stories, 'Brother Boniface', published in *Tales from Bective Bridge* (1942), Barney escapes the unending drudgery of money-making in his parents' shop to join a monastery where he hopes he will have more time to meditate on nature's beauties. The story turns on the irony that the relentless monastic routine leaves Boniface little time for contemplation. 'Brother Boniface' connects with one of Lavin's major themes, namely the danger of people's lives being absorbed by the tyranny of the workplace. She portrays men, especially middle-class men, who find their working identities so central to who they are as people that their emotional and spiritual life becomes damaged. This theme of paid work as a source of masculine identity, status and power must be set in the context of widespread unemployment and emigration in Ireland, which put added pressure on those with jobs to work hard in order to keep them. In other words, though Lavin's stories mainly explore internal pressures on the middle-class male professional, the unstated external pressures on them should be borne in mind too.

'A Woman Friend' (1951) is one of Lavin's earliest portraits of the professional man. A successful surgeon, Dr Lew Anderson is someone who, in a phrase that should alert us to danger in Lavin's world, is 'fully acclimatized to professional life'.[15] The price of Lew's professional success has been his emotional life. He takes Bina, the eponymous woman friend, for granted and has failed to mature emotionally so that when his career is threatened, he all but collapses. In his analysis of masculinity, Victor J. Seidler comments: 'men have rarely acknowledged the time and energy that goes into the emotional work that sustains a relationship'.[16] 'A Woman Friend' reverses James Joyce's story 'The Boarding House' for here, the young male is not entrapped by his landlady and her daughter but selfishly profits by their care and support. Bina and her mother look after Lew's comfort and bolster his self-esteem, acting, in Woolf's famous description, 'as looking-glasses possessing the magic and delicious power of reflecting the figure of man at twice its natural size'.[17] Bina persuades Lew that his habit of dropping off to sleep is not a weakness but shows 'some sort of superiority in him — some exceptional self-control or will-power — she'd ended by making him quite puffed-up about it'.[18] Bina is one of several portraits in Lavin's work showing women colluding in their society's belief in the dominant male.

With her portrait of James in 'A Memory' (1972), Lavin extends and deepens her study of the professional man who locates his identity in his work. A research professor, James rises early in order to give 'the best of his brain to work'.[19] His days are spent in relentless intellectual activity without even balancing relationships with students or colleagues for, since his elevation to research professor, he has lived in isolation in the country writing, ironically, on the creative process. Even James worries at times that all this intellectual activity may be siphoning off energy from his body making him less physically active, another important masculine attribute. Worrying about a possible loss of physical vigour but not about his inability to form relationships, James aptly fits Seidler's description of professional men who learn that time is a scarce commodity they must be careful not to waste and that to spend it on personal relationships is self-indulgence. Men, argues Seidler, 'learn that life is there to be got on with, not really to be reflected upon … time and energy given to relationships is time taken away from our own projects'.[20] Waged time is the only time that counts. Anthony Clare, an Irishman, described imbibing similar messages about masculinity from the society around him: 'I learned very early on that what a man does; his work is as important as, even more important than, who he is; that a man is defined in modern capitalistic society in terms not of being but doing … My career, particularly my medical career, was always portrayed and interpreted by others as much as by myself, as more important than spouse, family, friends.'[21]

In 'A Memory', James similarly thinks in terms of individual achievement. His youthful relationship with Emmy failed despite his powerful feelings for her because he was unwilling to subordinate his career to marriage. For ten years, Myra has served as his form of relaxation between work. Myra, an independent professional woman who earns her money through freelance translation, plays by James' rules, bolstering his self-esteem and colluding in the notion that the world of work is more valuable than the domestic sphere. She knows that for James emotional independence is crucial so she makes no demands on him, adjusts her life to accommodate the amount of time he wants to see her and has gradually suppressed in herself any trace of behaviour that might seem 'wifey', a word they coin 'to describe a certain type of woman they both abhorred'.[22] James fits very easily into Chodorow's analysis of masculinity as defined by internal suppression of the feminine and devaluation of women in the social world. Fearing the feminine in himself, James loathes any sign of womanliness, so Myra relinquishes her former domestic skills of embroidery and baking and restricts her domesticity to ordering takeaways, which they pay for separately. For James, her flat has taken on 'a marvellously masculine air'.[23] Their situation is very akin to the patriarchy as described by Anthony Clare:

> That power of patriarchy, that set of relations of power that enable men to control women, is grounded in the belief that the public takes precedence over the private. Women struggling to escape the constraints of patriarchy are drawn into a tacit acceptance of the superior value of the public, the business, the profession and the office, and a devaluation of the private. Men, as a consequence, feel little need to reassess the priority they give to the public; indeed, the very desire of women to establish their own public legitimacy is interpreted as further proof that the public is indeed superior and the private is legitimately regarded as inferior.[24]

For James, and for Myra under James's influence, emotions are seen as an indication of weakness and self-indulgence but the cost to Myra of suppressing her instinct for domestic life is hinted at: 'It was — she said — as if part of her had become palsied.'[25] One evening, after a spectacularly casual piece of behaviour by James, Myra's feelings erupt. She claims she has 'denatured herself for James'.[26] James, for whom emotional control is a mark of masculinity, dismisses Myra's outburst as 'a performance' and 'hysterical'. When he prepares to leave, Myra tries physically to stop him by throwing out her arms in 'an outrageous gesture of crucifixion'.[27] The image, though strong, does not seem inappropriate. Myra has indeed crucified her emotional life for James' sake. She has recently undergone a hysterectomy and been so shaken by it that James is led to wonder whether she had wanted children all along, despite his own abhorrence of them.

Although on one level Lavin's story skirts essentialism in the notion that there is an essential female nature that Myra has sacrificed, on another level, the story may be read as an allegory with Myra representing all that Lavin believes the workplace excludes — intimacy, warmth, self-giving. In the end, 'A Memory' is less about gender difference than about the tyranny of an assertive job culture, internalized by James, that does not accommodate the world of emotions and families. Lavin was thus decades ahead in laying bare the masculinist structures of the workplace and the damage done by them to men as well as to women. In this she may have been influenced by Woolf who also pointed out the deforming nature of the professions upon character. Woolf's ideal college, outlined in 'Three Guineas', would 'explore the ways in which mind and body can be made to co-operate'.[28] In a powerful section of this essay, she describes the lives of men — barristers, bishops, politicians, doctors, journalists – so consumed by their professions that they cease to find any joy in life, making us question, she says, 'the value of professional life — not its cash value; that is great; but its spiritual, its moral, its intellectual value'.[29] Professional life, Woolf argues, is so organized as to militate against time for friendship, travel, leisure and art and she warns women, just then beginning to enter the professions, against adopting male attitudes. Instead, she advocates keeping a critical distance from the dominant power structures, posing the question: 'How can we [women] enter the professions and yet remain civilized human beings?'[30] Myra fails to maintain the necessary critical distance and becomes sucked into James' world whereas what Woolf wants is for women to enter the professional world bringing with them the values they have acquired in their private life.

Similarly, Lavin warns against concentrating on professional life to the exclusion of personal relations and her warning is to men as well as to women. For James suffers from his emotional repression: his insistence on devoting all his time to intellectual pursuits has impoverished his life. If he is unable to acknowledge Myra's emotional needs, he is also unable to tend to his own. Men, argues Seidler, 'dampen these emotions … because they come to be associated with the femininity we have rejected as part of our quest for masculinity'.[31] James remains locked within himself, unable to articulate, even to himself, what has gone wrong in his life. As he lies dying of, ironically, a heart attack, the rotting leaves filling his mouth are an apt symbol of his life. In retrospect, the opening sentence of the story, 'James did all right for a man on his own', seems very ironic and Lavin may be seen as writing here against Frank O'Connor's romantic positioning of the short story's protagonist as an outlaw figure 'wandering about the fringes of society'.[32] For Lavin, such figures are not heroes but lacking in humanity because they keep themselves apart from social relations.

In 'A Memory', Lavin lays bare the dark side of the solitary hero as leading to fear, insecurity, paranoia, and an inability to form loving relationships. Her males are seen most favourably when enmeshed in community and family. In 'At Sallygap', Manny is at his most sympathetic not as a solitary dreamer but when he responds with compassion to Annie. 'No man need regard himself as a failure if he has failed with women', O'Connor asserted in his chapter on Lavin.[33] In Lavin's stories, on the contrary, men are failures if they fail in their personal relationships, no matter how successful they are in their careers. In her own life, Lavin was famous for not separating the world of work from her family life, writing at the kitchen table or in the National Library with her daughters beside her doing their homework.[34]

In 'A Memory', James, repressing the feminine in himself, is nauseated by references to women's bodies, a common reaction amongst Lavin's celibate males. In 'Love is for Lovers', Mathew in his youth idealizes the golden girls on the posters while finding real young women 'coarse'. Like James, Mathew has devoted all his waking time to his work, a business in Mathew's case that he does not even own. Reaching 'the noncommittal age of forty-four', he suddenly starts to think about marriage but he is too fixed in his celibacy and too caught up in romanticizations about women, while being repelled by the physicality of their bodies, to change.[35] Men may be more powerful than women in the outside world but in Lavin's fiction they often pay a terrible price in terms of personal isolation and sexual immaturity.

Similarly, in 'The Lucky Pair' (1962), Andrew Gill, auditor of the students' law society, can scarcely bring himself to mention his sister-in-law's miscarriage. At the student dance he holds himself aloof from the pleasures of the dancers and prominently displays his auditor's red ribbon and other medals in a way that Woolf mocked men for in 'Three Guineas'.[36] Andrew is ambitious, prejudiced against women, and afraid of marriage ruining his career. He is scathing of a fellow medical student caught up in a passionate relationship: 'How can he hope to make a success of his profession with all that strain and stress?'[37] The title of the story is ironic for if the lucky pair is Andrew and his unnamed girl, they are about to embark, as the girl is aware, on a marriage without passion.

A late story, 'A Marriage', published in 1985, portrays a James who this time has married his Emmy. James is another of Lavin's professional males, so consumed by work that he is unable to take a day off. He fails to understand Emmy's desire for greater intimacy when she tells him: 'We could have taken better care of our love.'[38] This is in line with Anthony Clare's observation that women are often concerned about the quality of their married lives, whereas 'men appear quite content just to be married'.[39] James is unable to talk about his exhaustion or even admit that he needs help: Lavin's men sometimes behave as if illness and parenthood were women's issues or at least a sign of weakness. James displays all the symptoms of what George Yudice has called 'overresponsibility', involving feelings of being overworked and exhausted, but believing that no one else is capable of doing the job properly.[40] Such feelings are far from empowering, though the James of 'A Marriage' is portrayed more sympathetically than his predecessor in 'A Memory', an indication that by this time Lavin had thought more deeply about the pressures of men's professional lives.

If Lavin's middle-class male professionals adapt all too well to society's expectations, she also portrays men who do not fit easily into masculine stereotypes. In 'At Sallygap', a very Joycean story of impoverished Dublin lives, it is Annie who wants her husband, Manny (the diminutive is significant), to be more stereotypically male, even to the point of violence. If there was widespread silence in Ireland over the subject of men's domestic violence until the feminist movement got started in the 1970s, it was only in the 1990s that silence over domestic violence by women against men was broken by commentators such as John Waters in his columns in *The Irish Times*.[41] In 'At Sallygap', it is Annie who equates manliness with violence to women and children and Manny who fears Annie's future violence. In depicting Annie's longing for violent quarrels that might in some way make up for the passion that is missing in their sex life, Lavin is strangely prescient of later feminist work on female sexual fantasies that incorporate violence.[42] As Annie yearns for violence, Manny yearns for adventure. 'At Sallygap' is a story of male entrapment in the home and in a menial job that allows no time for reflection or the expansion of the soul that Manny finds briefly at Sallygap, looking down over the city. 'At Sallygap' was first published in 1943 but substantially revised by Lavin to make Manny less of a comic figure.[43] In the final version, Manny is tragic, not only because he cannot fulfil Annie's needs for a passionate relationship, but because he lives in a society that extols masculine physicality and makes men like himself, decent, hard-working, compassionate, if limited, feel inferior.

If the male character is distorted by the demands of celibacy on her priest characters and by relentless career demands on her middle-class professionals, it is economics that shapes the lives of her lower middle-class shopkeepers. Lavin's stories display sympathy for shopkeepers like Manny and the two Daniels in 'Posy' and the Grimes' sequence, trapped in an unvarying routine and repressed by women in the family. In 'Posy', Daniel Dogget's elder sisters and their firm awareness of their place in the social hierarchy of their town, dominate his life. Marriage is only appropriate in their eyes if it is for social advantage, to move up into the professional classes. The story turns on the irony that in his youth Daniel had the possibility of escape but since it was with their despised serving girl, Posy Mallow, he lacked the courage to resist his sisters' scorn. Unlike the young Mallows, reared in poverty in Meadow Lane, Daniel has not had the courage or the energy to make something of his life, remaining trapped in his sisters' sterile and snobbish view of life. Though the Mallows started life below the Doggets in social status, many of them have since prospered. Posy herself has done well enough to turn her son into someone Daniel recognizes as a member of the professional classes his sisters wanted him to marry into. The Mallows are associated with nature and energy whilst Daniel's name suggests a dogged pursuit of an unending daily round. Only at the end is there a momentary epiphany when Daniel transcends his environment and his own petty caution in a sudden impulse of generosity as he rejoices that Posy has escaped 'petty provincial existence' and flown to freedom. Unlike Bedelia Grimes in 'The Little Prince', a life of petty cares has not entirely dried up his heart.

Lavin is often more generous to her male than to her female characters and perhaps this is a residue of her relationship with her father. Women like Daniel's sisters and Bedelia Grimes are presented as rigid enforcers of social hierarchy and public opinion. In 'The Little Prince' (1956), Daniel is more humane than Bedelia, giving credit to people in need, despite Bedelia's objections. Starting out life as a shop boy, Daniel knows that he has been fortunate to marry Bedelia, the owner's daughter. Within the small room for manoeuvre granted to him, he has exercised some compassion, putting aside Tom's share of the profits each month. In middle age he understands the limited range of options that have been open to him. If he had left Grimes and Son, he acknowledges that he would likely have ended up behind a similar counter, 'probably in the same town'.[44]

Loyalty is often an attribute of Lavin's male characters: Jamey Morrow in 'A Gentle Soul' (1951) and Robert in 'A Happy Death' (1946) display both sensitivity and tenderness in their determined love of one woman. In portraying feminized male characters like Jamey and Robert, Lavin disrupts the conventional link between masculinity and power. In a sense Robert's desire to cling to his independence by continuing to work despite his fragile health arises out of a false pride in the fiction of the male breadwinner. Yet in another sense he is right to insist on working for at home he is gradually robbed of his self-worth by his wife, Ella, who runs a profitable lodging house and sneers at his paltry wages when he is demoted from assistant librarian to stockman. Being out of the house is necessary to Robert in ways Ella does not understand. Possessing less authority in the home than even his own children who have long since stopped calling him father, Robert has turned into a 'hollow-faced nonentity that stole apologetically in and out of the house, and ate his meals in the darkest corner of the kitchen'.[45]

Ella is obsessed with appearance of respectability. She married Robert for his feminine looks and, in an interesting reversal of gender stereotypes, it is his lost looks she most regrets. Gender stereotypes are further reversed when Ella wants Robert to give up work and help her, not by working alongside her, but by dressing in smart clothes and sitting on a bench outside in order to raise the tone of her boarding house. Treating her husband as an object of display and showing insensitivity to his need to have work of his own in order to enhance his self-esteem, Ella believes his looks will enhance her business. Robert's solipsistic love for her endures and allows him, in spite of all her ministrations, to have a happy death. Ella, however, never understands all she has missed by her concentration on money-making and rising in the world, and by refusing to share power within the home. Lavin's stories recognize that if public life empowers certain kinds of men, inside the home women like Bedelia and Ella have too much power. This in itself is a comment on the 1937 Constitution relegating women to home and family. What is needed, her stories imply, is a balance of power both in the home and in the workplace.

There is one Lavin story that seems to herald the 1990s 'new man'. In 'The New Gardener' (1962), Clem is a single father who works flexible hours in order to care for his four children and is tenderly considerate to all creatures and plants. Clem gives the kind of detailed care to his children, stopping work early to fetch them from school or to cook them a hot meal, that his society generally associates with women, a fact highlighted in the narrator's remark: 'if Clem was a good father, he was a still better mother'.[46] The story ends with Clem being taken away by detectives and the reader surmises that he has murdered his wife because of her physical abuse of their small daughter. Nevertheless, the strikingly modern portrayal of his abilities as a father remains.

Masculinity is constantly evolving. Many men nowadays base their definition of masculinity not on strength, aggression and dominance, but on the quality of their friendships and their relationships with partners and children.[47] In 1969, Lavin married her long-standing friend, Michael Scott, a former Jesuit priest. He features in several of her later stories as a cultured and educated priest. In 'The Lost Child' (1969), Father Hugh was prepared to take on board women's opinions on the teachings of the Catholic Church. In 'Happiness' (1968), Father Hugh is shown in domestic scenes surrounded by Vera's daughters drying their hair and clipping their nails while their mother runs out of the bathroom in her slip. He is described as first visiting them to help them through the death of their father but he ends up lavishing thwarted paternal love on Vera's daughters thus filling, the narrator explains, the 'cavity in his own life'.[48] The story reveals Lavin's continuing doubts over the celibate life. A profession, even that of a priest, cannot make up for the lack of a domestic life. 'Celibacy was never meant to take all the warmth and homeliness out of their lives' Vera insists.[49] Father Hugh is humanized by family life. He gains happiness from being with Vera's children and exercises almost maternal care in his relationship with Vera, worrying about her and preventing her from exhausting herself. His manliness is revealed not so much in his professional priestly role as in his domestic.

Lavin was arguably ahead of her time in portraying masculinities. In her short stories she displays awareness of the stress involved in the maintenance of the masculine façade. She recognizes male vulnerability and the pressure men come under to maintain their masculinity. Her writing reveals that masculinity is not just about men but about women's attitudes as well since women like Annie and Myra are portrayed as colluding in masculinist values. In 'The Widow's Son' (1946), the widow's harshness arises out of fear that in the absence of a male role model the neighbours will say that she has brought up her son to be soft. The widow knows what kind of masculinity her society expects and that it will be difficult for her son to survive if he is seen as coddled. Very much in line with Nancy Chodorow's later analysis, the widow represses her emotions and damages her relationship with her son in a bid to produce the type of man her society requires.

Lavin's male characters are often stoics who have learned to put up with things since, whether from choice or through economic circumstances, they have centred their lives and identity in the world of work. There are many different ways of being male in her work, from authoritarian priests to workaholic professionals, from steadfast but limited shopkeepers like Manny and Daniel, to caring father figures like Father Hugh. She describes men like Robert, Father Hugh and Clem, comfortable with expressions of intimacy, in ways generally excluded by traditional masculinities. By portraying varieties of masculinity in her work, Lavin complicates the stereotypes of Irish masculinity being propagated by church and state and challenges the notion that the world of paid work, still largely in the period when she was writing occupied by Irish men, is more valuable than the life of the home. By creating male characters who move between work and home,

Lavin's fiction contributes to a breaking down of public/private distinctions, as Woolf at the end of 'Three Guineas' imagines women and men working together to dismantle patriarchal structures of public life. Lavin portrays men as well as women struggling to protect the world of personal relationships against the tyranny of the world of work. By exposing contradictory ways of being male, her writing leaps over the feminist protests of the 1970s and 1980s to a postmodernist recognition of the fluidity of gender roles. If there are 'masculine' women in her work, like Bedelia, Ella, and Myra, there are also feminized males like Manny, Robert, Clem, and Father Hugh. In its destabilization of gender stereotypes and deconstruction of false dualisms between mind and body, culture and nature, masculinity and femininity, Lavin's work may be regarded as political in a way it rarely has in the past. Certainly her fiction displays a very modern recognition that men suffer from investing emotionally in their work to the detriment of friendships and family. Analysis of the portrayal of masculinities in her short stories reveals that valuing the personal, the intimate and the social is essential to what was a constant preoccupation of Lavin, namely how to achieve happiness.

Endnotes

1   A crisis in Irish masculinity has been acknowledged recently with concerns raised about high levels of aggression, poor communication skills, depression and suicide among young Irish men. Boys, particularly in single sex schools, were perceived to need help to improve their interpersonal and social skills and to be given a positive understanding of male roles. Fine Gael TD Brian Hayes called for a commission on the status of men and the government was sufficiently concerned to develop an Exploring Masculinities programme during 1997—98 in nineteen boys' schools. It ran into opposition, however, from parents concerned that the programme was not underpinned by Catholic values and from certain influential journalists who perceived a feminist agenda behind the programme. The programme was launched in 2000 but lost momentum because of these criticisms, see O. McCormack, 'Exploring Masculinities — The Sequel', PhD Thesis, University of Limerick, 2010. In literary criticism, Irish masculinities have begun to be studied in such works as B. Singleton's *Masculinities and the Contemporary Irish Theatre* (New York: Palgrave/Macmillan, 2011) and C. Magennis and R. Mullen (eds), *Irish Masculinities: Reflections on Literature and Culture*, (Dublin: Irish Academic Press, 2011). An earlier volume edited by E. Walshe, *Sex, Nation and Dissent in Irish Writing* (Cork, Cork University Press, 1997), looked at the way the privileging of a particular form of masculinist nationalism suppressed dissenting voices.

2   M. Kimmel, 'Masculinity as Homophobia: Fear, Shame and Silence in the Construction of Gender Identity', in H. Brod and M. Kaufman (eds), *Theorising Masculinities* (London: Sage Publications, 1994), p.120.

3   J. Butler, *Gender Trouble: Feminism and the Subversion of Identity* (New York and London: Routledge, 1990).

4   N. Chodorow, *The Reproduction of Mothering: Psychoanalysis and the Sociology of Gender* (Berkeley and Los Angeles: The University of California Press, 1978), p.181.

5   D. Dinnerstein, *The Rocking of the Cradle and the Ruling of the World* (London: Souvenir Press, 1978).

6   V. Woolf, *A Room of One's Own. Three Guineas*, M. Shiach (ed.), (Oxford: World's Classics, 1992), pp.49–50.

7   M. Kaufman, 'Men, Feminism, and Men's Contradictory Experiences of Power', in Brod and Kaufman (eds), *Theorising Masculinities*, p.148.

8   L. Segal, *Slow Motion: Changing Masculinities, Changing Men*, 3rd edition (New York: Palgrave/Macmillan, 2007), p.xxiv.

9   Kaufman, 'Men, Feminism', p.145.

10 L. Levenson, *The Four Seasons of Mary Lavin* (Dublin: Marino Books, 1998), p.43.

11 A. Clare, *On Men* (London: Chatto and Windus, 2000), p.177.

12 For the hyper-masculine Northern Irish male, see J. Jeffers, *The Irish Novel at the End of the Twentieth Century: Gender, Bodies, and Power* (New York and Basingstoke: Palgrave, 2002), p.25; G. Meaney, *Gender, Ireland, and Cultural Change: Race, Sex, and Nation* (New York: Routledge, 2010), pp.169–180; essays by J.W. Foster, M. Davey, N. Rea and K.A. Parson in Magennis and Mullen (eds), *Irish Masculinities*.

13 T. Brown, *Ireland: A Social and Cultural History, 1922–2002* (London: Harper Perennial, 2004), p.22.

14 M. Lavin, 'The Shrine', in *The Shrine and Other Stories* (London: Constable, 1977), p.31.

15 M. Lavin, 'A Woman Friend', in *The Stories of Mary Lavin, Volume 2* (London: Constable, 1974), p.182.

16 V.J. Seidler, *Unreasonable Men: Masculinity and Social Theory* (New York and London: Routledge, 1994), p.146.

17 Woolf, *A Room of One's Own. Three Guineas*, p.45.

18 Lavin, 'A Woman Friend', p.179.

19 M. Lavin, 'A Memory', in *A Memory and Other Stories* (London: Constable, 1972), p.162.

20 Seidler, *Unreasonable Men*, p.147.

21 Clare, *On Men*, p.1.

22 Lavin, 'A Memory', p.188.

23 Ibid., p.165.

24 Clare, *On Men*, p.8.

25 Lavin, 'A Memory', p.165.

26 Ibid., p.195.

27 Ibid., p.198.

28 Woolf, *A Room of One's Own. Three Guineas*, p.200.

29 Ibid., p.258.

30 Ibid., p.262.

31 Seidler, *Unreasonable Men*, p.148.

32 F. O'Connor, *The Lonely Voice: A Study of the Short Story* (Cork: Cork City Council, 2003), p.5.

33 O'Connor, *The Lonely Voice*, p.144.

34 Levenson, *The Four Seasons*, pp.138–42.

35 M. Lavin 'Love is for Lovers', in *Tales from Bective Bridge* (London: Faber and Faber, 2012), p. 95.

36 '… to express worth of any kind, whether intellectual or moral, by wearing pieces of metal, or ribbon, coloured hoods or gowns, is a barbarity which deserves the ridicule which we bestow upon the rites of savages'. Woolf, *A Room of One's Own. Three Guineas*, p.179.

37 M. Lavin, 'The Lucky Pair', in *In the Middle of the Fields and Other Stories* (London: Constable, 1967), p.43.

38 M. Lavin, 'A Marriage', in *A Family Likeness and Other Stories* (London: Constable, 1985), p.65.

39 Clare, *On Men*, p.82.

40 G. Yudice, 'What's a Straight White Man To Do?' in M. Berger, B. Wallis and S. Watson (eds), *Deconstructing Masculinity* (New York: Routledge, 1995), pp.267–83.

41 For example, J. Waters, 'Bending facts to prop up myths about male violence', *The Irish Times*, 7 January 2002. In 1997, Mary Cleary founded AMEN, a voluntary group that provides help to male victims of violence.

42 As recorded, for example, in N. Friday, *My Secret Garden: Women's Sexual Fantasies* (New York: Pocket Book, 1974).

43 A.A. Kelly, *Mary Lavin, Quiet Rebel: A Study of Her Short Stories* (Dublin: Wolfhound Press, 1980), pp.156–9.

44 M. Lavin, 'The Little Prince', in *In a Café. Selected Stories*, E. Walsh Peavoy (ed.) (Harmondsworth: Penguin, 1999), p.271.

45 M. Lavin, 'A Happy Death', in *The Stories of Mary Lavin, Volume 1* (London: Constable, 1964), p.187. 'A Happy Death' has echoes of 'The Will', based on the life of Lavin's favourite aunt who was thought to have married beneath her. Ella and Robert reappear as Lally and Robert in 'A Bevy of Aunts' (1985).

46 M. Lavin, 'The New Gardener', in *Happiness and Other Stories* (London: Constable, 1969), p.37.

47 See Clare, *On Men*, p.100.

48 Lavin, 'Happiness', in *Happiness and Other Stories*, p.10.

49 Ibid.

3 | Discontinuities: *Tales From Bective Bridge* and the Modernist Short Story

Anne Fogarty

The title of Mary Lavin's debut volume of short stories, *Tales from Bective Bridge*, published in 1943, is deliberately, even mischievously, deceptive.[1] It promises cohesive and interlocking stories located in an ascertainable provincial setting. Yet, it quickly transpires on reading the contents that the comforting demarcations and reassuringly rounded plots apparently heralded never materialize. Lavin's volume thus plays with notional expectations of the Irish short story and uses a seeming conventionalism to mask its singular and jarring nature. This essay sets out to investigate the contexts of Mary Lavin's experimentalism, to pinpoint and tease out aspects of her radical aesthetic, and to interpret and cross-connect the diverse, unsettling stories with their Gothic sub-currents that she included in her inaugural publication.

Lavin, it is well known, broke off a PhD dissertation at University College Dublin on Virginia Woolf to embark on a writing career. This doctoral work, it must be noted, was itself pioneering as it was undertaken in the late 1930s, a period at which criticism of Woolf was still in its beginnings.[2] As she herself described it, her first short story, 'Miss Holland' (1939), was written on the back of the discarded pages of her thesis.[3] This professional *volte-face* suggests that she began to find herself as a writer by pointedly abandoning her plans to investigate the fiction of Woolf. Symbolically, a breakage with the tradition of modernism and academe were necessary departure points for her own creativity. But she also disclosed that it was a chance conversation in which a woman talked about having had tea with Virginia Woolf that prompted her decision to take up writing.[4] The realization that the writer, however august, is not simply a figure apart but rather embedded in the casual everyday flow of life transforms her concept of the artistic vocation. The fact that her initial work was inscribed on the reverse of sections of her unfinished thesis intimates further that Woolf acted as a hidden motivating force and an abiding role model.

This essay will argue that Lavin at once departs from and carries forward aspects of the modernist experiment with the short story. In particular, she continues, whilst also making her own, the formal innovations of James Joyce, Katherine Mansfield, Anton Chekhov and Virginia Woolf. Her stories in *Tales from Bective Bridge* set out to jolt and discomfit the reader in the same manner as those in Joyce's *Dubliners*. But she veers away from Joyce's achievement in choosing a very different literary terrain, those precisely rendered aspects of Ireland that can be viewed from Bective, County Meath. A seemingly nondescript midlands milieu provides the envisaged fundament of Lavin's first endeavour at self-invention and at the staking out of a distinctive authorial domain. Even though the stories in her first volume stray across several different Irish locations which are often unspecified, they are nonetheless conjoined by the dislocating perspective of a woman writer who views things otherwise and seeks to capture facets of the stifling realities of mid-century Ireland and of an inhospitable provincial environment in a fresh and startling manner. Bective, it will be seen, acts at once as a cipher for Lavin's unflinching and often lacerating vision of Irish society and for the sphere of difference with which her writing concerns itself formally and thematically. In a manner akin to Dublin in Joyce's fiction, Bective in Lavin's writing designates a vividly apprehended world and the zone of the imagination in which she sites her distinctive and unsettling narratives. It is a reinvented Ireland at once familiar and utterly estranging.

Many accounts of Lavin's work define it by dint of what it omits. Frank O'Connor's influential but fundamentally uncomprehending assessment of her achievement described the unease her oeuvre caused in her male readership: 'An Irishman, reading the stories of Mary Lavin is actually more at a loss than a foreigner would be.'[5] The title of the final chapter of *The Lonely Voice*, 'The Girl at the Gaol Gate', in which he broached her writing pointedly positioned her as outside and ancillary to the normative male tradition with which his survey of the Irish short story concerns itself.[6] Even though he, like several other critics, pertinently noted her attempt to deal with 'life that goes on underground', he concentrated on what her fiction excluded, including most glaringly for him the nationalist struggle and the armed conflicts and political strife that had dominated life in the country during the War of Independence and the Civil War.[7] Lavin's interest in what he labelled the 'life of the kitchen', by contrast, seemed aberrant to him and exemplified the Otherness of the female author from which he self-evidently recoiled.[8] As my argument will show, O'Connor polemically overstated the degree to which Lavin deviated from the naturalism of the Irish short story in the mid-twentieth century or indeed from his own precepts that this form is a vehicle for the 'members of a submerged population' and for figures that are isolated from society.[9] The unassuageable loneliness that O'Connor pinpointed as a facet of the short story form is a marked characteristic of her tales. However, his hostility to Lavin may ultimately be deemed to stem from his rejection of modernism, a foundational premise of his study of the short story.[10] Those aspects of Lavin that make him uneasy are as much a result of her continuation of modernist techniques and concerns as with the feminist undercurrents of her work.

Picking up on some of O'Connor's recognitions, Augustine Martin, Declan Kiberd and Maurice Harmon also drew attention to the themes that Lavin eschewed and to her highlighting of domestic subject matter. However, they dealt more sympathetically with her work and were more successful at pinpointing its difference and perplexing energies. In his afterword to a reprinting of Lavin's second novel, *Mary O'Grady*, Martin cogently contended that her fiction as a whole is 'outrageously private', but akin to O'Connor he located the drama of her writing in 'domestic quotidian things' and in the 'humblest of events and objects.'[11] Kiberd, in his assessment of her writing, also observed that it refused the grand themes either of 'nation or of female destiny'.[12] Lavin, in his view, retreated to the subject of the family in her fictions as a means both of escaping social proprieties and of investigating issues that were repressed or papered over by the pieties and moral conventions overtly determining forms of social intercourse in the country. Perceptively, he observed that her fiction hinged on alternating moments of revelation and of secrecy and that her stories aimed to uncover structures of feeling rather than to show aspects of character. Yet, ultimately he deemed that her radicalism was muted as it was masked by the accommodations that she arrived at with the constrictions of Irish society. Maurice Harmon determined that moralism was the driving force of Lavin's work and that her stories, moreover, posited a correlation between character and style.[13] He argued further that the staging of momentous moral choices is a recurrent scenario in her fictions and that Lavin is centrally concerned with probing the values by which people live their lives and the ways in which they compromise their happiness and well-being. Lavin, in Harmon's view, emerged winningly as a low-key but dogged existentialist who closely scrutinized the values of the flawed protagonists she created.

The burden of this essay is that Mary Lavin is a more overtly radical writer than has regularly been discerned and that a different critical lens is necessary in order to excavate the patent tensions in her stories and to recognize the degree to which they breach taboos. The frequently iterated perception that she concentrates on feminine themes such as the domestic and the family tends to confirm the assumption that the stereotypically female qualities of gentility, circumspection and even quaintness are likewise characteristics of her work. Yet, in my eyes, it would be difficult to overstate the ferocity and jarring dissonances of her literary debut, *Tales from Bective Bridge,* and its merciless but invigorating energies. The accomplished and self-reflexive stories in this collection, deliberately play with modernist methods and preoccupations while also conjuring with and making over forms such as the folk tale and the fable associated with the Literary Revival and with late nineteenth-century Decadence. Lavin, moreover, in prolonging the artistic experimentalism of the early decades of the twentieth century may be aligned with what critics now dub 'intermodernism', a belated modernism that is practised by writers between the two world wars into the 1940s and 1950s and beyond, and takes on characteristics of its own.[14]

Even a brief rehearsal of the subject matter of these tales alerts us to their oddity and extremism: a family feud about the value of a dungheap ('Lilacs'); a *Liebestod* or death pact wherein a woman fatefully claims her right to be buried with her husband, thereby precipitating their joint drowning ('The Green Grave and the Black Grave'); the savage scapegoating and murder of a woman by her brothers who have connived in her prostitution and forced her to act as a servant to them and the three children she has borne out of wedlock ('Sarah'); a guileless, simple-minded monk who is cruelly kept from self-realization ('Brother Boniface'); a loveless marriage which turns out to be founded on hatred and sadomasochist urges ('At Sallygap'); the intertwining of bestiality, eroticism and predatory female power ('Love is for Lovers'); an amoral theft as a recompense for local hostility ('Say Could that Lad be I?'); a community fetishism for scarred female bodies ('A Fable'); a lonely spinster who moves to a boarding house following her father's death and is ostracized by the other lodgers; ('Miss Holland') and a mother terrified and physically disfigured by the ghost of her soldier son who died in the First World War ('The Dead Soldier'). This is a volume, in sum, in which Lavin self-consciously makes manifest the dangerous and unaccommodating nature of her art and also begins to realize the symbolic potential of a disruptive, free-floating subaltern and feminist point of view. The primitivist *élan* of her writing, moreover, sets it apart at once from the superstition and puritanism of Irish Catholic culture in the 1930s and from the hopeful beliefs of a secular humanism in the possibility of moral good and social accord. The fictional worlds that Lavin depicts are riven by conflict and never permit decorous endings or a neatly orchestrated closure.[15] The perpetual play of unruly and wayward recognitions is the basis of her discomfiting vision. The searing hold of devastating truths, moreover, rarely suffices to offset the engulfment that frequently awaits her figures.

In a letter to David Garnett on 26 July 1917, Virginia Woolf noted that one of her earliest short stories, 'The Mark on the Wall' (1917), was produced 'all in one flight', thus contrasting with the continuing toil of composing a novel.[16] Woolf is both accounting for the speed with which short fiction may be written and reflecting on the formal openness that attracted her to this mode. Her description of the experience of creating 'The Mark on the Wall' chimes with Lavin's oft-cited claim that the short story is an 'arrow in flight'.[17] Indeed, as this essay will propose there are many compelling intersections between Lavin's work and that of Woolf.[18] Lavin, it will be claimed, from her initial volume is intent on continuing, but also making her own of, modernist experiments with time and narrative form and on seeking to capture the quintessence of sentience and of everyday, lived experience. The anonymous female protagonist of 'The Mark on the Wall' considers how life is defined by its lack of coherence and by the objects we lose and discard. She reflects further:

> Why, if one wants to compare life to anything, one must liken it to being blown through the Tube at fifty miles an hour — landing at the other end without a single hairpin in one's hair! ... Tumbling head over heels in the asphodel meadows like brown paper parcels pitched down a chute in the post office! With one's hair flying back like the tail of a racehorse. Yes, that seems to express the rapidity of life, the perpetual waste and repair; all so casual, all so haphazard.[19]

The woman writer in Lavin's 'A Story with a Pattern' (1945) exhibits a similar insight into the chaos of existence. She gets embroiled in a quarrel with a disapproving male critic who laments the lack of substance in her work and refutes his views with a rueful account of the inchoate nature of life: 'Life has very little plot, I said. Life itself has a habit of breaking off in the middle.'[20] Akin to Woolf, Lavin is interested in the permutations and challenges of the plotless short story with its tendency to start and end *in medias res*.[21] Her fictions are never linear; instead, they are built around breaks, interruptions, digressions, reversals, gaps and incompletions. Woolf in her essay 'The Russian Point of View' (1925) attempted to pinpoint the distinguishing qualities of Chekhov's stories whose skill she admired and sought to emulate. She observed that his tales frequently trail off or culminate simply with a mystifying 'tone of interrogation'.[22] Lavin, in keeping with her affinity with modernist forebears such as Chekhov, Joyce and Woolf, introduces just such a note of interrogation into her works whereby meanings accrete but never cohere into stable patterns. Like Woolf, she is never simply interested in the arc of the story and more often than not dismantles or blocks it.[23] Hers is an aesthetic of disjunctions, incongruences, teasing ironies and tangents. Open-endedness and inconclusion are signatures of her narratives rather than consequential resolutions.

The Joycean notion of the epiphany is apposite for describing the dispersed and layered meanings that Lavin's stories set out to convey. Albeit often erroneously understood to mean insight, epiphany for Joyce actually had the opposite import and was associated initially with what he termed 'mere straws in the wind', little errors or gestures by which people betrayed what they intended to conceal.[24] Epiphany is thus a means of signposting but not fully articulating masked psychological realities. Joyce gradually evolved his theory of epiphany to encompass several conflicting forms, including moments of dramatic irony on the one hand, and of lyrical outpouring on the other. In all of its manifestations, complex meaning is caught in an oblique manner. While the epiphanies Joyce collected as an apprentice writer were purportedly vital snatches of reality, they are qualified by their elusiveness and their resistance to assuming any kind of narrative shape. Analogously, the climactic moments that intersperse and punctuate Joyce's *Dubliners* rarely issue in apprehensions that can easily be grasped or transmuted into convenient moral reckonings or rounded psychological disclosures. Lavin, it will be seen, inherits Joyce's techniques but gives them a peculiar stamp. The most crucial recognitions in her narratives are often a prelude to silence, negation and the muffling over of all reaction.

One of the signal ways in which Lavin's work intersects with that of her modernist predecessors is in its problematization of the self and its fascination with the vexed subject of inwardness. Woolf was particularly concerned in her novels and short fiction with conveying the elusive motions of the mind and with creating a sense of the immediacy and unstemmable flow of existence. However, the attempt to delve into emotions or to render inward states served only to underscore the intractability of the self. Thus, in 'An Unwritten Novel' (1920), a narrator inspired by the unhappy expression of a woman sitting opposite her on the train projects her story and imagines her to be impoverished, lonely, childless and cruelly rejected by a lover.[25] At the end of the journey, however, she discovers that her inventions about Minnie Marsh and the fickle James Moggridge have been entirely wrong, as the woman is met by her adult son with whom she engages in amicable conversation. The story retrospectively is shown to be a fantasia that allowed us to follow the flow of thought of the narrator but that brought us no closer to knowing the inner promptings of the self or to fathoming the life of a fellow traveller.[26] At one point the narrator ponders on the nature of interiority: 'But when the self speaks to the self, who is speaking?'[27] She contends in response that what we perceive when self-communing is 'the entombed soul, the spirit driven in, in, in to the central catacomb; the self that took the veil and left the world'.[28] It is this entombed self, banished from the world, that seems particularly to fascinate Mary Lavin. She exploits the liminal perspectives of the radically disempowered or uses a dislocating female vision in order to sketch out forms of estrangement that issue in death or ever more privatized forms of inwardness.[29] The individual is indivisible from society in her stories and the self is knowable only if viewed in correlation with counter-selves. The nondescript provincial lives that Lavin depicts may be seen as mirroring the insular and inward-looking nature of Irish society under Éamon de Valera. Conceived in this manner, her work appears to be impelled by a naturalist impetus and also to be concerned with delineating and critiquing the values of conservative Irish families and communities through its pointedly placed ironies.[30] However, her texts always exceed these objectives, especially to the degree that they evince an experimental focus on states of diminution and relinquishment. Her stories centre less on individuals than on attenuated selves and regularly fasten on voided scenes that become increasingly subjectless. Negation, silence and absurdity are as much fundaments of her writing as of that of Samuel Beckett.

'Lilacs' (1942), the opening narrative of *Tales from Bective Bridge*, establishes many of the techniques and preoccupations of the volume as a whole. Lavin's singular vision is at once evident in the rapid mutations of the central images, the unexpected leaps and tangents in the plot and the degree to which the key subjects fuse with their social world or are blotted out from view at important junctures. The sentimental title stands in ironic apposition to the central subject of the story: dungheaps. Startlingly, from the initial sentence, excrement is established as the overriding theme. Lavin daringly constructs a vision of a family that centres not on harmony but on ordure. The malodorous manure, which is the mainstay of Phelim Mulloy's farmyard business, is counterposed to the prospect of the sweet-smelling lilacs for which his wife, Ros, and daughters, Kate and Stacy, long. The latter unite in their passive opposition to the dungheaps and variously express their disapproval of their stench. Stacy's headaches and refusal to leave her bed on delivery days concretize their feminine resistance to what is seemingly a male imposition. Phelim's stubbornness and refusal to relinquish his patriarchal sway over them are as much a source of his daughters' condemnation as the piles of dung amassed outside the windows of their home.

Yet, Lavin subtly shifts grounds throughout the narrative, drawing out the complexity of this family conflict and upturning our assumptions about its nature. The dung, which initially appears to betoken the oppressiveness of material reality, economic necessity and male authority, also becomes an index of hidden emotion, the lyricism of the natural world, human desire, and the peculiar erotic bond between Ros and Phelim Mulloy. Phelim's sudden death prompts Ros to recall the circumstances of their courtship and to recollect his poetic account of how he used to drive around the countryside in his father's trap and relish looking down at the 'gold rings of dung dried out by the sun, as they flashed past underneath the horses' hooves'.[31] She correlates his love of dung with his physicality and opposition to the prurience of those around him. In this light, his daughters' discountenancing of his way of life is revealed to have its basis in snobbery and to result from their weak-willed acceptance of a code of shame rooted in a dubious denial of the realities of the material world and bodily existence. Lilacs, flowers usually associated with springtime renewal, hence take on an inverted meaning. Though they act throughout as a floating signifier for the ineluctable nature of female desire, they also acquire a decidedly unpoetic cast by contrast with the vividly described dung. In characteristic fashion, Lavin's guiding metaphors are charged with ambivalence.

If the male vigour of Phelim's enterprising way of life is preferred to the insubstantiality of female dreams of lilacs, the decision to abide by his principles appears nonetheless to exact a price. While the dung is used to enrich the roses in the gardens of middle-class women, Rose herself is restyled Ros by him and shorn of her bloom and expectations. The 'pink dog-roses' of the country laneway in which Phelim courted her cede to the unseen flowers raised in small-town gardens.[32] The acceptance of a second-order existence devoted to the maintenance of the lives of others involves a relinquishment. Fulfilment is dogged by lack. In one of the several swerves away from the initial conflict between a man and his wife and daughters that the story undertakes, the spotlight moves to Ros' life as a widow. In a *volte-face*, she determinedly pursues her husband's business but simultaneously wastes away under the force of her grief. The manure heaps now become a bone of contention between herself and her daughters who view her all-consuming devotion as misplaced. The dungheap re-assumes its resonance as an emblem of patriarchy and has furthermore acquired a malign force as it appears to drain Ros of life and to precipitate her demise. After Ros' death, the conflict stages itself anew as a dyadic struggle between the two sisters, Stacy's airy romanticism being played off against Kate's self-serving pursuit of marriage. Neither vision of the world is ultimately vindicated, although Kate's greed and materialist exploitation of sexuality are shown to be necessary survival skills. Stacy, who assumes sole possession of the family home, is reminded by the local solicitor in the final lines of the story that, notwithstanding her dream of a fragrant garden, she needs the dunghills to survive. Her response is unrecorded as, in the manner of such charged epiphanies in modernist narratives, meaning is simply evacuated at this juncture. Stacy's point of view is suspended and rendered null; the female desire for which the lilacs have acted as vehicle has been finally obliterated.

The following story continues the subversive reimagining of traditional female roles undertaken in 'Lilacs' and the concomitant questioning of conservative views of sexuality. 'The Green Grave and the Black Grave' (1940), the most experimental tale in the volume, suggestively reworks the denouements of J.M. Synge's *Riders to the Sea* (1904) and *The Playboy of the Western World* (1907). It is composed in a rhythmic language designed to replicate the motion of waves and of west of Ireland speech patterns. Implicitly, this language too is an example of *écriture feminine* and an embodiment of the contrary energies that fuel Lavin's writing. The body of Eamonn Buidhe Murnane is discovered by island fishermen at the start of the story. The physical exertions needed to load his body into their boat and then to drag it ashore render plastic the starkness of death. 'The live glitter of the dead eyes' of the corpse distresses his rescuers and obliquely alerts us to the Gothic elements of this tale.[33] Eamonn Buidhe, contrary to the custom of island men, we learn, has taken an inland wife who is seen as alien and disruptive of local ways. The savage intensity of their liaison is depicted as the conjoining of two violently opposed worlds. Their warring union is particularly borne out by their clashing attitudes towards death. Eamonn Buidhe, in keeping with his culture, longs for death in the green grave of the sea, while she prefers the prospect of burial in the black grave of clay on land. She disparages the virginal isolation of the green grave that he seeks and declares that 'the black grave is for lovers'.[34] For her, eros and death are intertwined. Despite their denunciations of her, the uncanny potency of the inland woman is recognized by the islandmen who note that she seems to borrow her power from the elements and even to exert control over the sea itself.

Having dragged the body on land, the men go in search of Eamonn Buidhe's wife in order to tell her of his death and to force her to accept the role of widow as dictated by tradition. They assume uneasily that she has indirectly got her way as her husband's corpse has been reclaimed from the sea and must be buried on land. But they are foiled in their efforts to dragoon her for widowhood as she is not to be found and the body too disappears from the shore. We discover in the final paragraph that Eamonn Buidhe has got the death he sought but only after a fashion, as he is 'held fast in the white arms of his one-year wife, who came from the inlands, where women have no knowledge of the sea but only a knowledge of love'.[35] The iconic grief and fatalistic suffering of Maurya at the end of Synge's *Riders to the Sea* are cancelled out here. Likewise, Pegeen Mike's loss of Christy Mahon at the close of *The Playboy of the Western World* is suggestively re-scripted. The female protagonist in Lavin's tale is no longer a foil to the dead or absconded male figures through whom she is defined. Nor is she forced to do the work of mourning on their behalf. The Otherness of erotic love as envisioned by a woman is fully and disturbingly realized in the unexpected ending. The demonic energy of the inland woman's possessive love is eerily captured in the image of their drowned bodies caught in an everlasting embrace. Lavin leaves her readers with a disquietingly ambivalent scene redolent of the destructive force of the female vision that impelled it. The pointed reversal of well-known scenes in Synge's canonical plays effected by this resolution also advertises the revolutionary force of the feminist counter-aesthetic that Lavin implicitly articulates in her inaugural publication.

'Sarah' also deals with a taboo subject in foregrounding a protagonist who upsets conventional expectations of female propriety. Like several other tales in *Tales from Bective Bridge*, it is a study in impersonality, a formalist technique counterpointing its key themes of primitive passion and savage retribution. Sarah Murray, the central figure, is an unmarried woman who engages freely in sexual liaisons and has had three children outside of marriage. She becomes pregnant a fourth time in the course of the tale by Oliver Kedrigan, whose wife has engaged her as a housekeeper. In response, her brothers throw her out of her home and she dies in a ditch along with the baby to whom she has given birth. The details of Sarah's life prior to the events of the story are unceremoniously announced in the opening paragraph, thus brusquely bypassing the Catholic sensibilities that would have objected to such subject matter. Indeed, in an ironic gesture towards the reigning pieties in Ireland in the 1940s, Sarah is represented as winning the acceptance of her fellow villagers because of her exemplary domestic skills and her religious devotion.

The unfolding of the story depends on unexplained gaps and blanks, the overriding omission being an elaboration of Sarah's views on events. Her struggles and her sexual freedom can be intuited but they are never made explicit. Similarly, her domination by her brothers who force her to keep house for them and her children is not elucidated, merely recounted with glacial impartiality. Female subjugation to the point of enslavement is depicted as a matter of course in this merciless community. A veil is drawn over the circumstances of her fourth pregnancy by Oliver Kedrigan, and the reasons as to why it should be seen by her brothers as a greater *contretemps* than all of the previous ones are also occluded. Through carefully weaving together these ellipses, Lavin skilfully renders resonant the silences that subtend her story.[36] Kedrigan is linked with masculinist control of the natural world as borne out by the 'forty lambing ewes' that he is in charge of and the 'predatory vixen' that is he is planning to tackle.[37] He is attracted to Sarah's vitalism which contrasts with his wife's pallor and her inability to bear children. The ambiguous animal sexuality that allures him to her is captured obliquely in his clumsy comparison of her red complexion to the raddle that he uses to mark his sheep. This ruddiness acts at once as a sign of Sarah's difference and of her victimization.

Her Otherness marks her out as a scapegoat in this village in which untrammelled female sexuality, even though superficially tolerated, is in actuality ostracized. Her brothers confront her in relation to this pregnancy, it would appear, because it came about through a sexual assignation that was not arranged by them. It is intimated that they had connived in her prostitution in the case of all the earlier pregnancies. In the final lines, Sarah's death is triumphantly reported on by her rival, the now pregnant Kathleen Kedrigan, who relates that she was found 'dead as a rat' in the ditch alongside her baby.[38] Sarah herself is an aporia at the end of this narrative. Her angered responses to Oliver Kedrigan's leering overtures and her brothers' accusations are noted. But she vanishes from the plot after she has been physically dragged by her older brother from the family home. Her interiority and the anguish of her final night fall outside the boundaries of the story. Their censored weight gives traction to the narrative, even though the reader can never succeed in fully piecing together the buried biography of this tragic heroine who so completely defies the norms of Irish society. Lavin's readers are enjoined to become attuned to these silences and to interpret the gaps in her narratives. 'Sarah', furthermore, exemplifies the author's subversion of the cohesiveness of the single-effect story, as it constantly redirects our attention between the empowered actions of the heroine, the growing vindictiveness of the villagers, a half-glimpsed rural primitivism, the unstable relationship of the Kedrigans, the embattled, sickly pregnancy of Kathleen Kedrigan, and the Murray brothers' possessive and ultimately murderous manipulations of their household and their sister's sexuality. The epiphany at the end of the narrative is, as a consequence, layered and its ironies manifold. Kedrigan's angry request that his wife give him the raddle is laden with ambiguity. It hints both that he feels a continuing bond with the outlawed and flagrantly amoral Sarah and that the brutal male prerogative to violently dominate women still holds full sway.

Disjunctiveness is also a feature of 'At Sallygap' (1941) and 'The Dead Soldier' (1942), which both wholly overturn sacrosanct Irish institutions — marriage and maternity — while expertly confounding the narrative expectations that they initially build up. They uncover the forms of alienation that characterize modern life and show these to be features as much of rural as of urban existence. Above all, they lay bare the disaffection of the female characters and reveal this to be all-consuming and unmitigated. Female hysteria and imbalance are pivotal in both these stories and become the foundations of Lavin's radical aesthetic. 'At Sallygap' appears initially to be a Joycean story centring on the paralysis of Dublin, the 'indistinct city' in which Manny Ryan, who has traded the prospect of a career as a musician in Paris for a safely domesticated marriage to Annie and life as a shopkeeper, feels trapped.[39] However, during a brief business trip to Sallygap, which he turns into a pallid soul-searching excursion, Manny seems to reach a fatalistic accommodation with his narrow existence. He determines that occasional outings to the country will compensate for his sense of privation.

His quietism is, however, blown apart when, in an unforeseen shift, Lavin refocalizes the narrative around Annie, thus abruptly relocating her story beyond the limits of the male-centred, Joycean tale that she had apparently been imitating. Spurred by Manny's uncharacteristic absence, Annie's lurid and erotically charged fantasies, in which she delightedly refashions her timid husband as an abusive alcoholic or envisages his suicide by drowning, entirely scotch the bourgeois belief that marriage and the home can be places of accommodation or fulfilment. Further, her perverse longing for violence and excited elicitation of the horror of his 'sodden corpse, white and hideously swollen' unflinchingly expose the sadomasochistic underpinnings of their relationship.[40] Deviant sexual desires rather than romantic rural dreams are indicated to be at the heart of a modern Irish marriage and to typify Annie's disturbingly histrionic projections. Exposed to his wife's taunts and cruelty on his return home, Manny sees himself ultimately as 'imprisoned forever in her hatred'.[41] Like Mathew Simmins in 'Love is for Lovers' (1942), he appears to accept the narrowing-in of his existence and the sacrificial diminution of self that it entails, but Lavin, in averting to the words of his wife that he has failed to register in the final sentences, redirects our attention to the unspeakable femininity that has rent a gaping hole in this tale.

'The Dead Soldier', a hybrid text that conflates the modernist ghost story with a traditional folk tale about the spectral return of a beloved, also centres on an uncanny femininity which is revealed at the denouement and reverses the initial premises of this text about the unswerving nature of maternal love and the ritualistic devotion to death in traditional Irish society. The unnamed old woman in the story, who has lost her son in the First World War, keeps a lonely and eerie vigil for him beside the hearth on All Soul's Night. Her confident expectation of his ghostly return converts to horror at an unnamed vision that assaults her during the night. Even though retrospectively the narrative scotches any Gothic intimations as the ghost is discovered to have been a neighbour who looked through the window in response to the light he saw there, this merely reinforces the sense of the inexplicable. Fear and love are revealed to be adjacent emotions in this story. The old woman's face has become permanently twisted into a grotesque mask, we learn, as a result of her conjuration of her son. Her horrified grimace, which turns her face into a skull, signifies all the unspeakable subjects averted to but never wholly articulated in the narrative. Encompassed in this uncanny domain are the horror of war, the violent demise of the soldier son, the nullity of death and the unappeasable nature of female and specifically maternal desire. In keeping with the indeterminacy of Lavin's modernist tales, the ghost of the son hovers between meanings and is represented severally as a figment or non-event, a deep-seated aspect of the primitive yearnings of this grieving mother and the *horror vacui* that typifies contemporary life.

'Miss Holland', the first story that Lavin composed, may be seen partly as an artistic manifesto, as well as the representation of an attenuated persona who gradually realizes the extent of her isolation from those around her and disappears in the final lines into an even more all-enveloping solitariness. The unflinchingness with which Agnes Holland 'takes one good, hard look'[42] at the fellow boarders who have shocked her with their coarse vulgarity epitomizes the flinty imagination at the core of Mary Lavin's inaugural volume of short stories, with its daring expression of taboo themes, its foregrounding of violent and sexually insubordinate female figures, its experimentation with impersonality and subjectless selves, such as Ros Mulloy, Brother Boniface, Sarah Murray, the inland woman and Mathew Simmins, and its critical perspectives on a modern Ireland in which the boundaries between the provincial village, the country and the city are purposefully blurred. *Tales from Bective Bridge* is anything but a gauche debut; it knowingly draws upon and extends the arsenal of techniques of the modernist short story as practised by James Joyce, Virginia Woolf and Katherine Mansfield such as the epiphany, ellipses, indeterminacy, fragmentation, plural and ramifying plot structures and ambiguously trailing endings. In these stories, Lavin skilfully orchestrates oscillating themes and captures the flux, negation and savagery that are central to her apprehension of the world. In *Tales from Bective Bridge*, Lavin claims a space for herself in the international literary tradition of the short story and announces herself as an Irish feminist intermodernist whose multifaceted work is distinctive, exacting and driven by an unrelenting ferocity.

Endnotes

1   M. Lavin, *Tales from Bective Bridge* (1943; Dublin: Poolbeg Press, 1978).

2   R. Gruber wrote the first PhD on Woolf in the US in 1932 which she subsequently published under the title, *Virginia Woolf: The Will to Create as a Woman* (1935; New York: Carroll and Graf, 2005).

3   See L. Levenson, *The Four Seasons of Mary Lavin* (Dublin: Marino Books, 1998), pp.47–49.

4   Levenson, *The Four Seasons*, p.48.

5   F. O'Connor, *The Lonely Voice: A Study of the Short Story* (London: Macmillan, 1965), p.203.

6   Ibid., pp.202-13.

7   Ibid., p.207.

8   Ibid., p.211.

9   Ibid., p.28.

10 For an account of O'Connor's hostility to modernism, see A. Hunter, *The Cambridge Introduction to the Short Story in English* (Cambridge: Cambridge University Press, 2007), pp.105–7.

11 A. Martin, 'Afterword', *Mary O'Grady* (1950; London: Virago Press, 1986), p.389.

12 D. Kiberd, *Inventing Ireland: The Literature of the Modern Nation* (London: Jonathan Cape, 1995), p.409.

13 M. Harmon, 'Mary Lavin: Moralist of the Heart', in B. Hayley and C. Murray (eds), *A Bountiful Friendship: Literature, History and Ideas* (Gerrards Cross: Colin Smythe, 1992), pp.107–23.

14 See K. Bluemel (ed.), *Intermodernism: Literary Culture in Mid-Twentieth-Century Britain* (Edinburgh: Edinburgh University Press, 2011). For a definition of intermodernism, see especially 'Introduction', pp.1–18.

15 Evelyn Conlon notes that one hallmark of Lavin's stories is her capacity to 'almost shrug off the drama of the situation'. See 'Introduction' in *Tales From Bective Bridge* (London: Faber and Faber, 2012), p.ix.

16 N. Nicolson (ed.), *The Question of Things Happening: The Letters of Virginia Woolf, Volume 2: 1912–1922* (London: Hogarth Press, 1979), p.167.

17 Lavin restated this perception variously throughout her life. For one formulation of this idea, see Levenson, *The Four Seasons*, p.54.

18 For instructive discussions of the links between Woolf and Lavin, see H. Ingman, *A History of the Irish Short Story* (Cambridge: Cambridge University Press, 2009), pp.170–71 and K. Laing, 'Virginia Woolf in Ireland: A Short Voyage Out', *The South Carolina Review*, 34, 1 (2001), pp.180–7.

19 V. Woolf, 'The Mark on the Wall', in S. Dick (ed.), *A Haunted House: The Complete Shorter Fiction* (London: Vintage, 2003), p.78.

20 M. Lavin, 'A Story with a Pattern', in E. Walsh Peavoy (ed.), *In a Café* (Dublin: Town House, 1995), pp.205–6.

21 On the distinction between plotted and plotless short stories, see C. Hanson, *Short Stories and Short Fictions 1880–1980* (London: Macmillan, 1985), pp.1–33.

22 V. Woolf, 'The Russian Point of View', in A. McNeillie (ed.), *The Essays of Virginia Woolf, Volume 4 1925–1928* (London: Hogarth Press, 1994), p.184.

23 On the dynamism of Woolf's stories and her utilization of strategies of interruption and fragmentation, see C. Reynier, *Virginia Woolf's Ethics of the Short Story* (London: Palgrave Macmillan, 2009), pp.36–59.

24 For an account of Joyce's evolving descriptions of epiphany, see A.W. Litz, 'Introduction', in R. Ellmann, A.W. Litz and J. Whittier-Ferguson (eds), *Poems and Shorter Writings: Including Epiphanies, Giacomo Joyce and 'A Portrait of the Artist'* (London: Faber, 1991), pp.159–160. For more extensive analyses of the multivalency of the epiphany and of the ambiguous and conflicting artistic forms it assumes, see M. Beja, *Epiphany in the Modern*

Novel (London: Peter Owen, 1971) and D. Head, 'James Joyce: The Non-Epiphany Principle', in *The Modernist Short Story: A Study in Theory and Practice* (Cambridge: Cambridge University Press, 2009), pp.37–78.

25 V. Woolf, 'An Unwritten Novel', in *A Haunted House*, pp.106–115.

26 Gillian Beer contends that Woolf endeavours to break down notions of the 'I' and the 'We' and to realize in their stead forms of impersonality and communality. See G. Beer, 'The Body of the People: *Mrs Dalloway* to *The Waves*', in *Virginia Woolf: The Common Ground. Essays by Gillian Beer* (Edinburgh: Edinburgh University Press, 1996), pp.48–73.

27 Woolf, 'An Unwritten Novel', p.114.

28 Ibid., p.114.

29 On liminality as a prominent feature of women writers' remoulding of the modernist short story, see C. Drewery, *Modernist Short Fiction by Women: The Liminal in Katherine Mansfield, Dorothy Richardson, May Sinclair and Virginia Woolf* (Farnham, Surrey: Ashgate, 2011).

30 For a suggestive account of Lavin's early volumes of short stories, which proposes that they undermine the realism of which they make use, see C. Wills, 'Women Writers and the Death of Rural Ireland: Realism and Nostalgia in the 1940s', *Éire-Ireland*, 41, (Spring/Summer 2006), pp.192–212.

31 M. Lavin, 'Lilacs', in *Tales from Bective Bridge*, p.21.

32 Ibid.

33 M. Lavin 'The Green Grave and the Black Grave', in *Tales from Bective Bridge,* p.43.

34 Ibid., p.46.

35 Ibid., p.57.

36 On the similar importance of silence in Virginia Woolf's fictions, see P. Ondek Laurence, *The Reading of Silence: Virginia Woolf in the English Tradition* (Stanford: Stanford University Press, 1991).

37 M. Lavin, 'Sarah', in *Tales from Bective Bridge*, p.60.

38 Ibid., p.68.

39 M. Lavin, 'At Sallygap', in *Tales from Bective Bridge*, p.91.

40 Ibid., p.108.

41 Ibid., p.113.

42 M. Lavin, 'Miss Holland', in *Tales from Bective Bridge*, p.188.

4 | Theatrical Trends in Mary Lavin's Early Stories

Giovanna Tallone

In her portrayal of the Irish middle classes, Mary Lavin sheds light on the often cruel impositions social conventions cast on sensitive characters. Manny in 'At Sallygap' (1941), Lally in 'The Will' (1944), and Rose in 'A Gentle Soul' (1951) are victims of a restrictive society based on materialism and class differences. In a world in which social hierarchy, class and family relationships act as determining forces, everyone must take up a fixed role. The shopkeepers, farmers and widows that are given voice in her stories are conscious of their place in society, and of the part they have to play.[1] Widowed and unmarried women alike in stories like 'In a Café' (1960), 'In the Middle of the Fields' (1961) or 'A Single Lady' (1951) are expected to act according to their social position, and in 'The Nun's Mother' (1944), Mrs Latimer wonders if she is to take up a new role now that her daughter Angela has entered the convent:

> Would she perhaps be obliged to assume an attitude? Expected to dress differently? More discreetly? To give up smoking? ... To put holy pictures even in her *downstairs* rooms? ... to punctuate her conversations with pious little tags like 'God willing', 'Thanks be to God' and 'God between us and all harm'?[2]

The assumption of roles within a restrictive social context is a recurring motif in Lavin's stories and within her realistic portrayal of Ireland a *fil rouge* of theatricality can be detected. In some stories of the 1940s, in particular, Lavin exploits the narrative situation of performing and role-playing to draw attention to the marginal position of women in a patriarchal society. These performances involve sensitive and lonely characters, who are unable to face life or to find their own place in life, and thus hope to gain a new or accepted identity in the role they assume. At the same time, however, the polarity between spectator and participant forms a recurring narrative pattern in these stories, ranging from a visual process of watching to the assumption of roles in a virtual or real performance.

In terms of stylistic devices and narrative organization, Mary Lavin's vivid use of description — in a way similar to stage design or stage directions — and of dialogue marks the intersection of drama and fiction. In some early stories, in addition, Lavin produces theatrical effects through narrative situations built around rehearsals, performances, and impersonations. An implicit theatrical effect also characterizes stories with a more openly oral quality, like 'The Green Grave and the Black Grave' (1940), in which dialogue and third-person narration reproduce the rhythm of the Anglo-Irish language.[3] Likewise, 'A Likely Story' (1957) is marked by patterns of oral storytelling[4] and its opening paragraph exploits a traditional formula: 'Once upon a time there was a widow who had one son. He was her only son: her only joy. His name was Packy'.[5] In the interaction between fiction and drama, 'dialogue scenes convincingly reveal the main character' while the structural elements of oral storytelling are reiterated by the use of repetitions and direct invocations of the reader.[6] An apostrophe like 'Do you know Bective?' suggests oral storytelling as ritual and performance in the interplay between public storyteller and audience.

The theatrical features of Lavin's fiction are also hinted at by Evelyn Conlon in her introduction to the 1996 reissue of *Tales from Bective Bridge*:

> Reading a collection of Mary Lavin can take a long time. The reader needs to take breaths, because quite often, days after reading the story, you realise that your original view was in fact only a minor part of what was going on. Quite like a play in which the action takes place before you, but the nuances take place later.[7]

The theatrical dimension of Lavin's stories does not just lie in stylistic features, such as dramatic dialogue or oral storytelling, but also in the explicit or implicit theatrical situations that mark a number of her stories. Theatricality is here understood in a very general sense, as relating to the theatre, being set in or around a theatre, or evoking theatrical situations. Thus, both thematic elements and formal aspects of Lavin's stories suggest a crossover of genres and highlight the nature of the short story as 'a mixed mode ... which most of the time blends the narrative and the dramatic form', so that stories can bear 'a formal resemblance with the script of a play.'[8]

Some early Lavin stories in particular are built around performances and impersonations. 'Miss Holland' (1939), 'Fogger Halt' (1944), and 'The Becker Wives' (1946) offer narrative situations in which the theatre plays an important role, from veiled references to role-playing in 'Miss Holland', over the dramatic element of impersonation in 'The Becker Wives', to the more explicit presence of a theatre, play and actors in 'Fogger Halt'. In all three stories, moreover, characters alternate between being spectators or actors. This interchange is presented as both a process of self-discovery and a form of persecution, since society is felt to dictate a role, whether old and established, or new and original.

'Miss Holland', 'Fogger Halt', and 'The Becker Wives' have other features in common as well: each story revolves around a female character who has to take up or interpret a role in order to survive in a hostile environment. Playacting in these stories is shown to be either a way of assuming a new role and identity, as in 'Miss Holland', or a way of escaping from one's identity and the monotony of everyday life, as in 'The Becker Wives' and 'Fogger Halt'.[9] Each of the protagonists in these stories might say, as Charlotte does in 'Fogger Halt': 'Do you not understand how I feel? I am shut up here like a prisoner'.[10] The characters seek a temporary way out of the trap of loneliness in performances, yet these are revealed in the end as only another form of claustrophobia.[11]

In 'Miss Holland', 'Fogger Halt', and 'The Becker Wives', the motifs of theatre and performance both sustain the psychological and social analysis at the heart of the stories and highlight Lavin's aesthetic principle of 'looking closer than normal into the human heart'.[12] This emphasis on detailed observation finds particular expression in these stories as they all develop around the act of perception. This is evident already in Lavin's first story, 'Miss Holland', which Seamus O'Sullivan, the editor of *The Dublin Magazine*, praised for 'its delicate restraints' in the portrait of a lonely, unmarried, middle-aged woman who has come down in the world.[13] Grown up in respectable gentility, Agnes Holland is a victim of her own social class. As a dutiful and submissive daughter, she has 'always stood aside', leaving decisions in everyday life to her father.[14] She has spent her life believing in art and beauty, but is totally ignorant of the more brute realities of life. After the death of her father, Miss Holland strives in vain to adapt herself to her reduced circumstances and to her new life in a lodging house where she 'tries desperately to be accepted' and loved.[15] She endeavours to overcome the barriers of class and her own shy disposition by taking up a role that is not hers, preparing and rehearsing a script with which to participate in the lodgers' conversation at mealtimes. The working-class background of the other lodgers, their coarse language and bad manners both attract and repel her — 'Oh, they were a lively bunch!' — and she finds herself busy studying them, becoming a spectator to their lives.[16]

From this point of view, the story recalls 'Miss Brill' (1920) by Katherine Mansfield, a writer Mary Lavin always admired and whose influence she often acknowledged.[17] Both Miss Holland and Miss Brill are lonely spinsters who try to turn their mediocre lives into acceptable fictions. Every Sunday Miss Brill goes to a park to listen to a band and to watch the people around her. At first she eavesdrops, 'listening as though she didn't listen, ... sitting in other people's lives just for a minute while they talked around her'.[18] Then, in her inner monologue, the real world becomes a stage as Miss Brill indulges in the fiction of reality: 'Oh, how fascinating it was! How she enjoyed it! How she loved sitting there, watching it all! It was like a play. It was exactly like a play. Who would believe the sky at the back wasn't painted?'[19] Miss Brill then comes to believe she has 'a part' in this play as well and she imagines herself 'an actress' for the 'old invalid gentleman to whom she read the newspaper four afternoons a week'.[20]

Like Miss Brill, Miss Holland is also a spectator who wishes to somehow be part of the show going on in front of her — that is, the other lodgers' conversation. In her perception of the other lodgers, fiction and reality overlap as Miss Holland tries to read the new world around her through the familiar lens of drama: 'They were such real men, not like some of her cousins who would deceive anyone when they played the female lead in Gilbert and Sullivan!'[21] Miss Holland's role as a spectator is introduced at the beginning of the story with recurring references to the act of looking — 'She saw [the cat]', 'the house seemed comfortable', 'the lady looked clean'[22] — and it is ultimately also the sight of the neighbours' cat that makes her decide to take the room.

When she finally enters her new home, the landlady's act of 'opening the door' is presented as a sort of curtain raising, disclosing the setting of her new life with the full apparatus of stage props. Miss Holland 'looked around the room', which will later set the stage for her rehearsals of the new parts she wants to play.[23] Wallpaper, counterpane, armchair, fireplace with its mantelshelf, all are examined in the detailed list of stage directions. When she turns her head to 'the view from the window', she is again a spectator watching the scene in the gardens outside, and when dinner time comes, impressions move from the visual to the aural: 'she heard voices ... in the room below'.[24] The voices are offstage, and they are not only a realistic detail of the arrival of the other lodgers, but anticipate the recurring motif of the 'babble of voices', which later becomes a 'babel of voices', clearly marking Miss Holland's position as an outsider, socially and emotionally.[25] Her wish 'to be included' never leaves her as 'Night after night she listened to the talk at supper time, and more and more she felt she'd never enter more fully into [the conversation] than by giving vigorous nods of her head.'[26]

Imprisoned in her own silence, Miss Holland looks for a script that can transform her from spectator into actress. Her lack of appropriate linguistic and communicative skills was already hinted at in the beginning of the story, where she is shown not to be 'adept at asking the kind of questions that would elicit facts necessary for finding out if a lodging house would, or would not suit her'.[27] This lack is further demonstrated by her inability to participate in the chaotic conversations that take place at dinner. For her, such 'torrents of talk, such tempestuous arguments' are a sign of life and liveliness which stand in stark contrast to the stagnation that characterizes her own existence.[28] Unlike the other characters, Miss Holland cannot speak because she has no appropriate script available to her. Even the landlady has her own script, speaking of the rent, the number of meals and the content of mattresses, while at the opening of the story Miss Holland has 'lost the bit of paper on which the agent had written' the name of the housekeeper.[29] These scribbled words are a co-referent for the script she will try to provide herself with, pathetically buying a newspaper so as to be able to participate in the conversation at dinner. 'Armed with a few telling comments gleaned from the editorial', Miss Holland 'prepare[s] to go down to supper that evening', casting herself into her role as an actress ready for her cue.[30]

Explicit references to theatre and acting become increasingly frequent as the story goes on. After her failed attempt to perform her part, Miss Holland rehearses her script in an imaginary performance: 'Later, in bed with the light out, she went back over things and in a whisper to herself she inserted her comment quite easily into the conversation! ... There were no interruptions, except when an imaginary Betty Stone said, in an aside to an imaginary Marge Moran, that it took a mature mind to get to the root of anything'.[31] The repetition of 'imaginary' emphasizes Miss Holland's distance from reality: rehearsing never becomes actual playacting as she is the actress who cannot face the audience, in spite of her almost ritualistic dressing up before mealtimes.

Theatrical images are also applied to the behaviour of the neighbours' cat. For Miss Holland, the cat represents the beauty of life she is sensitive to and finds lacking in the other lodgers. In her perception, the cat becomes an actor and his movements a 'performance', 'most likely put on for her benefit'.[32] It is this performance that provides Miss Holland with the script she has been looking for: 'She had already rehearsed what she would say, but she kept making small alterations, changing the order of her words, dropping a word or ... two words, here and there, where they seemed exaggeratedly ornate'.[33] She is especially concerned about finding 'an exclamation or an introductory word', a 'striking opening, [a] powerful beginning', wondering: 'How would she begin her recital? For ... she was determined to make her debut that very evening'. The cat's performance as 'he danced away into the shadows' gives Miss Holland the right phrase:

> 'He danced away' Miss Holland said out loud. 'Like a flamenco dancer', she added. And she knew she had her opening line. Glancing at her watch she decided to allow herself a moment for a last rehearsal ... She felt like an actress on a first night, with the curtain about to rise. Only this wasn't play-acting. This was real life.[34]

However, the divide between fiction and reality, between rehearsal and performance, sends Miss Holland back into her role as a spectator. When she was ready for her recital, 'she forgot the exact words she had prepared' and the sentence she improvised clashed with Mr Moriarty's similar phrase.[35] In his account of his shooting at the neighbours' cat, Mr Moriarty too resorts to the language of drama as he expects 'a round of applause' for putting 'a stop to [the cat's] concert for one night'.[36] Miss Holland's obsessively repeated rehearsal does not result in a performance and she is forced to leave the stage, but takes one final look — as a conscious spectator — at the ugliness the lodgers represent: 'I must take one good, hard look at them — she thought, so I'll never forget how awful they are, and so I can try to protect myself from people like them in the future'.[37]

'Fogger Halt', one of Lavin's most neglected stories, is a text in which theatre and performances play a literal as well as a symbolic role. While the plot of the story revolves around a play performed by a travelling company, the protagonist of the story, Charlotte, resembles Miss Holland in her role as spectator to the world around her. Like 'Miss Holland', in fact, Charlotte is an isolated character unable to adapt herself to a new environment. She too is caught in a moment of transition, when she leaves the Young Ladies' Academy to go back home, to the military camp where she is to keep house for her father. In other words, she has to take up an explicitly feminine role in a male community which she despises: 'Fogger was unsupportable'.[38] Fascinated by the world of drama as a better elsewhere, Charlotte blurs real life and the fiction of drama, a confusion which is also hinted at by the title of the story.

The two-part structure of the story also resembles a play, with the first part anticipating the performance of the travelling theatre company and the second part dwelling on the performance itself and its aftermath. The theatrical organisation of the text is also noticeable in the dominance of dialogue. The story opens with a direct statement addressed to Charlotte by her fellow students at the Academy: '"How we envy you, Charlotte," cried the other young ladies as they stood on the steps of their parting friend. Charlotte was leaving the Academy'.[39] All through the story, dialogue serves to enhance character revelation and Charlotte's speech in particular reveals her snobbish feelings of resentment at having to return to Fogger Halt. Her arrival itself is construed as a show for the soldiers: 'They were hanging out of the barrack windows when she came in the gates with her father.' Yet from the spectator position of her own room, which 'looked out on the courtyard', she only sees 'soldiers, soldiers, odious, odious soldiers', no one who shares her interest 'in art, in literature, in Life'.[40] In a dialogue between Charlotte and her aunt, the narrator makes fun of Charlotte's snobbery and her highbrow airs as she contrasts the misery of 'stupid people' and their 'stupid talk' with the intellectual stimulus of the Academy.[41] Like Miss Holland, Charlotte wants beauty, but she lacks sensitivity and is unable to see below the surface; in soldiers she only sees uniforms, a visible mark of their official role: 'Common soldiers and officers were all one to Charlotte. She could see no good under a gabardine tunic'.[42]

With the arrival of Captain Locke at Fogger, references to theatre and performance become more explicit and the Captain is introduced with the traditional features of the male lead: 'he was tall, and thin, and as neat as a whip, with curls like the main curls on a statue'.[43] Charlotte, however, only notices the corresponding stage props of his costume: 'his leather belt and his leather leggings and his bright brass buttons'.[44] For Charlotte, Captain Locke exists only in his role as a soldier. In a way, she has prescribed a script for him, fixing the Captain in a role. Annoyed at being 'pestered' by him as by the other soldiers, Charlotte looks for a hiding place in the summer house, a shelter and a stage at the same time, after 'taking an old cavalry coat belonging to her father, and wrapping it around her' as a form of disguise.[45]

The subsequent encounter with Captain Locke in the summer house is described in theatrical terms. Angry at having been found out, Charlotte says 'Please do not try to interpret me'.[46] Interestingly, the word 'interpretation' is used in different ways in the story, both as a synonym of explanation as in this instance, and in the theatrical sense of performance, as when one of the actors of the company asks: 'Did you like my interpretation of the part tonight?'[47] The connotation of drama and performance is thus included in the verb 'to interpret', whose ambiguity is then developed in a more openly theatrical dimension as it is Charlotte who gives a wrong 'interpretation' of the Captain's 'interpretation': 'Charlotte looked at him with disgust, because she thought that the Captain was affecting an amorous pose'.[48] Likewise, Charlotte plays the role of an actress for Captain Locke, so that each of them is at the same time performer and spectator: 'Something about the way Charlotte held her head, something about the way the cloak trailed in her wake, reminded Captain Locke of a tragedienne, walking across the boards of a stage'.[49] This is a turning point in the story as this 'interpretation' of Charlotte and Locke's 'interpretation' of her point forward to the performance of the travelling company which Charlotte and the Captain will attend night after night.

When attending the play, Charlotte and the Captain are staged as spectators and actors at the same time. In fact, sitting 'exactly in the centre' of the audience they can have 'a good view of the entire performance', but they are also under scrutiny, and aware of not being 'the only people in the hall'.[50] As a matter of fact, the dramatic situation of the play on stage reproduces the condition of contrasted love the Captain identifies as his own, so that the boundaries between fiction or illusion and reality become blurred. Gradually, the Captain's superficial observations on the stage props and the curtain create a new interest in Charlotte, who interprets the captain's statements as evidence of his artistic sensitivity: 'I am interested in your sensitivity to the painted scenery'. The actual performance of the play is thus anticipated by the Captain's own performance, as he has taken up the role Charlotte wanted him to have, that of the blunt soldier fascinated by the power of art.

On stage, a replica of the protagonists' story can be seen: the 'young girl in a white dress' and the 'young officer in a red coat with brass buttons' are clearly fictional reproductions of Charlotte and the Captain.[51] The young officer's part has him 'fl[i]ng down on his knees by her side', a script the Captain himself would be ready to act out. And yet, in this mediocre melodrama, a metadramatic element draws attention to both the fiction of drama in the story and the fiction of story as story: 'The moment the lovers left the stage the other officer turned to the audience. "Now I will play my part!" he cried, and then and there began to divest himself of his sword and tunic, revealing inside them a leather jerkin'.[52] The dressing and undressing of the actors on the stage thus highlights the continuous assumption of roles on the part of the protagonists of 'Fogger Halt'.

Conscious of Charlotte's admiration for the actors and their world, Captain Locke assumes an official role when introducing her to the actors she is eager to meet: '"I'll make an opening for you" said the captain' and asking one of the actors for light, he makes conversation possible.[53] Yet Charlotte's naive and idealistic vision of the theatre is shattered by her backstage visit. All actors look alike to her, and 'although the identity of these characters had stood out so clearly when they were upon the boards', now in the shabbiness of the backstage 'they were almost indistinguishable from one another'.[54] The actors only exist as masks and when these are taken off, their self-centeredness becomes visible: 'I believe that I have made something out of it by my new interpretation'; 'I am at home in any role'; 'I am chained to the grief that I portray on the stage'; 'But who else in this company could play Hamlet if I were not to play it?'; 'I alone, in this company, have the perfect figure'.[55] In this sarcastic accumulation of self-glorification, Charlotte's idealizing vision of the theatre as a supreme art form is gradually deconstructed. The story's narrative structure is circular: it closes with the departure of both the Captain and the actors just as it had opened with Charlotte's leaving the Academy and the Captain's arrival at Fogger. The latter leaves theatrically, as 'with all the grace of the Male Lead, he doffed his cap, bowed from the waist, and set off down the cinder path to the quarters of the unmarried officers ... as he walked away in the bright moonlight that illumined the courtyard like the floodlights of a theatre'.[56]

'Fogger Halt' develops Lavin's familiar theme of lack of understanding and communication between individuals in the context of a theatrical performance. Theatre is both a backdrop for the story and a metaphor for the fixed roles everyone seems to play. Soldiers, actors, male leads, sensitive young girls are trapped in the everlasting performance of their own lives. Charlotte's naïve admiration for the theatre as an alternative and better world fixes her even more deeply in the role she has chosen. Yet this identity of the young, sensitive intellectual is exposed as just another form of role-playing.

In the novella 'The Becker Wives', the fixity of social roles is challenged by a new member of the family who upsets the traditional order. The arrival of Flora, the new bride-to-be, brings the freshness of novelty and life into the mediocrity of the Becker family. A careful portrait of middle-class values and personal complexities, 'The Becker Wives' explores characterization through theatrical interpretation, as it is centred on the main character's acting skills. Flora, the many-sided and multi-faceted artist, does not fit into the materialistic middle-class world of the Becker family and with her gift of mimicry, she offers them a brief release from their stiff ordinariness.

The members of the Becker family are extremely conscious of their own social position and of the respectability they have acquired as corn merchants in the community, and they play their role accordingly. Yet, on public occasions in restaurants they are always only spectators, staring at the other dinner guests. The obsessive repetition of such phrases as 'they liked to stare', 'they stared at some one or other', 'their gaze wandered', they 'stare at strangers', 'gap[e] at other people', 'gaze at a prominent actor', and finally 'cran[e] their necks to see the judge' marks the members of the Becker family as spectators in a fixed position.[57] They are shown to be unable to move out of their fixed roles just as they are unable to go beyond their coarse, materialistic values to acquire what Theobald calls 'distinction'.[58] The family immobility comes to the fore in the visual impact of the Becker women, who soon become matrons closely resembling one another.[59] Their 'fur coats', 'fur capes, fur tippets, and fleece-lined boots' become a sort of uniform for the Becker wives.[60] Even their first names, Charlotte, Julia, Honoria, and the Becker daughter, Henrietta, recall middle-class gentility,[61] while Theobald's fiancée, Flora, seems to come from a different world of nymphs and fairies. While all the Becker wives are stout and solid, Flora is 'exceedingly small', 'fine-boned' and 'exquisitely proportioned' and everything in and around her makes her look like a bird.[62] She is eccentric, in the original sense of the word, and because she cannot become one of the Beckers, she conquers them with her 'impersonations'.

Her first introduction to the family is already staged in theatrical terms and disrupts traditional patterns and expectations. Theobald wants Flora to be a 'surprise' — the word is repeated six times in this section of the story — and in orchestrating her entrance, Theobald acts as a director carefully building up a scene and as an actor consciously 'intent on making his entry'.[63] The theatrical effect of Flora's arrival is further highlighted by the reaction of James, the eldest of the Becker sons, who makes a connection to the theatre environment as soon as he hears her name: 'at the sound of the name a vague memory stirred in him and gaudy and tinsel images pirouetted before his mind's eye. Hadn't there been an operetta in his youth called *The Flora Doras*?'[64] The reference to dance anticipates the light movements of the girl, while the word 'operetta' with its mixture of recital and music prefigures her voice, which has the effect of the *coup de théâtre*: 'To everyone's surprise the voice that sang out was as sweet and melodious as a bar of music'.[65]

As soon as she has the chance, Flora 'stages a trick' in a fake photographic session.[66] As a photographer, she is a 'maker of images', creating an illusion of reality.[67] Likewise, as an actress she reproduces the illusion of selves other than her own. As Vertreace has put it, 'As an artist, Flora carefully observes each person around her in order to reveal that person's character by imitation.'[68] So, unlike the Beckers, she observes not as a spectator but as a protagonist. When she notices the Beckers moving chairs to make room for her and Theobald, her exclamation sheds light on the potential theatricality of the scene: 'They look as if they are playing some game' which anticipates her authoritative suggestion 'oh how I wish I was a photographer .... Let's pretend that I am one'.[69] For Flora, the reality of the world outside and the reality of her imaginary games are one, so much so that at the end of the evening she is seen as 'pretending to pick up her photographic equipment, and when Theobald gave her his arm, she made as if she was changing it to the other arm'.[70] Pretending and role-playing create a new possible reality: 'It was exactly as if she was a real photographer.'[71] In the same scene Flora is also a director, telling the Beckers when to smile and how to pose. Captivated by Flora's magic, they obediently follow her instructions, thus becoming actors impersonating themselves.

In a process of endless metamorphosis, Flora is protean and literally becomes 'what she imagines herself to be', the various selves of her impersonations and performances.[72] In her 'pranks and antics', she 'depart[s] her body ... entering that of someone else': first she imitates a flame beginning 'to glow, to grow more vivid and more vital', then her attention turns to animals and people that apparently belong to 'a steady repertoire'.[73] The 'little green dragon' she claims to see is replaced by family members, first Charlotte's washerwoman that 'Flora could imitate to the life', then her husband Theobald and her sisters-in-law. These performances fascinate the Beckers who fall under the spell of such an unusual person, one who is so far from their standards as to be an alien: 'She's something new in our lives and no mistake'.[74] With their materialistic perspective, the Beckers objectify Flora, turning her into a 'something' rather than a 'someone'. Yet initially Flora changes the Becker world rather than being assimilated into it. Like a theatre director, she dictates what is to be done, involving the Beckers in her world made of performances and overturning the tastes of the Becker wives in terms of housing, furniture, art and vacations.

However, Flora's impersonations gradually become more serious. Instead of imitating different people, her attention turns obsessively to the pregnant Honoria. If this is at first considered 'side-splitting' by the other Beckers, they gradually come to regard it as 'a mockery of motherhood', unpleasant and disquieting.[75] Flora gradually gets lost in the labyrinth of her own deranged mind and 'becomes' Honoria. Perhaps she had wanted to be part of the family circle all along and only through impersonation and mimicry could she become a proper, childbearing Becker wife.

It is worth noticing that in her insanity Flora keeps a piece of paper with her name written on it: 'As long as I have my name written down on this bit of paper no one will succeed in getting me mixed up'.[76] The piece of paper, 'a blur of wretchedly bad handwriting', acts as a script for Flora to follow, yet her performing days have reached an end and Flora begins to dissolve as she no longer exists outside her impersonations. The conclusion of the story marks the circular pattern of 'The Becker Wives': 'Their brief journey into another world had been rudely cut short. They had merely glimpsed from afar a strange and exciting vista, but they had established no foothold in that far place'.[77] If they had been acting in some way, it was under the direction of Flora. Without her, the family endlessly remain spectators.

Flora's impersonations can be read both as an attempt to communicate and as an antidote against loneliness, just like Miss Holland's scripts and Charlotte's artistic ambitions. Nothing is known about Flora's past and background, apart from the final revelation of insanity in her family. Theatrical performances therefore provide her with a sense of self she does not seem to possess — but this sense of self is as illusory as Miss Holland's rehearsals and Charlotte's intellectual posing. In short, in 'Miss Holland', 'Fogger Halt' and 'The Becker Wives', acting is closely linked to the protagonists' loneliness. Theatrical metaphors and images are used to stage the isolation of individuals in unfamiliar or hostile environments.

Interestingly, Lavin also used theatrical images to refer to her own practice as a writer. In a conversation with Maurice Harmon, she said: 'There was a need to fill a vacuum with imaginary people. I remember at a very early age being tantalized by the longing to get inside the body of someone else to see if it felt the same as being me. This was almost an obsession'.[78] For Lavin, in other words, impersonation and acting are also at a more fundamental level connected to the act of writing. They form the basis of Lavin's aesthetics of 'looking closer than normal into the human heart'. In her stories about rehearsals, spectators, performances and impersonations, as I have shown, Lavin looks closer than normal into the hearts of lonely protagonists who try and mostly fail to break down barriers so as to find a script and a role of their own.

Endnotes

1   For a discussion of the rigid social context of Mary Lavin's stories, see H. Ingman, *A History of the Irish Short Story* (Cambridge: Cambridge University Press, 2009), A.A. Kelly, *Mary Lavin, Quiet Rebel: A Study of Her Short Stories* (Dublin: Wolfhound Press, 1980), Z. Bowen, *Mary Lavin* (Lewisburg, PA: Bucknell University Press, 1975), R.F. Peterson, *Mary Lavin* (Boston: Twayne Publishers, 1978), A. Martin, 'A Skeleton Key to the Stories of Mary Lavin', *Studies*, 52, 208 (Winter 1963), pp.393–406.

2   M. Lavin, 'The Nun's Mother', in *The Stories of Mary Lavin, Volume 2* (London: Constable, 1974), p.46.

3   Bowen, *Mary Lavin*, p.45.

4   M. Gottwald, 'Narrative Strategies in the Selected Stories of Mary Lavin', in B. Bramsbäck and M. Croghan (eds), *Anglo-Irish Literature: Aspects of Language and Culture, Volume 2* (Uppsala: Uppsala University Press, 1988), p.183.

5   M. Lavin, 'A Likely Story', in *The Stories of Mary Lavin, Volume 2*, p.364.

6   Gottwald, 'Narrative Strategies', p.183.

7   E. Conlon, 'New Introduction', in M. Lavin, *Tales from Bective Bridge* (Dublin: Town House, 1996), p.X.

8   L. Lepaludier, 'Theatricality in the Short Story: Staging the Word?', *Journal of the Short Story in English*, 51 (Autumn 2008), pp.17, 18.

9   Bowen, *Mary Lavin*, p.33.

10 M. Lavin, 'Fogger Halt', in W. Woodrow (ed.), *English Story* (London: Collins, 1944), p.87.

11 'Miss Holland' was published in *The Dublin Magazine* in 1939 before being included in Lavin's first collection *Tales from Bective Bridge*. 'Fogger Halt' appeared only in *English Story*, in 1944. 'The Becker Wives' was first published in the volume *The Becker Wives and Other Stories* in 1946. It was reprinted in *Twelve Modern Short Novels* and in the second volume of *The Stories of Mary Lavin* in 1974. It also enjoyed a single volume publication in 1971 and was included in Lavin's *Penguin Selected Stories* in 1981.

12 M. Lavin, 'Preface', in *Selected Stories* (New York: Macmillan, 1959), p.vii.

13 R. Burnham, 'Mary Lavin's Short Stories in *The Dublin Magazine*', *Cahier du Centre d'Études Irlandaises*, 2 (1977), p.103.

14 M. Lavin, 'Miss Holland', in *Tales from Bective Bridge* (Dublin: Poolbeg Press, 1978), p.170.

15 L. Levenson, *The Four Seasons of Mary Lavin* (Dublin: Marino Books, 1998), p.58; Kelly, *Mary Lavin*, p.24.

16 Lavin, 'Miss Holland', p.177.

17 Martin, 'A Skeleton Key', p.394; Ingman, *A History of the Irish Short Story*, p.6.

18 K. Mansfield, 'Miss Brill', in *The Collected Stories of Katherine Mansfield* (London: Penguin, 1981), p.332.

19 Mansfield, 'Miss Brill', p.334.

20 Ibid.

21 Lavin, 'Miss Holland', p.174.

22 Ibid., p.166.

23 Ibid., p.171.

24 Ibid., p.172.

25 Ibid., pp.177, 178.

26 Ibid., pp.175, 179.

27 Ibid., p.166.

28 Ibid., p.177.

29 Ibid., p.168.

30 Ibid., p.180.

31 Ibid., p.180.

32 Ibid., p.181.

33 Ibid., pp.182–3.

34 Ibid., pp.184–5.

35 Ibid., p.186.

36 Ibid., p.187.

37 Ibid., p.188.

38 Lavin, 'Fogger Halt', p.82.

39 Ibid., p.81.

40 Ibid., pp.82–3.

41 Ibid., p.83.

42 Ibid., p.82.

43 Ibid., p.84.

44 Ibid.

45 Ibid., p.85.

46 Ibid., p.86.

47 Ibid., p.101.

48 Ibid., p.86.

49 Ibid., p.88.

50 Ibid., p.91.

51 Ibid., p.93.

52 Ibid., p.94.

53 Ibid., p.101.

54 Ibid., p.100.

55 Ibid., pp.101–2.

56 Ibid., p.106.

57 M. Lavin, 'The Becker Wives', in *The Stories of Mary Lavin, Volume 2* (London: Constable, 1974), pp.306–8.

58 Ibid., p.320.

59 M.M. Vertreace, 'The Goddess Resurrected in Mary Lavin's Short Fiction', in M. Pearlman (ed.), *The Anna Book. Searching for Anna in Literary History* (Westport: Greenwood, 1992), p.161.

60 Lavin, 'The Becker Wives', p.304.

61 Kelly, *Mary Lavin*, p.21.

62 Lavin, 'The Becker Wives', p.328.

63 Ibid., p.329.

64 Ibid., p.328.

65 Ibid., p.329.

66 Peterson, *Mary Lavin*, p.118.

67 P. Meszaros, 'Woman as Artist: The Fiction of Mary Lavin', *Critique: Studies in Modern Fiction*, 21, 1 (Fall 1982), p.48.

68 Vertreace, 'The Goddess Resurrected', p.16.

69 Lavin, 'The Becker Wives', pp.329, 330.

70 Ibid., p.335.

71 Ibid., p.331.

72 Meszaros, 'Woman as Artist', p.47.

73 Lavin, 'The Becker Wives', pp.351, 148, 341, 342.

74 Ibid., p.335.

75 Ibid., pp.351, 353.

76 Ibid., p.361.

77 Ibid., p.363.

78 M. Harmon, 'From Conversations with Mary Lavin', *Irish University Review*, 27, 2, (Autumn/Winter 1997), p.287.

5 | 'Trying to Get the Words Right': Mary Lavin and *The New Yorker*

Gráinne Hurley

> Personally, if I wanted a job, I'd like to be an editor. An editor can turn a middling story into a good one. But he cannot make a good one out of a bad one.[1]

This essay explores new contexts for understanding Mary Lavin's work by examining her relationship with *The New Yorker* magazine. Lavin's affiliation with *The New Yorker* came about in 1957, by way of an introduction by J.D. Salinger, with whom she had been corresponding about American markets. In letters to her, he urged her to submit some work to the magazine:

> So far as I know, you've never done any short stories for The New Yorker. That's a pity. Couldn't you think about it? Short stories, reminiscence. They're terribly generous to contributors. And it's the only sane magazine to deal with in this country. X Frank O'Connor and Maive [*sic*] Brennan do good things for the magazine. Please think about it. Nobody Irish has done any intimate, reflective pieces for them. Some things out of England, but nothing really Irish. I don't mean to push, but I think you and the magazine ought to have a Relationship. I hope you'll think about it.[2]

Unbeknownst to Lavin, Salinger wrote to William Maxwell suggesting that she might be a prospective contributor.[3] The introduction resulted in a fruitful collaboration, with *The New Yorker* publishing sixteen of Lavin's stories over an eighteen-year period (1958–76). It also produced extensive correspondence between Lavin and the magazine, primarily with her *New Yorker* editor of sixteen years, Rachel MacKenzie.[4] This previously unexamined correspondence forms the basis of this essay, and reveals a wealth of information critical to the study and understanding of Lavin's writing processes.[5] It casts light on *The New Yorker*'s editing procedure and its shaping of Lavin's stories for publication, and examines how Lavin pursued her creative writing interests whilst writing within the confines of *The New Yorker*'s editorial requirements. Ultimately it demonstrates how Lavin develops as a writer and forms her own aesthetic through the editing process and interaction with the magazine.

The New Yorker first contacted Lavin in a letter of 27 November 1957, inviting her to submit fiction for consideration: 'We've had a note from Mr. Salinger telling us that you'd like to contribute to The New Yorker. Of course we're delighted to hear it, and of course we'd be delighted to consider any fiction you'd care to send us.'[6] Lavin was a widow of three and a half years raising three young daughters, caring for an ailing mother and managing a household and a farm. Although a successful and established writer, she had only recently returned to writing following her husband's death. Certainly it had not been a productive period for her, as she wrote to Edith Oliver:[7]

> I do not know if Mr Salinger told you that after the death of my husband I wrote nothing for four years. This was nothing of the writers block business which I hardly understand. It was just that I didn't think life itself worth living, and as I really think writing, or writers rather, could be defined as people who find life even <u>more</u> worth living than most people, you can, I am sure, understand how I did not write in tho [*sic*] years. But I started again about a year ago, and wrote <u>Assigh</u> [*sic*] and some others.[8]

Although the letter from *The New Yorker* made no promises to Lavin, as their 'requirements are peculiar and indefinable, we can never promise acceptance to any writer',[9] still it gave her a much needed boost and newfound confidence, and she credited the magazine with inspiring her to write again:

I was so pleased and so proud, and so anxious to have a story for you that I started to write immediately, and although my difficulties, the farm, the children, the <u>bills</u> were as bad as ever — no, I should say a bit worse than ever! the conflagration was started and nothing could stop it. In ten days I wrote over thirty thousand words, which, if you saw all I did as well, as mother, father, plumber, electrician, mechanic (and on occasion social nit-wit!) you'd realise that's a fair bit of work.[10]

The thirty thousand words comprised of two stories, 'In a Café' (1960), and 'Lemonade' (1961). Doubtful that the magazine will like them, Lavin writes that 'in spite of a desperate need I have of money, in spite of my feeling the great honour you have done me by asking to read them … in the end, what really matters to me, whether you take or reject them, is that through you, they got written'.[11]

The New Yorker was notorious for its swift rejection of pieces and scrupulous editing procedures. The magazine was seen to foster and cultivate a certain style, though it seemed almost impossible to define what that style was. Hortense Calisher in her introduction to the *Best American Short Stories 1981*, of which nine out of the twenty stories selected were originally published in *The New Yorker*, wrote:

Perhaps this is a good place to talk about the 'typical' *New Yorker* short story, since the proportion of my inclusions from that magazine will give pain to some. There is no typical one, really, but I can describe what people think it is: a story of suburbia or other middle-class to 'upper' milieu, which exists to record the delicate observation of the small fauna, terrors, and fatuities of a domestic existence, sometimes leveled in with a larger terror—a death, say, or a mortal disease—so that we may respond to the seamlessness of life, and of the recorder's style.[12]

The magazine's editors tended to deny that there was a *New Yorker* style, pointing out the broad range of writers in the magazine. Roger Angell, in an article published in *The New Yorker*, wrote:

'Are you looking for the typical New Yorker story?' someone else asks. 'Sure, lady', I want to answer back. 'The one that's exactly like Borges and Brodkey and Edna O'Brien and John O'Hara and Susan Minot and Eudora Welty and Niccolò Tucci and Isaac Singer. That's the one, except with more Keillor and Nabokov in it. Whenever we find one of those, we snap it right up.' [13]

In attempting to explain the *New Yorker* style, E.B. White said that 'If sometimes there seems to be a sort of sameness of sound in *The New Yorker*, it probably can be traced to the magazine's copy desk, which is a marvelous fortress of grammatical exactitude and stylish convention. Commas in *The New Yorker* fall with the precision of knives in a circus act, outlining the victim. This may sometimes have a slight tendency to make one writer sound a bit like another.'[14] William Maxwell acknowledged that 'something that *is* characteristic of the writers who appear in *The New Yorker* is that the sentence is the unit by which the story advances, not the paragraph, and the individual sentence therefore carries a great deal of weight and tends to be carefully constructed, with no loose ends. And style becomes very important.'[15] Although clearly the writers published in the magazine were an eclectic mix and differed in style, the editors cultivated and shaped the writing in order to conform to the elusive *New Yorker* house style.

By the time Lavin was submitting to *The New Yorker*, William Shawn was at the helm.[16] He did not appoint a chief fiction editor and had ultimate approval on all stories. Lavin's initial submissions to the magazine were handled by Edith Oliver and Mary D. Rudd. Lavin was continually prepared for rejection and anticipated and pointed out faults in her stories to the editors. The first of Lavin's stories to be submitted to *The New Yorker* was 'Asigh' (1959) but she had little hope for it, certain that it was 'excessively long' and 'a bit dull and slow' for the magazine.[17] The story was due to be included in a volume of Lavin's *Selected Stories* being published by Macmillan later that year. In another letter to Oliver, Lavin writes: 'Thank you for your letter. The mere sight of that tall-hatted gentleman on your letter-head cheers me. I have no doubt the magic will be sufficient to cast a spell over me, even when the rejection letter comes from the 'editors concerned' as I have no doubt it will, as the story is not everybodys dish of tea, and the New Yorker is!'[18] Her doubts were justified. Exactly one month after it was submitted, Mary D. Rudd wrote to Lavin that the magazine was rejecting it: 'Unfortunately, 'Assigh' [*sic*] is not right for us — as you suspected.'[19] Other early submissions promptly rejected included 'Distant Thunder', 'What's Wrong with Aubretia?'

(1959), 'Lemonade', and 'The Mouse' (1961). The rejection letters were all gentle and encouraging. Lavin was not disheartened and continued to submit stories to the magazine, anxious to 'make that high grade — a sale to The New Yorker'.[20]

Rachel MacKenzie took over as Lavin's principal *New Yorker* editor in 1958 and encouraged her professionally whilst also being sympathetic and supportive towards her various personal predicaments over the years. She worked tirelessly on Lavin's stories and was always pained at having to reject anything submitted by her. Lavin came to trust and confide in MacKenzie and greatly valued her judgement and editing of her work. A friendship and understanding developed between the two women, as revealed in their frequent and increasingly intimate correspondence.

Many of Lavin's stories required substantial revision for publication in the magazine. The majority of her stories needed to be significantly cut. Space was an issue for the magazine, and it was more difficult to find space for longer stories. 'The Lost Child' (1969) was problematic because of its length, as MacKenzie explained to Lavin:

> I figure it can be cut by about 15 pages (on a guess), but that still leaves it long enough to require what we call an all-fiction front. And we already have on hand over an eighteen-month supply of such stories. (We get an all-fiction front just once a month, and not always that often.) This means it will be somewhere between eighteen months and two years before we can use 'The Lost Child', and we can take it only if that long a wait is acceptable to you and the story is not going into a book before the summer of 1970. (Isn't that horrifying?)[21]

Lavin is happy for it to be cut and made stronger, but she is concerned about holding the piece as she feels it is 'topical now — with the birth control issues'. Although Lavin would rather the story be printed in *The New Yorker*, she seeks MacKenzie's permission to contact her literary agent, Phyllis Jackson, about it as she fears that it would be stale in 1970. 'The Lost Child' was consequently published in the *Southern Review* in January 1969. MacKenzie informs Lavin that unless her other stories are shorter, they will have the same difficulty with them: 'Scheduling is difficult all round these days, we have so many stories and so many book publication dates to meet.'[22]

The magazine also felt that Lavin's stories tended to be slow to start. It was an issue Lavin was acutely aware of; at an early stage, she commented to the editors of her story, 'The Living' (1958): 'I <u>fully understand</u> that, unlike a book, The New Yorker cannot always use a story that does not reveal its strength till near the end. In the case of my stories, several readers might have committed suicide long before the end.'[23] Space was not the only concern with respect to long stories; writers were paid for their number of words. The annual contract given to writers specified their minimum word rate payment for that year. However, there is no evidence from the correspondence that this is the reason that Lavin's stories tended to be heavily cut, or indeed why Lavin submitted such lengthy stories.

Lavin, for the most part, was amenable to *The New Yorker*'s editing of her stories, believing them to be generally improved and sharpened up as a result of it. Caroline Walsh remembers her mother being constantly on the phone with her *New Yorker* editors 'trying to get the words right'.[24] Lavin was always anxious to make a sale to *The New Yorker*, not only for the prestige of getting published in it, but also for the financial gain, which contributed considerably to her compliance with editing changes. In addition, Lavin did not give up easily on stories and she strove to salvage and resubmit stories rejected by the magazine. The fact that *The New Yorker* would not publish a piece previously published put further pressure on Lavin to produce new stories and rework rejected ones. There was added pressure, albeit self-imposed, to submit as many stories as possible in a given period, in order to make the magazine's quantity bonus.[25]

Lavin viewed her writing as a work-in-progress and continually revised and re-edited her stories, with usually up to ten versions of a story:

> You know I always am a bit sceptical of writers who claim to do fifty versions of a story etc, although I do about ten orfifteen [sic] sometimes, but I know that although a diabolic compulsion makes me often rewrite the entire story, the actual change is often a small one. And I do suffer from a need oftentimes to perfect the bit I am going to scrap. Its [sic] like a tailor — a crazy tailor — sitting crosslegged hemming the bits of cloth he has cut away from the pattern.[26]

Lavin also edited stories after they were printed and before they went into collections, explaining that 'Every time a story of mine is about to appear in a second edition, or an anthology, I feel obliged to take another bash at it … re-editing can be interesting and exciting.'[27] Caroline Walsh remarked that she was saddened by her mother's constant revisions, and the fact that she couldn't let go.[28] However ultimately for Lavin, the short story writing process was fluid, and revision was integral to her craft and mode of production.

Almost one year after the magazine's first letter to Lavin, the magazine printed its first story by her.[29] 'The Living', was a story Lavin liked, and in a letter to Oliver and Rudd she mentions that it is 'full of corpses and lunatics', but believes that if they read it to the end they will see that it is a 'story of love and sweetness'.[30] The editors 'have a great enthusiasm' for the story but they ask that Lavin revise it before a final decision. Their main concern is 'the fact that the corpse is that of a feeble minded child-man. This magazine has a feeling that amounts almost to a taboo against using mentally deficient or disturbed children in stories, and we are afraid that to ask for a decision on the manuscript as it now stands would prejudice the outcome.'

MacKenzie suggests that Lavin replace the son with the woman's husband in order 'for the children to regard his death, as they do here, with equanimity'. Also, while allowing that he could be 'mindless', they suggest that it be from a stroke or accident. MacKenzie seeks Lavin's permission in cutting the story.[31] Lavin is agreeable to altering it, adding that she could not 'blame a magazine from shrinking at the thought of publishing a story about a mentally deficient child. Indeed — is it not one of the problems of art itself — how far can we go in depicting the unbearable — & only if there is a catharsis is it justifiable at all.'[32] Lavin changes the story to a simple-minded man and credits the change with having remembered a story where a woman was asked at a dinner party if she had any children and responding that she hadn't, pointed to her husband and said, 'this is all the baby I got'.[33] In the story printed in the magazine the corpse was that of the husband but 'he was a class of delicate ever since he was hit by the train'. Despite being open to the suggested changes, Lavin writes that she will keep the original version when it comes to the collected form.[34]

MacKenzie says of 'The Living', that it is a story 'we shan't give up on easily, and we'll certainly try again if, by any chance, this revision shouldn't quite work'.[35] 'The Living', to Lavin's delight was accepted, as she desperately needed the money, although there were further revisions to be made to it. MacKenzie explained to Lavin that cutting was the main change and 'the New Yorker practice in punctuation has made a number of changes, and the difference in American and English usage, and the tidying up of repetitions, and so on'. MacKenzie informs her that the story is one that the magazine will be very proud to publish but they also want Lavin to be happy with it 'so if anything bothers you particularly, you must say so and we'll see what we can do to fix it as you would like'.[36]

The late 1950s and early 1960s proved a prolific and lucrative writing period for Lavin. The magazine purchased 'The Living' (November 1958), 'Second Hand' (April 1959), 'The Bridal Sheets' (October 1959), and 'The Great Wave' (June 1959) in the same twelve-month period which earned Lavin her first quantity bonus, as explained by MacKenzie on 13 March 1959:

> 15% added not only to the purchase price of the fourth piece, but to the three preceding pieces. A fifth piece bought within the twelve months earns the same 15% extra, and with a sixth piece the bonus becomes 35%, and that, too, is retroactive, with a payment of 20% added to the 15% bonus paid on the preceding five pieces. The 15% bonus will appear with the payment for 'The Great Wave'.[37]

The quantity bonus certainly incentivized Lavin to be productive, and she made every attempt to earn it. However, while money was a necessity and driving force for Lavin, it was not a purely financial exercise for her, as she later explained to MacKenzie that she did not care about the money but had a 'moral obligation' to try for the bonus in order to do her duty towards her family.[38]

In the same correspondence Lavin was also offered the first-reading agreement, a contract which paid the writer an annual bonus in return for giving the magazine first refusal of their work. However, there was no guarantee that the magazine would accept anything from them. MacKenzie explained the contract:

> The first-reading agreement is an arrangement we have with a number of our good regular writers (Frank O'Connor has had one for years). It works to our advantage in that it gives us first chance at any fiction, reminiscence, and casual essays you write within the period, and it works to your advantage financially ... a 25% bonus over the basic price paid for each piece bought, and a cost-of-living adjustment figured against the Department of Labor index for 1950. The latter is paid quarterly and has been averaging over 30% of the basic purchase price; it is not absolutely guaranteed but has been paid now for a number of years and, unless something unforeseen occurs, we expect will continue.[39]

Lavin was so overwhelmed by the offer of the first-reading agreement that a paralysis came over her and 'spread to cover all my intellectual efforts, and I did nothing but dig in the garden'.[40] Lavin was 'honoured and pleased' to accept the agreement. The contract greatly eased Lavin's tensions and gave her a sense of worth and security with the magazine. However, it also made her anxious in case she couldn't continue to produce good work and make it worthwhile for the magazine. The magazine was delighted that she signed the agreement and MacKenzie explained to Lavin that it was 'not intended to exert pressure of any sort. It is only meant to help you write'.[41] The combination of the financial, aesthetic, and moral pressures produced an energy and creativity within Lavin.

Sometimes Lavin's stories had to be tweaked for *The New Yorker* audience's understanding. For example, the magazine had concern with the mention of the island in 'Bridal Sheets' (1959), as MacKenzie explains: 'For one thing, American readers need the island given a name since Ireland is an island, and they need the Midlands explained — we ignorantly jump at once to the English Midlands and then are confused when they turn out to be Irish.'[42]

Lavin practised self-editing and showed regard for the American reader when she writes to MacKenzie of her concern for her choice of characters' names in 'The Great Wave' (1959): 'And lastly a problem I found for myself, and which I tink [*sic*] was in my mind all the time, pushed back in the hurry and excitement of writing. Are you all happy about the names? There are THREE diminutives, which even for Ireland, seems a bit much.'[43] The names in question are Marteen, Seoineen and Jimeen. Lavin suggests that Marteen could become Martin, or indeed Liam or Peadar: 'what do you think? I'm so used to him as Martin … but the reader is not!' Lavin would like to keep the names Seoineen and Jimeen and debates:

> More serious however is the similarity between Seoineen and Jimeen. Now for me this was deliberate, suggesting at one and the same time their differences and likenesses. I like the idea of His Grace, James XX Bishop of … (Galway I suppose, or Tuam) being once called Jimeen. I thought of putting in some reference but the story got written without it, and I might be a hen trying to put a bit more yoke into an egg after it was laid. I couldn't break the shell anywayrere [*sic*][44] without damage. But I like the name Jimeen for him. I also like Seoineen and simply cannot imagine him by any other name.[45]

Also of concern for Lavin is her inkling that 'there is a common noun in use among American Irish with regard to a fellow called a SHONEEN I think it would mean sort of a no-good. Now the point is this — even if there is this connotation, does it matter. It may even have been because of this vague suggestion that I chose the name.' The magazine changes Marteen to Martin, but the names Jimeen and Soeineen remained the same.

Other changes made to suit the American reader included a drapery shop becoming a draper's shop in 'In Loving Memory', 'since drapery in American means curtains'.[46] 'The Yellow Beret' was heavily cut by the magazine, and they wanted to fix the location of the story by using Dublin in the title of the paper referred to in the story. While Lavin thinks it an excellent idea, she explains that there is no such paper:

> The Irish Times is virtually a metropolitan paper, but is circulated (ineffieintly [sic]) in the provinces. I mean it is not a city paper it is only that it is circulated inefficiently. Anyway people out of Irleand [sic] could not possibly know this anyway, so that is no help either. I wonder if you would be satisfied with a reference to the Irish Times which would place the locale in Ireland and leave it to the atmospehere [sic] of the paragraph, breakfast table, husband and wife, early morning paper etc to suggest a city? Or is [sic] you want a specific reference to Dublin we could say 'After all murders are not two a penny in Dublin like they are in London' or 'are not all that pentiful [sic] in Dublin yet'[47]

Lavin does not want to fabricate a title. The magazine responds that 'if there isn't a paper that fits our needs, of course the suggestion's no good. You place it any way you like.'[48] In the story printed in the magazine, the *Irish Times* is referred to and it includes the line 'Dublin was a small city for two murders in one night', by way of placing the story. Modifying her stories for *The New Yorker* reader was a learning experience for Lavin as a writer. She managed to keep the Irishness of her stories whilst very subtly adapting them for a cosmopolitan audience's comprehension.

William Shawn proved as uneasy as his predecessor, Harold Ross, with references to sex and bodily functions in the magazine, and included in his list of words that he would not permit in the magazine were 'balding' and 'pimples'.[49] The bloodiness of Lavin's 'The Lost Child' presented a problem because 'it made

Mr. Shawn sick', but MacKenzie 'assured him we could drain a good bit of it off in the editing'.[50] Lavin responded: 'I feel so bad about Mr. Shawn feeling sick. All I can say is he'd feel worse if I'd enlarged on the baptism bit & I may yet! But not necessary in <u>your</u> version.' When editing Lavin's short story 'Trastevere' (1971), MacKenzie writes to Lavin that the 'the cut of the baby with wet diapers like an udder has to do with Mr. Shawn's great sense of delicacy. He knows those babies are different, but he feels that three references to babies wetting are excessive. His real choice I'm sure, would be to have none. Not that he hasn't been around babies; he has. He just wants such matters referred to as little as possible in this magazine'.[51] MacKenzie takes comfort that Lavin can include it in the book version. While the magazine could be quite arbitrary and prudish in its editorial interventions, Lavin proved more modern in such matters and knew that she could still use her suppressed material in another version.

The magazine also did not like to publish stories about writers, as Lavin was to discover when she submitted 'In a Café'. 'In a Café' was chosen by the magazine for inclusion in the collection *Stories from The New Yorker, 1950–60*. It was William Shawn's favourite story of Lavin's. However, the story was initially rejected by the magazine.[52] It was a story that Lavin didn't particularly like and she didn't think the magazine would like it either. Despite believing it to be 'quite powerful', the reasons for rejection included that they felt the story 'would have to be drastically cut and speeded up before it could work out for this magazine. And after such major surgery, we aren't sure what would be left of 'your' story.' Also, they had an issue with the main character being a writer: '(By the way, I should tell you, for the future, that we prefer not to publish stories about writers and writing, although we do occasionally make exceptions. I put this in parentheses because it is not an important point in this instance)'. This harks back to Wolcott Gibbs' tenth rule in his essay 'Theory and Practice of Editing *New Yorker* Articles': 'To quote Mr Ross again, "Nobody gives a damn about a writer or his problems except another writer." Pieces about authors, reporters, poets, etc. are to be discouraged in principle. Whenever possible the protagonist should be arbitrarily transplanted to another line of business. When the reference is incidental and unnecessary, it should come out.'[53]

Lavin agrees with the magazine's decision on the story but does not give up hope on it, writing to Rudd: 'You are so right about In a Café. Of course I must cut it drastically & possibly re-shape it.'[54] The magazine is open to seeing a revised version and MacKenzie again highlights their concerns with the story:

Our criticism of it was twofold, as I remember: we felt that it was much too long and slow in pace (particularly slow getting under way); and we felt that its quality was uneven — some of it extraordinary and powerful, some of it banal. A very minor problem for us was that its central character was a writer — we avoid as much as we can stories about writers. In this story it wouldn't seem really to matter; she could be made something else without the story's being affected in any way.[55]

Lavin continued working on the story and four months later sent in an altered version of it.[56] She reduced it by twenty pages and removed the reference to the woman being a writer and believed it to be improved. However, she doubts that anyone will see what she was trying to achieve in the story 'to show how a ray, a small ray of human feeling, vague, perhaps vaguely lustful too, but above all a human feeling, broke through the aridity of [an] older womans [sic] mental attitude? I may not have done it at all.'[57]

Lavin was not precious about the story and was willing to revise it further — a sentiment she reiterates: 'Naturally I will be glad if you do happen to think In a Café will work out — or if you have any other changes to suggest. A few occur to me, but after all you are not running a writers school I know, & for my part, time presses & there is I feel a limit to what you can give to a story specially [sic] looking over your shoulder — like this.' MacKenzie also believes the story to be greatly improved and the magazine works on cutting it prior to making a decision on it.[58] Almost seven months later the story is accepted, and MacKenzie informs Lavin that everyone is 'enthusiastic about the new version of 'In a Café', and we are delighted to have it. Mr. Shawn thinks it is one of your best. I am so happy, for this is a story I have liked enormously and been moved by from the beginning ... Oh, I am so pleased it has worked out.'[59] There was still further editing to be done on it.

'In a Café' was eventually scheduled for a December 1959 issue but was pulled due to a scheduling emergency. They hoped to use it in a winter or early spring issue: 'That would seem to fit in with the fire in the cafe and the rawness outside, and the only change we feel is needed (we are so seasonal in our scheduling!) is to remove the sentence on the next-to-last galley about the birds in their secret nests making faint avowals of the last of the day. That would not be appropriate here for winter weather. Do you approve? We don't want to hold the story for next fall. Your work on the author's proof was fine, by the way —all problems resolved.'[60] Another rule formulated early at *The New Yorker* was that stories and poems that occurred at a particular time of year must be published at that time of year. While there is usually little resistance from Lavin in terms of revisions, she is rather reluctant to make this change that fits in with *The New Yorker*'s seasonal scheduling. Nevertheless, she acquiesces: 'I feel bad about cutting out the birds, which really were put into my mind by the line of Yeats about Dublin and the linnet wings. But I will do so very soon.'[61]

MacKenzie writes to Lavin that 'In a Café' is scheduled for the 27 February 1960 issue,[62] although it was actually printed in the 13 February 1960 issue, almost two years after it was initially submitted. The reference to the birds was still omitted. In later versions of the story, Lavin restores the birds nesting.

The magazine also changed the title of Lavin's story, 'The Kiss', to 'In the Middle of the Fields' (1961):

> Here's the check for what came in as 'The Kiss' but is going out to you as 'In the Middle of the Fields' — and don't you think that's a lovely title? If by some miserable chance you don't, would you suggest another one? I've forgotten just why everyone felt that 'The Kiss' doesn't do the story justice, but everyone did, and I do remember that I agreed with them.[63]

Lavin must have been happy with the title change as she kept it for all future publications of the story, and its title was used for a collection of her short stories published in 1967.[64]

Being published in *The New Yorker* introduced Lavin to a wider international audience and she was to reap the benefits association with the magazine earned her, in the United States particularly. Some of her stories originally printed in *The New Yorker* featured in the anthologies of *The Best American Short Stories* of 1960, 1962, 1965, 1966, 1969, and 1974.[65] 'In a Café' was selected for a collection, *Stories from The New Yorker 1950–1960*.[66] Also included in the collection of 47 stories were works by Frank O'Connor, Vladimir Nabokov, J.D. Salinger, John Updike, Mavis Gallant, William Maxwell, Philip Roth, Elizabeth Bishop, Tennessee Williams, Benedict Kiely, Dorothy Parker, Maeve Brennan, Jean Stafford, and John Cheever. Lavin also sold her manuscripts to American universities, did readings at various American institutions, and was engaged as writer-in-residence at the University of Connecticut for 12 weeks. Among other achievements, she was awarded the Guggenheim fellowship in 1959 and 1961, the Katherine Mansfield Prize in 1961, the Ella Lyman Cabot Award in 1972, and the Irish-American Foundation Literary Award in 1979.

MacKenzie suffered from ill health over the years and underwent open-heart surgery in 1970, which she described in her short story, 'Risk', which was published in the magazine.[67] In 1975, she took the year off to concentrate on her own writing.[68] Charles McGrath took over as Lavin's editor. Lavin continued to submit stories to the magazine, but she was to have only one more story published in it, 'Eterna' ('Perpetua'), in the 8 March 1976 issue, although she continued to have a contract with the magazine until 1984.[69]

MacKenzie died in 1980. Her *New Yorker* obituary observed: 'Those who had the good fortune to be introduced to the editing process by Rachel MacKenzie were quickly enlightened and reassured. Her genius was a combination of absolute friendship and a shared love for the work in progress.'[70] Certainly for Lavin this sentiment rings true, as she wrote to MacKenzie: 'Sometimes pondering over the proofs I feel I should be paying The New Yorker a fee not vice-versa! And to think of all a poor author hears about editorial interference & destruction. I am a willing witness for the defence.'[71]

MacKenzie championed and cultivated Lavin as a *New Yorker* writer. Through working with MacKenzie, Lavin gained a first-hand insight into *The New Yorker's* editorial procedures. Her stories evolved through the magazine's editorial process, and were pared down, tightened, and sharpened up but it was always in collaboration and agreement with Lavin. This is evidenced when Mackenzie, working on the story 'Happiness' (1968), writes to Lavin that she would: 'like to go ahead as we did with 'One Summer,' with me cutting and getting it into tighter shape, and you working over the surface of that cut version. Is this agreeable?'[72] In a later letter, she writes that the same story 'could rest — if you like — until you are here in the fall, when we could go over it together, as we did 'One Summer.''[73]

It is significant to note that both Lavin and MacKenzie's time with *The New Yorker* practically concurred, and Lavin's career at *The New Yorker* was inextricably tied with that of MacKenzie's. While MacKenzie's departure coincided with, and perhaps contributed somewhat to the end of Lavin's stories being published in the magazine, it is important to note that the magazine was accepting fewer of Lavin's stories prior to MacKenzie's departure in 1975. On 15 April 1972, Lavin, in sending another story to MacKenzie, wrote that 'It's been so long since you've liked one I feel a great lack of confidence, except that I rewrote all the others & they've gone into my new book — due in June.'[74] MacKenzie subsequently rejects Lavin's 'A Mug of Water' (1974),[75] and 'The Shrine' (1974),[76] but advises Lavin that they may be suited to one of the literary quarterlies and afterwards a book collection. MacKenzie comforts herself 'with the knowledge that the collections are reaching a wider audience in this country now that Houghton Mifflin are bringing them out'. When rejecting 'The Shrine', MacKenzie writes to Lavin: 'I hate sending stories back to you; I'd save them all and have a Mary Lavin Annual Supplement — or something.'[77]

'Lavin's story 'Tom' was accepted on 1 August 1972. Lavin was greatly relieved and wrote to MacKenzie:

> It was <u>deeply</u> reassuring after all the failures to sell one to you — was it eleven! in a long row. I've rewritten most of them & I'll send you the book. They are coming out in on [*sic*] Sep 5. The rest I will work on over the winter but I know now they were far too long — not just for you but for their own good! I have never in my life written as much as in the past 18 months — I think I feel I must get it all down — & prune later — except Tom which just shaped itself.[78]

'Tom' was published in *The New Yorker* in January 1973. However, Lavin's reassurance was short-lived. In December 1973, she became increasingly anxious that nothing had been published since 'Tom', and that her first-reading agreement was never returned: 'I am writing more than ever in my life but I seem to be writing myself further & further from the New Yorker, but I don't think anyone really cares ... I've reached the age where nothing matters very much anymore except for learning that fact and it's a big, big, living fact.'[79] MacKenzie returns the first-reading agreement and consoles Lavin by writing to her: 'Of course we care about you — as a writer and a person, too — and I've been sadder than you probably realise that so many recent stories have had to go back to you.'[80] In a later letter, MacKenzie writes to Lavin:

> I know your prestige as a writer does not rest on <u>The New Yorker</u>, but I feel that you have enhanced our prestige as a literary publication and it fills me with sadness that we have not taken a story from you in such a long time. My comfort is that the stories <u>do</u> get published and that they have an unfailingly intelligent and appreciative critical reception, and readers. Small comfort! No, it is; we seem not to be the magazine for a number of stories that I wish we published.[81]

Regardless of whether Lavin's stories were improved or not by *The New Yorker*'s editorial intervention, ultimately they would not have been published in the magazine without it. Also, Lavin proved to be a commercial writer, and as early as 12 February 1958, prior to having a story accepted by *The New Yorker*, wrote to the magazine, naively perhaps, that she was writing a story 'directed straight at the New Yorker target too, even if it misses', whatever Lavin perceived that audience to be. Lavin was savvy and practical. She needed to make money and knew that she could always revise even a published story for any further publications. The fact that she was already a great reviser of her stories aided this process.

The New Yorker was the first to publish significant works of Lavin's, and all of the stories published in *The New Yorker* were published again in various collections of short stories, perhaps indicating their popularity and prestige. Ultimately *The New Yorker* has to be credited with inspiring Lavin to write again after her husband's death, and J.D. Salinger given recognition for having introduced them, as acknowledged by Lavin in a letter to the magazine:

> You are so kind to me. And as I have said before, but could not say too often, if you NEVER take a story you have done a great deal by your encouragement, and I will never cease to be grateful to you, nor to be amazed at the fact that my friend Mr. Salinger should go to the trouble of bringing us together.[82]

Endnotes

1   C. Murphy, 'Mary Lavin: An Interview', *Irish University Review*, 9, 2, (Autumn, 1979), p.219.

2   Mary Lavin Papers, James Joyce Library, Special Collections, University College Dublin, Ireland: 29 May 1957.

3   *The New Yorker* Records, Manuscripts and Archives Division, The New York Public Library. Astor, Lenox, and Tilden Foundations, 11 September 1957.

4   Rachel MacKenzie was a fiction editor at *The New Yorker* from 1956 until her death in 1980.

5   This correspondence is contained in *The New Yorker* Records. The records were consulted in October 2009.

6   *The New Yorker* Records, November 27 1957.

7   Edith Oliver (1913–1998) began contributing to *The New Yorker* in 1947 and joined the staff in 1961 as a movie and theatre critic. She retired in 1992.

8   *The New Yorker* Records, 12 February 1958. (Lavin's dates are clearly confused. Her husband died in May 1954.)

9   *The New Yorker* Records, 27 November 1957.

10 *The New Yorker* Records, 12 February 1958.

11 Ibid.

12 H. Calisher, 'Introduction', in H. Calisher and S. Ravenell (eds), *The Best American Short Stories 1981* (Boston: Houghton Mifflin, 1981), p.ix. Hortense Calisher was also a contributor to *The New Yorker*.

13 Roger Angell (1920–) has been a regular contributor to *The New Yorker* since 1944. He became a fiction editor in 1956 and now is senior editor and staff writer at the magazine. R. Angell, 'How do you get published in *The New Yorker*? After six thousand stories in print and a few hundred thousand rejections, our fiction editors are still looking for the answer', Onward and Upward with the Arts, 'STORYVILLE,' *The New Yorker*, 27 June & 4 July 1994, pp.104–9.

14 E.B. White, 'The Art of the Essay No. 1', *The Paris Review*, 48 (Fall 1969). Online: http://www.theparisreview.org/interviews/4155/the-art-of-the-essay-no-1-e-b-white.

15 W. Maxwell, 'The Art of Fiction No. 71', interviewed by John Seabrook, *The Paris Review*, 85 (Fall 1982). Online: http://www.theparisreview.org/interviews/3138/the-art-of-fiction-no-71-william-maxwell.

16 Harold Ross (1892–1951) was the founder and chief editor of *The New Yorker*. William Shawn (1907–1992) succeeded Ross as managing editor in 1952.

17 *The New Yorker* Records, 14 January 1958.

18 *The New Yorker* Records, 12 February 1958.

19 *The New Yorker* Records, 20 February 1958.

20 *The New Yorker* Records, 25 April 1958.

21 *The New Yorker* Records, 10 May 1968.

22 *The New Yorker* Records, 21 May 1968.

23 *The New Yorker* Records, 27 February 1958.

24 'Mary Lavin — A Personal Perspective', lecture by C. Walsh, Trevor/Bowen Summer School, Mitchelstown Literary Society, 25 May 2008.

25 The quantity bonus scheme gave a bonus to writers who sold more than a set number of pieces to the magazine in a twelve month period.

26 *The New Yorker* Records, 10 September 1960.

27 Murphy, 'Mary Lavin: An Interview', p.219.

28 'Mary Lavin — A Personal Perspective', lecture by C. Walsh.

29 M. Lavin, 'The Living', *The New Yorker*, 22 November 1958.

30 *The New Yorker* Records, 27 February 1958.

31 *The New Yorker* Records, 2 May 1958.

32 *The New Yorker* Records, 15 June 1958. Lavin explains that she did not open their letter until over six weeks after receiving it, having mistaken it for a manuscript from her agent.

33 *The New Yorker* Records, 21 June 1958.

34 *The New Yorker* Records, 15 June 1958.

35 *The New Yorker* Records, 23 June 1958.

36 *The New Yorker* Records, 13 October 1958.

37 *The New Yorker* Records, 13 March 1959.

38 *The New Yorker* Records, 27 and 28 June 1961.

39 *The New Yorker* Records, 13 March 1959.

40 *The New Yorker* Records, 7 April 1959.

41 *The New Yorker* Records, 10 April 1959.

42 *The New Yorker* Records, 13 January 1959.

43 *The New Yorker* Records, 7 April 1959.

44 Lavin might have meant either 'anywhere' or 'anymore here'.

45 *The New Yorker* Records, 7 April 1959.

46 *The New Yorker* Records, 29 July 1960.

47 *The New Yorker* Records, 10 September 1960.

48 *The New Yorker* Records, 12 September 1960.

49 B. Yagoda, *About Town: The New Yorker and the World It Made* (New York: Scribner, 2000), p.296.

50 *The New Yorker* Records, 10 May 1968.

51 *The New Yorker* Records, 18 October 1971.

52 *The New Yorker* Records, 7 April 1958.

53 J. Thurber, *The Years with Ross* (Boston: Little, Brown and Co., 1959), p.114.

54 *The New Yorker* Records, 25 April 1958.

55 *The New Yorker* Records, 23 June 1958.

56 *The New Yorker* Records, 29 October 1958.

57 Ibid.

58 *The New Yorker* Records, 16 December 1958.

59 *The New Yorker* Records, 7 July 1959.

60 *The New Yorker* Records, 9 December 1959.

61 *The New Yorker* Records, 19 January 1960 (Lavin misdated it 1959).

62 *The New Yorker* Records, 28 January 1960.

63 *The New Yorker* Records, 12 April 1961.

64 M. Lavin, *In the Middle of the Fields and Other Stories* (London: Constable, 1967; New York: Macmillan, 1969).

65 M. Foley (ed.), *The Best American Short Stories* (Boston: Houghton Mifflin). These stories were 'The Yellow Beret' (1960); 'In the Middle of the Fields' (1961); 'Heart of Gold' (1964); 'One Summer' (1965); 'Happiness' (1968); and 'Tom' (1973).

66 Anon. (ed.), *Stories from The New Yorker 1950–1960* (New York: Penguin, 1965).

67 'Risk', *The New Yorker*, 21 November 1970.

68 MacKenzie's first novel, *The Wine of Astonishment*, was published in 1974.

69 In 1985, S.I. Newhouse's Advance Publications took over *The New Yorker* magazine and promised that nothing would change. Shawn was fired in 1987.

70 Obituary of Rachel MacKenzie, *The New Yorker*, 14 April 1980.

71 *The New Yorker* Records, 30 April 1959.

72 *The New Yorker* Records, 11 April 1967.

73 *The New Yorker* Records, 19 May 1967.

74 *The New Yorker* Records, 15 April 1972. The book Lavin referred to was probably the collection *A Memory and Other Stories* (London: Constable, 1972; Boston: Houghton Mifflin, 1973). The collection included the stories 'Tomb of an Ancestor,' 'Asigh,' 'Via Violetta,' and 'A Memory', all of which had been rejected by *The New Yorker*.

75 *The New Yorker* Records, 25 April 1972.

76 *The New Yorker* Records, 26 May 1972.

77 Ibid.

78 *The New Yorker* Records, 5 August 1972.

79 *The New Yorker* Records, 26 December 1973.

80 *The New Yorker* Records, 4 January 1974.

81 *The New Yorker* Records, 27 February 1974.

82 *The New Yorker* Records, 27 February 1958.

6 | The Irish-American Dimension of Mary Lavin's Stories

Theresa Wray

Catalogued as an Irish writer within academic syllabi, libraries and bookshops, Mary Lavin's American heritage is often a secondary consideration to readers. Indeed, her distinguished career supports her reputation as an Irish writer and distances itself to some degree from the transatlantic move. Yet Mary Josephine Lavin was born in East Walpole, Massachusetts, USA on 10 June 1912 and this dual American/Irish heritage is a significant underlying influence on specific areas of her writing.[1] It is true that the majority of Lavin's short stories are set in Ireland. Her focus there is on the middle classes, below stairs workers, farming and fishing communities and small-town populations of Irish origin. Lavin herself recognised that the particularity of place was something that she had come to focus on as a result of her move from America. As time went on, Ireland inevitably became the 'backdrop' from which her characters could emerge.[2] Yet Lavin moves beyond any perceived limitations (such as those raised by A.A. Kelly), arising from her use of socially defined settings.[3] Her American connections do have a particular bearing on a specific subset of stories and include a broader national engagement with the Irish narrative of emigration; in addition, they rework a more localised literary focus on the Big House environment. As the genesis of these fictions lies in the Lavin family experience, these experiences should be recognised as essential empirical evidence in a reading of her short stories; in these fictions, as elsewhere, the actions of an individual are acutely observed as part of a greater social pattern.

Lavin's drive is authenticity. She made that clear during an interview in the early 1980s: 'My interest is in recording and preserving the real life of living Irishmen and women whom I have known and seen with my own eyes ... I'd like to preserve them, rather than the diluted culture that is being shown by tourist bodies and agencies — all good and no bad.'[4] This authenticity is not essentialist; it is not driven exclusively by the story of Lavin's life; nevertheless, that personal narrative hugely informs her depiction of Ireland in the mid-twentieth century. Lavin's preface to *Selected Stories* (1959) also reveals a pragmatic, understated approach to her writing that underscores this wide-reaching objective. She writes: 'Short-story writing — for me — is only looking closer than normal into the human heart. The vagaries and contrarieties there to be found have their own integral design.'[5] This almost surgical pursuit of deep-rooted diversities through the abstraction of a primary organ in human beings translates well into her short stories, contributing to a better understanding of the individual and the community from which they came. The inter-connected nature of Lavin's construction of realism, for that is what she is talking about, can be read in Raymond Williams' terms in that 'Every aspect of personal life is radically affected by the quality of the general life, yet the general life is seen at its most important in completely personal terms.'[6] Lavin's focus on individuals, and their relationship with wider circles of the people and locations of Irish communities, offers a clear depiction of this correlation. Lavin subtly redraws the boundary between the personal and the public to reveal these substantial linkages in that she makes use of autobiographical material which maps onto a broader social landscape. It is within this framework that her short stories can be most usefully read. The following examination of Lavin's narratives crosses the boundary between autobiographical and fictional experience, and is mindful of the valuable wider connections made in the process.

Although the American dimension of the fictions has been marginalised in favour of Lavin's advertised presence as an Irish writer, biographical summations have, as a matter of accuracy, always acknowledged the facts of her birth. Intellectually, Lavin does not appear constrained by the potentially parochial nature of national labelling; rather, by successfully locating global human interests within micro-universes, she transcends any presumed provincial classification. Lavin saw herself as following in the broader traditions of Western literature, citing Chekhov, Flaubert, Joyce, Tolstoy, Edith Wharton, George Sand and Sara Orne Jewett as major influences on her writing.[7] However, this does not rule out the inclusion of local interests, as the work of Orne Jewett in particular demonstrates.[8] Nevertheless, the demands of more specific loyalties in her personal life prioritise a local and national engagement and must factor into a reading of her work.

In 1945, close to the time of his death, her father Tom Lavin asked that she retain her American citizenship; her parents greatly valued their naturalised status and Mary Lavin agreed to Tom Lavin's request, respecting his wishes. It was not until 1981 that she finally relinquished citizenship, recognising that all her family, past and present, were Irish and that she herself had remained in Ireland for sixty years. She identified herself as an Irishwoman.[9] Nevertheless, over thirty-five years her connection to America was also strengthened through her time as writer in residence at the University Of Connecticut at Storrs, and also a number of readings at other institutions. There was also a return visit to East Walpole. Yet although Lavin spent this time in the United States, she remained an Irish writer to her readers.

Tom Lavin's long-term working relationship with his employer, Charles S. Bird Senior, a philanthropist, local industrialist, and the owner of the family paper mill in East Walpole, is unquestionably the catalyst for short stories such as 'Magenta' (1946), 'The Joy Ride' (1946) and 'Scylla and Charybdis' (1956).[10] Early on after his arrival in America sometime in the 1890s, Tom Lavin worked on the Endean Estate there. As part of his employment with the Bird family in an increasingly industrialised pocket of small-town America, Tom Lavin travelled back and forth to Ireland to purchase horses for Endean, which is how he originally met his wife Nora.[11] After a lengthy courtship, Tom and Nora were eventually married in 1911 in Waltham, Massachusetts.[12] On their return to Ireland, Tom had enough money saved through investments to enable the purchase of a house in Dublin and he later managed the Bird family estate, Bective House in County Meath. This latter development in the Lavin history significantly highlights reclamation of a Big House through an American meritocracy. Mary Lavin's knowledge of estate systems and management finds its way into the resulting Big House fictions as both she and her first husband William Walsh had taken on a number of supervisory and administrative responsibilities on the estate during Tom Lavin's illness and after his death.[13] As part of the corpus of her work, the emigration narrative and the Big House study are inextricably linked to the fusion of this heritage. The emigration sub-genre evolves from an unashamedly semi-fictional exploration of her parents' return to Irish shores, as she admitted in discussion with John Quinn.[14] In the case of the Big House stories, historical tension between the long-held literary picture of decay and inefficiency is balanced against a real-life, influential, transnational modernity that is a product of her father's working association with a wealthy American family. The oppressive decay of the house in

'Magenta' draws attention to the demands of upkeep on an estate that Lavin was so familiar with, and household hierarchies are reinforced in 'The Joy Ride' and 'Scylla and Charybdis'.

Reorienting the weighting of experience from an *a priori* Irish rationalization to an American perspective does not preclude the former; it is essential that both emerge as useful contexts for these narratives. Lavin's drive for authenticity cannot ignore autobiographical material if the short stories are to offer 'the real life of living Irishmen and women' as she said. However, this is measured. The transposed inter-location of public and private emotional, historical and political interests in particular within the scope of these short stories is handled deftly and with enormous empathy by Lavin, signposting older anxieties alongside newer concerns. It is significant then that Lavin's testimony to the Irish emigration story is an important element of her corpus of work. Lavin even explores the anticipated yet thwarted story of the journey in 'At Sallygap' (1941); this appears in her first collection *Tales From Bective Bridge* (1942). It offers a European dimension to the picture of emigration and Joyce's influence is clearly marked by the echo of 'Eveline'.[15] Lavin may well be revisiting the story as a marker in the lineage of emigration narratives: in both 'Eveline' and 'At Sallygap', the longing to travel away from home is in the end outweighed by hesitation, fear and social obligation. In Joyce's short story, the main protagonist Eveline experiences the same longing for change as young Manny does in 'At Sallygap'. Eveline's predicament is a tension between the burden of responsibility placed upon her to care for her bullying drunkard of a father and her desire for marriage and respect. Entrapment for her is bound within social expectation and personal reserve: as a woman, she is confined within the domestic sphere and is the preferred carer of an aged relative, destined to remain within the home whatever the provocation. Eveline is more obviously driven to escape from the outset of the narrative because of her father's behaviour: she has already gone against his wishes and in secret continued her relationship with a young sailor named Frank.

In 'At Sallygap', we are initially led to believe that Manny is in control of his life; there is an assumption of patriarchal confidence and control in his easy-going conversation on the bus as he travels from Dublin to the countryside. Yet Manny is equally burdened by his own lack of confidence and the responsibilities he holds in an unsatisfactory marriage. As we eventually discover in each story, Eveline and Manny both reached the docks intending to travel but each stalled. We never know how Eveline's life continues as there is no closure in the narrative. With Manny the reality of remaining in Ireland is at least clear to us and he returns to the restrictions of his life in Dublin.[16]

In a much later narrative, 'The Little Prince' (1956) tells the more generic, well-trodden and problematic account of the Irish traveller gone forever. 'Lemonade' (1961) and 'Tom' (1973), however, reflect upon the personal ramifications of the return to Ireland from America, suggesting the influence of her father's history. In these short stories, Mary Lavin moves cautiously, neither dismissing nor over-eulogising the enormity of enforced travel, although she clearly recognised the historical foundation for such a significant exodus and its imposition upon the nation, marking that 'before the British came we owned the land. We were forced against our will into becoming a nation of emigrants'.[17] Elsewhere, Lavin appears keen to conserve accurate detail about those she may have known or observed in some form, such as Lally in 'The Will' (1944). She revealed: 'I was afraid someone in the family would recognise traits of my aunt in the fictitious character. But of course, no-one did — Lally was only an objectification of a concept'.[18] Lavin points out that this aunt 'pitted herself against her mother, her family and the Church, at a time when to do so was very uncommon', but stressed that the aunt had merely 'embodied the concept of a certain kind of person'.[19]

Whilst Lavin offers authentic depictions of the relentless drudgery of small-town living rather than offer a diluted form of the Irish to outsiders, there is a curious ellipsis in the physical transatlantic journey of Irish emigration itself in 'Lemonade' and 'Tom'. It would be expected that some memories of the voyage to Ireland might have been relocated into her writing; after all, Lavin conscientiously specifies the names of the vessels on the journeys. Yet 'Lemonade', which clearly engages with a child's experience of the return journey to Ireland, does not document the transatlantic shift in detail. Even in a radio interview, Lavin occludes her own journey to Ireland, contracting the experience to seeing her father driving away from the SS *Winefriedian* in the docks, with one phrase: 'travelling across the Atlantic Ocean brought home the vastness of the gulf between my father and me'.[20] Yet she recalls life on land in Walpole, writing: 'I was ten when I left East Walpole, a good age, because I kept enough remembrance of one country to stimulate a never ending comparison between it and the new country.'[21] Despite this gap on-board, an implicit historical and national consciousness constructs and invests meaning in entrances and exits, arrivals and departures on each journey.

The short stories address the journey in different ways. In 'Lemonade', the fictional Delaney family's history is relayed through an omniscient narrator, with the child Maudie at the centre of experience in America and Ireland. 'Lemonade' focuses on a child's life before and after the long journey of emigration, with the motif of the sugary drink charting young Maudie's experience of secrets: it is a 'grown-up' drink, masking the power of whiskey to numb disappointment in America; in Ireland, it is also a treat for a dead child at the expense of the living. The interweaving of social convention with an individual's emotional instability, loss and pain through the offering and receiving of refreshment takes precedence in a story that sidesteps the enormity of transatlantic separation between father and daughter; yet the journey did take place.

At the traditional wake the night before travel, Lavin alludes to class consciousness among the emigrant population, to snobberies about steerage passage and to one-way tickets that denote a final decision between husband and wife regarding a sense of where home is. The collective wistful investment of the crowd at the travel wake is at once a social occasion and an opportunity to restate allegiances, where 'They were all Irish, but not born-Irish, and so taking part in this leave-taking of Dinny's wife and child had a two-fold nostalgia for them, a nostalgia for the old country, but also for the old people, now dead and gone, through whose eyes, only, they had ever seen that lost land.'[22]

As the wake continues, Dinny Delaney expands his storytelling about former passages across the Atlantic to reveal the chaos of his travel in steerage:

> To give you an idea of the way we used to be tossed about in those days, I must tell you there used to be a rim around the tables to prevent the cups and saucers from sliding off on the floor — No! Wait a minute. I think that must have been on later crossings altogether — in the real early days, when I was a young lad making my first voyage — the cups and saucers were chained to the tables — they were enamel cups, of course, or tin maybe[23]

His wife is embarrassed by the public revelation that he travelled in the lowest class of passage. In an effort to distract the attentions of some of the women there who wish to examine the luggage labels on *her* steamer trunks for evidence of similar transport, Mrs Delaney forces the labels towards them, defending the price of her passage. Her abhorrence of steerage is well-placed; in a report in *The New York Times*, steerage conditions were deemed unsafe and unsanitary.[24]

The confusion of separation is far more explicit in the short story 'Tom', classified as 'semi-fictional' by Lavin in a radio interview.[25] A first-person narration, it fictionalises Tom Lavin's memories of his emigration to America but interestingly the strength of the story is not so much in that but in a much later return to Roscommon where contemporaries seem to have aged unrecognisably. Lavin uses the generic labels 'old-timer' and 'old woman' to intimate distance between the locals and those returning from America.[26] Recognition between former neighbours and classmates is distorted by the gulf in their experience: those who travelled appeared to be sustained by some elixir of youth, strengthened by new opportunities; those left behind had a hard life, and aged quickly. In 'Tom', Lavin illustrates her father's story through the landscape that he left behind, where 'All he took with him to America were the memories of the boy he had been, running barefoot over the bogs and the unfenced fields of Roscommon with a homemade fishing rod in his hand, or maybe a catapult … [she adds significantly] My father had made his memories mine.'[27]

Lavin's final phrase echoes the sense of inherited nostalgia in 'Lemonade'. Here in 'Tom', as Levenson notes, Nora Lavin's reminiscences are also lodged in the superficiality of the journey across the Atlantic with its shallow focus on entertainment and social status: Tom Lavin's frequent travels in steerage had been upgraded in the fiction, and 'mother' had a state-room in cabin class.[28] Games of quoits, reading on deck — all this reduces the impact of the journey, and is a far cry from publicised steerage conditions. In 'Tom' and 'The Little Prince', the traditional iconic emigration entry into New York is translated to an understated arrival in Boston. In 'Lemonade', the first sight of Ireland is reduced to time ('four o'clock in the morning') and merely imagined substance: 'if there were any daylight to see it, the coast of Ireland could have been seen, like a thin string of seaweed drifting on the horizon'. 'The Little Prince' offers no statuesque vision of Lady Liberty; rather, 'sirens were screaming' adding to a greater cacophony of noise.[29]

Lavin's abridged fictionalised versions of her parents' life stories sit alongside actual ellipses in the narratives: specific travel to and from the dockside is glossed over in favour of the next stage in the plot, reminding the reader of the artificiality and creativity of fiction. These are, after all, carefully constructed sequences and are not just a simple retelling of personal accounts. By crossing from fiction into that hinterland of autobiography in order to engage with the potential difficulties of relocation, Lavin risks being dismissed as derivative or unimaginative. Neither is true. Lavin's affirmation of the artistic process makes that clear when she writes that 'there is artifice needed to reduce or raise a detail to the proportion proper for making it striking or appealing'.[30]

James Ryan highlights the surprisingly limited representation of the emigration experience in fiction from the 1940s and 1950s even though the demographic shift to outside of Ireland was significant. This makes 'The Little Prince' noteworthy.[31] Ryan's examination points, for instance, to struggles Mary Lavin had in recreating this population transfer, but he does not include this short story as his primary interest lies in the frustrations Mary Lavin had with the theme. 'The Little Prince' falls into the abyss of emigration bereavement that we can deduce from Louise Ryan's analysis of how we come to terms with goodbyes. Ryan reminds us that 'Migration takes many forms — temporary and long-term, individual and familial, internal and external — and is often conceptualised in terms of permanent separation and loss.'[32] Any absences from the discourse surrounding emigration, particularly when examining a writer's approach to the theme, may not be easily recognised as contributing to the wider narrative. Nevertheless, absence as well as presence provides a marker of emotional and intellectual rationalisation of the event.

Lavin's generic construction of sibling division and migration, 'The Little Prince', is one of a series of Grimes family stories. 'The Little Prince' explores concerns about enforced emigration, highlighting sacrifices made as strategies of survival. Disparate personalities and inheritance concerns drive one sibling from the other, across the Atlantic, never to be heard from again. Bedelia, sister of Tom, is the primary worker in the family shop, and intends to marry Daniel, an employee there. As their father is nearing the end of his life, Bedelia resents Tom's *laissez-faire* attitude towards the family business and his over-generous nature towards 'idlers and spongers' who, as she puts it, 'knew they had only to rub you down with a few soft words, and they were sure to have their bellies filled with drink'.[33] She is concerned that her fiancé and herself will somehow lose out financially, and in a tense exchange, following her accusation that Tom is drinking (when he is not), she suggests that her brother move to America, the 'obvious place ... A new country, a fresh start'.[34] Tom leaves and never contacts them again. Bedelia's justification for his exile is that he:

> ... would not be the first black sheep to be sent across that ocean
> ... Many a young man like him went out in disgrace to come home
> a different man altogether; a man to be respected: a well-to-do
> man with a fur lining in his top-coat, his teeth stopped with gold,
> and the means to hire motor cars and drive his relatives about the
> countryside. Might not Tom make good there too?[35]

Two brief sightings of him by the daughter of a previous family servant suggested he was fine, although perhaps not in the highly-paid position that Bedelia might have wished for her brother.

For nearly thirty years Daniel puts a share of the shop profits aside for Tom, but it is never claimed. When reports come that a man with Tom's name has been brought to hospital 'from a lodging-house in a poor quarter of the town', Bedelia and Daniel travel to Belfast to board the SS *Samaria* bound for Boston.[36] The bigger picture of sibling rivalry, loss and estrangement is what 'The Little Prince' is focused on, yet the emigrant passage is given some substance here, characterised briefly by poor weather, seasickness and a coffin in the hold. Although this is in connection with an Englishman being repatriated to his adopted homeland of America, it is a conceit that resonates with famine history. The journey is fruitless though, as Bedelia fails to recognise her brother who has died whilst she travels over; when she attempts the identification, she thinks: 'if it was her brother, something had sundered them, something had severed the bonds of blood ... if it was I who was lying there, she thought, he would not know me'.[37] In 'The Little Prince', what I deduce as a form of emigration bereavement from Louise Ryan's work is realised through the physicality of the dead man, if indeed it is Tom, although the complex emotional imbalance between Bedelia and Tom from the outset suggests that this loss is manifested far earlier in the narrative, once Tom leaves the family home.

Lavin's move to Ireland and her father's subsequent employment generates a new frame of reference in Westmeath. Her marginal connection to a particular kind of Big House, through her father, introduced her to an alternative lifestyle. The resulting narratives are noteworthy because of some fictional distance from the locations of the middle-class, mid-range economy that she focuses on so well. Instead, Lavin's version of the Big House knowingly references the point of view of servants and other employees: housekeepers, a lawyer, overseers and other below stairs staff hold key interest for the reader as their points of view can be read as markers of discontent bound to the margins of a decaying Ascendancy. In foregrounding the rituals of futile domesticity through servants, Lavin charts a declining influence of absent owners. The inevitable frustration of the mid-to-lower classes is then played out against a questioning of the old order such as in 'The Joy Ride'. Big House narratives do depict such revolts against the establishment but this is usually tinged with an inherent respect for institutional authority. In stories such as Lavin's 'The Joy Ride' and 'Magenta', there is unmistakably a new-found confidence at the expense of this older system. A declining control over household staff that are more likely to opt for employment in the town or city suggests the beginning of a more dispassionate, professional connection between servant and master. Servants might have other opportunities to consider.

Her father's employment tangentially connected Lavin to the history and politics of Ascendancy Ireland. Once Tom Lavin was appointed estate manager, Bective was to play a significant role in Mary Lavin's life and to influence her distinguished body of writing. The title of her first collection, *Tales From Bective Bridge*, positions her writing in the local topography.[38] Bective was purchased by the Bird family on Tom Lavin's recommendation. The Bird family were already familiar with the demands of running a large estate as their own house Endean in Walpole, Massachusetts was part of a substantial development that was forged from a successful business dynasty where the family employed a large number of the local population.[39] They were social philanthropists, active in politics and keen sportsmen and women. The Birds maintained an estate income with traditional sporting and farming ventures. A successful breeding and racing stock programme was managed by Tom Lavin.[40] Fortunately, Bective House remained intact during the Civil War when other Big Houses were burned down in the area. Caroline Walsh attributes this survival to a 'legacy of good will left by the Boltons [who built Bective House circa 1850] which the owners that followed did their best to sustain'.[41] Yet as Walsh notes in her interview with Jack Horan in the same article, there was still some 'Republican activity' alongside Black and Tan patrols at the time and therefore a serious risk of attacks on these properties.

Tom Lavin's letters record life at Bective House. In correspondence with Howard Gotlieb, Mary Lavin talks quite candidly of her father's letters; she had read them in the past and reread them before passing them on to Gotlieb. Every detail concerning the horses, livestock and upkeep of the property was relayed back to America on a regular basis, sometimes with only days between each report. Everything was documented, from feed bills to maintenance costs, local intelligence and preparations for weekend and hunting parties, alongside more personal local news — and Mary Lavin observed this. Such close association with the running of a large estate, and its effect on her and her writing, manifests itself in a number of letters Mary Lavin wrote herself. In one to the editor of the *Atlantic Monthly* commiserating upon his ill health and the recuperative power of more comfortable American homes, she deviates from the topic (her thanks for the *Atlantic* accepting a story and the possibility of perhaps writing a novel) and offers general reflections upon the ugliness of Irish houses which, she says:

… (with the exception, of course, and always, of fine old residences like Bective) [*sic*] is something that always keeps me looking out windows. In a small way it was something of this that I tried to express in Lilacs — the way, in Ireland, there is a constant effort to resist the advances of beauty in any form, whether it is a new pattern on a tea-cup or or [*sic*] a minute difference of shading in a coat of yellow paint. I believe that this hurts me more than most people ~~and~~ but also I am able to bear it better, because I believe that it dates back to a time when people in Ireland actually were afraid to show any sign of prosperity, even by a new tea-cup, or a new coat of paint, in case their taxes would have been raised by the absentee landlords [*sic*] vigilant agent.[42]

This section of the letter reveals a number of things: an objective, dispassionate and critical view of an Ireland that Lavin understands; also an artistic sensibility and insecurity that self-diagnoses emotional pain, yet intellectually is able to rationalise a rejection of beauty in favour of a security and practicality conditioned by colonial rule. It is apparent that her keen understanding of that historical climate of fear is shaped somewhat by her time on the Bective estate. Lavin's interest in looking out of windows and her dislike of 'the ugliness of Irish houses' provides a fascinating context for her Big House narratives and the reference to 'Lilacs' makes it clear that Lavin fully grasps the social and economic forces that have shaped Irish history.

Zack Bowen and Richard Peterson both recognised that Bective was one of the early influences in Lavin's life but neither develops the correlation with her writing to its fullest extent.[43] For instance, Peterson (who has produced the most comprehensive overview of Lavin's work so far) is disappointed with the narrator's intrusion in the Big House narrative 'Scylla and Charybdis', and Bowen merely uses the short story to comment on Nora Lavin's own social pretensions. This is a missed opportunity as the social categories and tensions surrounding the boundaries of employer/employee relationships and Lavin's own position as daughter of the estate manager are imaginatively recreated in 'Scylla and Charybdis', which offers some insight into the lonely existence of a servant's child.[44] Here, a 14-year-old named Pidgie hovers on the margins of Big House living; she is liked by staff but unrecognised in the main by the young ladies of the household, destined to join the ranks of the below stairs staff once she leaves school. Her aim is to be 'a lady' and she subsequently enters into a quasi-apprenticeship, stealthily observing the young women with the aim of assimilating into the role at some point. One day she is drawn into the tennis match the young ladies of the house are playing, to act as ball girl. From then on during the summer she accompanies them on excursions, revelling in her new role as 'friend'. Pidgie's enthusiastic assumption that she has entered into a realm where she truly belongs is manifested in fantasies, where Miss Gloria would ask her father to release her into their care 'to have her become really one of us — like a sister!'[45] She daydreams of having a room at the front of 'The House' and explaining her good fortune to the other staff: 'She for her part, was resolved to be very kind to them and not abuse her new position.'[46] The story cannot end like this, however; Lavin's narrative shapes a potential move for Pidgie, anticipating a transition from servant to lady, only to abruptly undercut the dream. Her father reminds her 'You know very well that they wouldn't bring you in to eat with them! ... You may not have noticed it, but that's one thing the like of Those People never will do, and that is eat with their Lessers. Anything but eat with them! Even Mr Sims, the lawyer, gets his meals on a tray in the library.'[47]

And so it is proved as Pidgie's imagined social elevation remains unfulfilled. The significance of the story's title is somewhat overplayed by Lavin's depiction of the mythological monstrous female in the forms of gentrified conservatism and inverted snobbery yet we can forgive this as readers. Pidgie's private cravings for an ambitious existence of promotion to life above stairs are stunted by her marginalisation, while her adolescent epiphany engenders a reaffirmation of that above/below stairs division. 'Scylla and Charybdis' signals resistance, aspiration and a momentary blurring of boundaries, a transition if you will from the old order to new. It demonstrates the enormity of the task Lavin undertook in condensing and reshaping the Ascendancy narrative. Despite the restrictions of form, and the breadth of documented historical subject matter, Lavin eloquently uses the short story to chart a stage in the decline of Big House authority. It is also fair to say that Lavin's short stories complement the class sagas in M.J. Farrell's *Full House* (1935), *The Rising Tide* (1937) and *Two Days in Aragon* (1941), successfully creating a layered environment of decline.

As indicated previously, 'The Joy Ride' and 'Magenta' also contain clear references to the Big House tradition.[48] Both suggest the diminished nature of that social existence, and the dichotomy of moving on from the faded grandeur of the past to the liberation of a newer, more modern existence. The framing of these narratives within the short story is significant, as technical constraints of the genre do not easily support the temporality of dynastic decay. 'The Joy Ride' presents a traditional hierarchy of absent owner, overseer, two butlers and servants and implies faithful observance of the Big House genre, although what Vera Kreikamp describes as the 'archetypal image of a declining social class' is subverted on one count, as the Big House is well maintained.[49] 'Magenta' offers an almost wholly female domain, with two head maids/guardians in Miss Perks and Miss Budd and a scullery maid, Magenta. In his study, Zack Bowen also notes a sense of irony in the details surrounding the overseer and his aspirations.[50] The overseer in 'The Joy Ride' here believes 'the best preservative for anything was constant use' although this may be self-interest in planning the purchase of an ongoing business in the estate as he is biding his time until he can afford to buy out the old property (or so the rumours go).[51] Bowen's ironic reading may be counterbalanced with the genuine engagement that Lavin herself felt with the potential of estate life. We are told the fictional estate stood on '400 acres of best land in Meath', echoing to some extent Bective's own acreage (including woodland).[52] The fictional estate also had a well-stocked cellar which was to be the locus of disaster.

The overseer Malcolm and the butlers Purdy and Crickem are the main focus of the narrative. Crickem represents a younger, liberated generation. Purdy is 'about forty [with a] vulnerability that comes to people who have been a great many years in the same employment and who have come to feel that their security is dependent on a single thread'.[53] He is also a terrible drunk. There are obvious echoes of Maria Edgeworth's *Castle Rackrent* (1800) from the character 'type' set out here. Purdy, in unquestioningly maintaining a traditional life of servitude, is stifled of imagination. When the younger butler suggests that they both take an unofficial day off when the overseer is away, he declines at first for fear of reprisal. As Purdy begins to remember what it was like to think independently, they formulate a plan for a ride into the country, a picnic and, potentially, the company of a pretty young woman on the way.

Here Lavin appears to play with the popular desire for nostalgia that Clair Wills has identified in the period but as Wills notes, with a a 'sting in the tail' often found in Lavin's depictions of rural life.[54] With its strange mixture of past memories and present desire for change, the day is a testimony to failure. The picnic, with its symbolic connection to childhood and a desire to return to the past, makes them ill; they flirt with women as they ride along but do not stop. When they are close to home later that evening, they discover that the house they should have kept watch over has burnt to the ground. The reader understands just before Purdy does that it was his fault: he had stolen some sweet liquor from the cellar for their picnic, and he had dropped a lit match whilst searching for the drink. The unexpected recklessness borne out of years of subservience, which had engendered their absenteeism, is both bitter and sweet. The reader is left to wonder at the outcome as Purdy and Crickem literally vanish from the pages of the short story at the end, perhaps signifying a new egalitarian future. The open-ended narrative rejects the more traditional frame of retribution; it suggests a modernist disruption and unrestricted freedom from consequences as the reader is left to imagine life beyond the Big House.

'Magenta' conforms to the more familiar patterns of decay and isolation in the genre and is included here briefly as illustration. Trustees of the estate and a solicitor act as external assessors, a man works in the garden while Miss Perks and Miss Budd offer general housekeeping to prevent the residence from fading. They have a keen eye for observing the tasks necessary for the upkeep of the house and grounds but very little appetite for drudgery, and so Magenta performs the heavy tasks. True ownership of the property is never mentioned; the dysfunctional family genealogy is not evident, and neither is the direct usurping of land by an agent, yet Lavin still demonstrates that the absence of the owner allows a false sense of ownership and pride in the guardians. The women have become its public face in the locality. It is clear that Lavin's engagement with certain conventions of the genre is complicated by her own experiences, as other expectations are displaced.

The patterns of movement around the Big House that Gearóid Cronin identifies in Elizabeth Bowen's work appear here, to some extent, although deliberately modified to express slow decline and apathy.[55] Messages are delivered to the house by the postman and the locals; minor estate repairs are attended to. However, the two women remain entombed within its boundary except for Sunday mass. They are depicted as the living dead with pale skin: 'The damp and the passageways had blenched their skins till they had at last the same waxen pallor as the faces that peered out from the dark canvasses in the upper galleries of the house.'[56] There is the sense that the house will survive where they will not, in stark contrast to the manor house at the beginning of 'The Joy Ride'; nevertheless, at the centre of both narratives is a concern for survival of the workforce, perhaps marking a vested interest in authenticating and scribing Lavin's own family experience. Magenta's new life in the city is not a panacea for drudgery in the country; neither does it immediately annihilate connections with the old order. It suggests that the transition itself is only one step forward.

Lavin's stories consciously review expectations surrounding the Big House narrative as they form part of a much wider appraisal of human life. A much later short story, 'A Memory' (1972), hints at a regeneration of the Big House through new Irish money, but here Lavin initially shifts narrative emphasis to the city where she explores tropes of isolation and change through the experiences of her main protagonist James.[57] In fact, in 'A Memory', the Big House is sited on the periphery of events until its landscape becomes the setting for James' death: emotionally inept and brutally cautious with social interactions, it is fitting that James is alone at the end of his life. He is marginalised in the modern world, as 'out-of-date' as a Big House and its accompanying infrastructure in twentieth-century Ireland. Where his death is located at the cusp of change (this property is being renovated), Ireland moves on, but he is at odds with this progress.

Lavin's interest in transposing the Big House narrative into the short story format is a development of an established, if somewhat limited, tradition and engages with much earlier attention to the genre: Elizabeth Bowen's 'The Back Drawing Room' (1926) or Seán O'Faoláin's 'Midsummer Night Madness' (1932) are noteworthy examples.[58] However, Lavin obviates direct interpretations of the political or supernatural in her Big House fictions and so is located beyond what appeals to Bowen's or O'Faoláin's readers. Instead, in shape-shifting these fictions with a specific auto/biographical matrix, there is something far more personal here. Lavin's connection to a new form of Big House living during her childhood and early married life was undoubtedly the catalyst for a subset of her fictions. Her familiarity with that environment, and her knowledge of the close working relationship between her father and the Bird family can be read in the short stories. Lavin's nuanced understanding of the topographical and social milieu also contributes a distinct picture of Irish life at a particular juncture. However, this familiarity is only present because her father, Tom Lavin, travelled to America. That particular set of circumstances determined the outcome of future writings.

The creative process of fiction has always driven Mary Lavin. Whilst Lavin has never denied the manifestation of the Lavin family experience that lies at the heart of the short stories explored here, that experience has yet to be given full credit elsewhere in readings of her work. That family history, in part mirroring the histories of so many other Irish men and women, informs the national narrative and in particular shapes those fictional emphases that Lavin places on the transatlantic shift and the rebuilding of a new life in Ireland. It also contributes a distinct richness and depth to Lavin's own fictions. It is for these reasons that readers should be informed by Lavin's personal history.

Endnotes

1   The 1912 Walpole Census, East Walpole Historical Society Archives, Massachusetts, USA.

2   C. Murphy, 'Mary Lavin: an Interview', *Irish University Review*, 9, 2, (Autumn 1979), pp.207–24, 210.

3   A.A. Kelly, *Mary Lavin, Quiet Rebel: A Study of her Short Stories* (Dublin: Wolfhound Press, 1980), p.170. Kelly suggests that Lavin works 'within a limited artistic field, geographic, sociological and emotional in order to concentrate on the dramatic representation of feeling'.

4   L. Robert and S. Stevens, 'An Interview with Mary Lavin', *Studies*, 86, 341, (Spring 1997), p.46.

5   M. Lavin, *Selected Stories* (New York: The Macmillan Company, 1959), p.vii.

6   R. Williams, 'Realism and the Contemporary Novel', in D. Lodge (ed.), *20th Century Literary Criticism. A Reader* (London; New York: Longman, 1972), p.584.

7   M. Lavin, 'Writer at Work: an Interview with Mary Lavin', *St Stephens* 12, p.22, (1967).

8   Sarah Orne Jewett, *The Country of the Pointed Firs and Other Stories* (1896; New York; London: W.W. Norton and Company, 1994).

9   Declaration dated 17/6/81 relinquishing citizenship, Mary Lavin Papers, James Joyce Library, Special Collections, University College Dublin, Ireland, Folder 4.

10 Dating for all stories is for their first publication and based on Heinz Kosok's dateline in 'Mary Lavin: A Bibliography', *Irish University Review*, 9, 2, (Autumn 1979), pp.279–312.

11 J. Quinn (ed.), 'Mary Lavin', in *A Portrait of the Artist as a Young Girl* (London: Methuen, 1987), p.82.

12 L. Levenson, *The Four Seasons of Mary Lavin* (Dublin: Marino Books, 1998), p.18.

13 Correspondence between Mary Lavin, William Walsh, Tom Lavin and the Bird family during the 1940s illustrates the close connection between these individuals and the working of the Bective Estate: The Howard Gotlieb Archive, Boston University, USA; Mary Lavin Papers, James Joyce Library.

14 Quinn, *A Portrait*, p.81.

15 M. Lavin, 'At Sallygap', in *Tales From Bective Bridge* (London: Michael Joseph, 1943); J. Joyce, 'Eveline', in *Dubliners* (London: Paladin, 1988).

16 See also G. Tallone, 'Elsewhere is a Negative Mirror: The "Sally Gap" Stories of Éilís Ní Dhuibhne and Mary Lavin', *Hungarian Journal of English and American Studies*, 10, 1-2 (2004), pp. 203–15. Tallone's insightful reading of Lavin's 'At Sallygap' locates the geographical space of the mountain route as 'a new home for alternate readings of individual lives' and identifies another stage in emigration discourse through Éilís Ní Dhuibhne's 'At Sally Gap'.

17 Robert and Stevens, 'An Interview with Mary Lavin', p.47.

18 Murphy, 'Mary Lavin: An Interview', p.209.

19 Ibid., pp. 209, 208.

20 Quinn, *A Portrait*, p.85.

21 Letter dated 30 January 1940, Ellery Sedgwick papers, Massachusetts Historical Society, Boston, USA: Mary Lavin folder. Permission granted by the Lavin family to use this quotation here.

22 M. Lavin, 'Lemonade' in *The Great Wave and Other Stories* (New York: The Macmillan Company, 1961), p.75.

23 Ibid.

24 'Women in Steerage – Conditions called appalling', *The New York Times*, 14 December 1909.

25 Quinn, *A Portrait*, p.81.

26 M. Lavin, 'Tom', in *The Shrine and Other Stories* (London: Constable, 1977), pp.67, 71.

27 Lavin, 'Tom', p.52.

28 Levenson, *The Four Seasons*, p.17.

29 Lavin, 'Lemonade', p.79; 'The Little Prince', in *The Patriot Son and Other Stories* (London: Michael Joseph, 1956), p.239.

30 Lavin, *Selected Stories*, p.viii.

31 J. Ryan, 'Inadmissable Departures: Why did the Emigrant Experience Feature so Infrequently in the Fiction of the Mid-twentieth Century?', in D. Keogh, F. O'Shea and C. Quinlan (eds), *Ireland: The Lost Decade in the 1950s* (Cork: Mercier Press, 2004), pp.230–1.

32 L. Ryan, '"A Decent Girl Well Worth Helping": Women, Migration and Unwanted Pregnancy' in L. Harte and Y. Whelan (eds), *Ireland Beyond Boundaries Mapping Irish Studies in the Twenty-first Century* (London; Dublin: Pluto Press, 2007), p.137.

33 M. Lavin, 'The Little Prince', p.203.

34 Ibid., p.207.

35 Ibid., p.199.

36 Ibid., p.231.

37 Ibid., p.251.

38 M. Lavin, *Tales From Bective Bridge* [1942], (London: Michael Joseph, 1945).

39 Walpole Historical Society, *Images of America: Walpole* (Portsmouth NH: Arcadia, 1998, 2004). The history of the Bird family is written and privately supplied by Elizabeth M. Cottrell, article, 2008, untitled. Lavin recalls her father's suggestion to Charles Sumner

Bird Jr. in Quinn, *A Portrait*, p.88.

40 Newspaper articles document the successful racing career of Heartbreak Hill, a horse owned by the Bird family and trained by Tom Lavin; his own letters detail racing successes and Tom Lavin's obituary notes his presence at local shows: *The Irish Times*, 4 October 1945.

41 C. Walsh, 'Bective: once you belong you belong', *The Irish Times*, 20 June 1978.

42 Letter dated 25 April 1940, Ellery Sedgwick Papers, Massachusetts Historical Society. Mary Lavin's reference is to 'Lilacs', *Tales From Bective Bridge* (1942). Permission to use the quotation here is granted by the Lavin family estate.

43 Z. Bowen, *Mary Lavin* (London: Associated University Presses, 1975; Lewisburg, USA: Bucknell University Press, 1975); R.F. Peterson, *Mary Lavin* (Boston: Twayne Publishers, 1978).

44 M. Lavin, 'Scylla and Charybdis', in *The Patriot Son and Other Stories* (London: Michael Joseph, 1956). This is the only collection in which this short story appears.

45 Ibid., p.39.

46 Ibid.

47 Ibid., p.38.

48 M. Lavin, 'The Joy Ride' and 'Magenta', in *The Becker Wives and Other Stories* (London: Michael Joseph, 1946).

49 V. Kreilkamp, *The Anglo-Irish Novel and the Big House* (Syracuse, NY: Syracuse University Press, 1998), p.21.

50 Bowen, *Mary Lavin*, p.25.

51 Lavin, 'The Joy Ride', p.79.

52 Ibid. Bective was reputed to have 300 acres including woodland, although estate agent particulars (undated) put it at 178 acres: Howard Gotlieb Archive, Boston University, MA.

53 Ibid., p.80.

54 C. Wills, *That Neutral Island: A Cultural History of Ireland during the Second World War* (London: Faber and Faber, 2007), p.297.

55 G. Cronin, 'The Big House and the Irish Landscape in the Work of Elizabeth Bowen', in J. Genet (ed.), *The Big House in Ireland: Reality and Representation* (Dingle, Co. Kerry: Brandon Books, 1991), pp.143–62.

56 Lavin, 'Magenta', p.185.

57 M. Lavin, 'A Memory', in *A Memory and Other Stories* (London: Constable, 1972).

58 E. Bowen, 'The Back Drawing Room', in *The Collected Stories of Elizabeth Bowen* (1980; London: Penguin Books, 1983); S. O'Faoláin, 'Midsummer Night Madness', in *Midsummer Night Madness and Other Stories* (1932; London: Penguin Books, 1982).

7 Blind Faith and Class Distinctions in Mary Lavin's 'The Small Bequest' and 'The Mock Auction'

Jeanette Shumaker

Mary Lavin's short story 'The Small Bequest' (1944) and her novella 'The Mock Auction' (1967) question the blind faith that retainers were traditionally expected to have in their employers.[1] Emma Blodgett of 'The Small Bequest' and Miss Lomas of 'The Mock Auction' look at themselves as members of their employers' families rather than as the employees they in fact are. In other words, Emma and Miss Lomas are outsiders who regard themselves as insiders. Emma is well-paid as her employer's companion, but she spends her salary on gifts for her employer's family, rather than saving for her retirement. Unlike Emma, Miss Lomas is unpaid; yet as the caretaker of a substantial farmhouse, Miss Lomas commands a maid, lives in the farmhouse's best bedroom, and, at her employer's behest, buys herself clothes befitting a lady. Miss Lomas thinks she is 'above money'[2], while Emma's generosity suggests she possesses a similar disinterest in preparing for old age. Images of a neglected, decaying house and garden help readers envision each woman's predicament after her employer dies. Lavin's works dramatize the painful, ambiguous position of the once-privileged, aging dependent who is neither a servant nor a master.

Critics of Lavin remark that the lack of political content, especially nationalism, in her stories explains the neglect of her work compared with that of male contemporaries such as Frank O'Connor.[3] 'The Patriot Son' (1956), Lavin's only story about nationalism, condemns it. In 2008, Elke D'hoker commented, 'Her work cannot be placed comfortably in the framework of Irish literature in general and the Irish short story in particular, nor does it allow for an easy recuperation in a feminist tradition, which has hampered a potential revival of her work in the context of feminist literary studies.'[4] Jacqueline Fulmer observes that 'The severity of censorship in Lavin's time, coupled with that era's hardened attitude towards opportunities for women, caused her to step so lightly sometimes that her shocks take some effort to reveal.'[5] I argue for placing Lavin in what Gerry Smyth calls 'the counter-tradition of ... Irish [fiction] which can be understood as an attempt to escape the limitations of the nation's colonial heritage and the manner in which it was forced to construe the world in terms of rigidly defined, oppositional categories — Irish and English, woman and man, national and alien'.[6] Through their optimistic female protagonists, 'The Small Bequest' and 'The Mock Auction' question such rigid dichotomies, especially in terms of class. I will draw upon the theories of René Girard, Julia Kristeva and others to illuminate the class dichotomies in Lavin's works.

While in 'The Mock Auction' Miss Lomas shares the role of outsider with a young man, Christy, in 'The Small Bequest' Emma Blodgett is the only outsider. Both stories critique Ireland's constricting snobbery, which Lavin, as the daughter of a steward to a large estate, had experienced herself.[7] 'The Small Bequest' focuses upon three elderly spinsters living in a household that, to the female narrator who lives next door, initially appears idyllic. Lavin's narrator is like a detective trying to solve a mystery about the secret conflicts between her neighbours: wealthy Adeline, her paid companion Emma, and Adeline's maid Hetty. By creating a narrator who tells a mystery story tongue-in-cheek, Lavin produces both suspense and amusement. Lavin distances readers to allow them to smile at Adeline's subtle struggles against Emma. This, in turn, prepares readers to be shocked by the story's dark ending. In these two Lavin stories, rivalry occurs between insiders and outsiders, as defined by their class. In *Deceit, Desire and the Novel*, René Girard explains that vanity is what motivates rivalry, and 'that same vanity demands [the rival's] defeat'.[8] Adeline Tate's grandniece Lucy remarks that her elderly aunt's vanity is as pronounced as that of 'a young girl'.[9]

Girard defines internal mediation as rivalry; by contrast, external mediation involves worshipping someone. Adeline's resentment of Emma fits Girard's notion of internal mediation since she sees Emma as her rival for the younger Tates' affection. By contrast, Emma, at first glance, seems to exemplify external mediation regarding Adeline, for Emma 'worships [her] model openly and declares [herself her] disciple'.[10] As Adeline's disciple, Emma wears an imitation silk dress of the same blue as Adeline's real silk gown. However, when Emma reports that shopkeepers take advantage of Adeline whenever she buys real silk at twice the price of the artificial silk that Emma considers identical, she no longer sounds like her mistress' disciple.[11] Here, as in calling the Tates by their childhood nicknames, Emma's error, from Adeline's point of view, lies in daring to take liberties with her so-called betters, whether through holding her own opinion about fabric or publicly claiming intimacy with her employers.[12] However, the narrator challenges Adeline's snobbery when she argues that it is 'natural' for Emma to use nicknames for the adult Tates given that she helped raise them: Emma started working for Adeline twenty-seven years ago, at age 33.

Another example of Emma's overstepping, in Adeline's judgment, occurs when Emma warns Adeline not to lean over too far while weeding. Instead of acting like an upper servant, Emma behaves more like a niece or a friend, daring to nag Adeline for her own good. But unquestioning obedience is what Adeline wants from Emma, not intimacy. When Emma calls her employer 'Aunt Adeline' and spends her ample salary on gifts for the Tates as though they were her own family, she defies class distinctions, albeit in an unusually gentle way. Unintentionally then, if we agree with the narrator that Emma is at times 'obtuse'[13], Emma provokes rivalry in Adeline over who has the best judgment and who most deserves affection from the young Tates.[14]

Girard explains that when a rival embraces internal mediation, 'all that interests him is a decisive victory over his insolent mediator'.[15] Adeline decides she will vanquish Emma from beyond the grave, after she no longer needs Emma's services. Adeline cleverly uses Emma's own words to hurt her when Adeline wills her thousand pounds to her 'fond niece Emma', who, according to the family's lawyer, doesn't exist.[16] Thus the deceased Adeline punishes Emma for having dared to claim a close relationship with her.

Adeline may be jealous of Emma's relative youth — for Emma, at 60, is twenty years younger than Adeline. Maybe Adeline resents Emma for being likely to outlive her. Adeline also seems to resent Emma's superior hearing and the affection that the kindly companion inspires in the young Tates: Emma 'had dangled most of them with as much affection, and a great deal more energy, than Miss Tate had ever done'.[17] At times, Adeline acts as though she were grateful towards Emma, but at other times, Adeline displays what Girard might call 'the most intense malice'.[18] The narrator is troubled by her glimpses of Adeline's hostility towards Emma. Adeline indirectly admits to her capacity for malice when she tells the narrator that the Tates have a 'bitter streak' in them that Emma, with her 'kind heart', lacks.[19]

'The more intense the hatred the nearer it brings us to the loathed rival', Girard argues.[20] Throughout the story, Adeline increases her engagement with Emma through shooting 'arrows' of anger that are the converse of Cupid's barbs of love. Paradoxically, though Adeline tries to convince the narrator that Emma is totally unlike Adeline's relatives, the intensity of Adeline's resentment of Emma is more like that of a jealous elder sister than an employer. As Girard writes, 'The sadist's violence is yet another effort to attain divinity.'[21] Like a Pharaoh, Adeline makes her chief minister Emma die with her in a metaphorical sense. Anger is an animating emotion; perhaps in old age Adeline feels most alive when she is sneering at Emma. Adeline's will is her only long-lasting shot at Emma; contemplating it probably gave Adeline secret pleasure during her last years. By speaking of Emma with apparent love in her will, Adeline makes herself sound benevolent while she is in fact robbing Emma of her well-deserved retirement. Adeline's actual bequest to Emma is poverty.

Girard reports that 'the mediator's apparent hostility does not diminish his prestige but instead augments it'.[22] When Adeline sneers at Emma for calling her 'Aunt Adeline', for example, Emma apparently doesn't notice. Emma also shows her tolerance of her employer's black moods by distracting Adeline from feeling irritated when she is unable to understand the young Tates due to the deterioration of her hearing at age 80. Despite her increasing shabbiness after Adeline dies, Emma refuses to think of Adeline as vengeful for leaving her without a bequest. Instead, Emma worships the memory of the Aunt Adeline she wished she had had, falling for the pretence of affection in Adeline's will. Ironically, she makes it impossible for Emma to forget her, for Emma doesn't have the means to move on. Emma might be compared to Job, since she is steadfast in her faith in a harsh divinity. Seeming to embody an ideal employee, Emma is masochistic in accepting Adeline's harshness which culminates in the pettiness of her will. Emma regards Adeline's supposed error of calling Emma her niece in her will as proof of Adeline's unstinting affection. For if Adeline really had regarded Emma as her niece, Emma would have become a Tate in feeling if not in fact, and would no longer be a member of what Girard calls 'the race of the accursed'.[23]

When Adeline shows the Tate family photographs to the narrator, she treats them as relics. Girard comments that 'The object is to the [external] mediator what a relic is to a saint.'[24] The photos are in similar 'silver and filigree frames' that denote not only their value but that they are to be regarded as a family group. The narrator comments: 'One after another [Adeline] rammed the silver frames into my hands, but snatched them away again almost as quickly, so that I had hardly time to do more than glimpse them.' Adeline's speed and roughness in presenting each photo comically suggests that she is not interested in familiarizing the narrator with the individuals pictured, but in teaching the narrator to recognize familial traits. When Adeline asks the narrator whether she noticed 'how strong the likeness is all down the line', she answers her own question by pointing out the abundance of 'aquiline noses' in the photos.[25] Ironically, Adeline is proud of those pronounced noses stereotypically associated with aristocrats, and also that Tate men are tall and the women small, with fine ankles.

The narrator sees Adeline look at Emma's 'fat ankles' with 'that glance of hatred' after praising the delicacy of the Tate ankles.[26] Did Adeline pick Emma for her companion in part because Emma is larger than herself? Emma's easy-going attitude enables her to overlook Adeline's jibes in a way the perceptive narrator cannot. Most likely, Adeline hired Emma so that she could enjoy feeling superior to her on a variety of counts.[27] Emma 'had a mass of grey hair, strong, straight, and unruly. Her figure was stout, too.'[28]

Augustine Martin praises Lavin's insight into the Irish middle class, while Thomas J. Murray observes that Lavin's characters are often 'the small crabbed people one associates with small dingy shops'.[29] Adeline might not belong to the middle class, but her fear of being considered one of its members motivates her prejudice against Emma. Stallybrass and White's argument about the motives behind middle-class snobbery applies to Adeline: 'The bourgeois subject continuously defined and redefined itself through the exclusion of what it marked out as 'low' — as dirty, repulsive, noisy, contaminating.'[30] Sublimation of 'low' desires may be the middle class' way of enforcing its supremacy. Even though the Tate family contains titled personages, it comes from 'plain' origins, and Adeline herself has no title, unlike some of her relatives. Adeline solidifies her aristocratic identity through ostracizing Emma, a symbol of ordinary carnality.

As if she is the protagonist of a doppelganger written in an unusually light vein, Adeline assigns her double, Emma, her own physical functions. When the young Tates bring candy or cakes, it is Emma who eats them for Adeline: 'the bodily appreciation of the gifts fell entirely to Miss Blodgett'; here Emma might be comparable to a dog who eats treats from its mistress' plate.[31] Yet Emma is no glutton in terms of her service to the Tates, whatever physical appearances she has to the contrary. Emma's 'surprisingly maternal bosom' is in accord with her generous love for Adeline.[32] Such love exceeds the role of a paid companion, growing beyond it, like Emma's ample figure. Emma may look like a Caliban compared to Adeline or Hetty's Ariel, but appearances are misleading. The narrator's frequent mistakes about which neighbour is which increase the readers' confusion about who deserves the most sympathy — Emma, Adeline or Hetty.

Lavin makes readers wonder whether markers of class such as the quality of a woman's clothes and visiting cards matter as much as the narrator and Adeline believe. Regarding silk quality, the narrator agrees with Adeline that real silk is superior to artificial silk because Adeline's real silk 'delicately rustled' while Emma's imitation silk rather comically 'creak[s]'.[33] Similarly, Adeline and Emma's visiting cards seem 'equally white', but Adeline's is engraved, whereas Emma's is handwritten, and Adeline's is on thicker stock than Emma's.[34] The spectre of the nineteenth-century stage Irishman and of the working-class Irish as simian creatures underlie Adeline and the narrator's contempt for the socially climbing Emma.

But Adeline and the narrator are not the only snobs. Emma's view of Hetty as low appears in her pleasure at ordering Hetty around as though Emma, not Adeline, were the mistress. At the story's end, Emma tells the narrator that since Hetty was 'only a servant', she meant 'nothing' to Adeline.[35] Of course, the irony here is that Emma still doesn't see that to Adeline, Emma was also a servant, and that's why her employer resented Emma acting like a relative.

By contrast with Emma, Hetty is small and slim like Adeline. Having served the Tates for fifty years, Hetty wears Adeline's old gowns and hats and at a distance, the narrator sometimes confuses the two. Hetty's resemblance to Adeline doesn't bother her mistress. This contrasts with Adeline's anger when Emma claims kin by calling her Aunt. Perhaps Adeline reacts differently because she and Emma share social territory that Hetty never enters. For example, when Emma and Adeline answer a niece's question at the same time and in the same words, it irritates Adeline. Twice, the narrator abruptly moves from comparing Hetty and Emma to comparing Hetty and Adeline; this shift confuses the reader, showing that distinctions of appearance and class are arbitrary. The narrator remarks: 'with her blue gown hidden under an old-fashioned apron, I would never have mistaken poor old Hetty for Miss Blodgett. Indeed, no two people could have been more dissimilar in many ways, although as a matter of fact in physique Hetty and Miss

Tate were not altogether unalike.'[36] Later, the narrator again compares two of her neighbours, then suddenly switches her subjects of comparison, creating three unstable dyads of similar yet different women:

> There could be no doubt that this charming old figurine [Adeline] was the result of careful selection and breeding. Yet, it was surprising to see how a generation or two of poverty and privation too could accelerate the pace of bone refinement, because there was undoubtedly something fine and compelling in old Hetty's clear and angular face. All the same, it was stupid of me to have mistaken Hetty for Miss Blodgett.[37]

The narrator sounds like she may be mocking heavy Emma in claiming to confuse her with thin Hetty. This is the sort of underhand thing Adeline might do. Perhaps in calling herself 'stupid' for engaging in a sarcastic comparison between Emma and Hetty, the narrator reminds the reader how easy it is for anyone to fall into petty ways of thinking like Adeline's.

Yet in linking Emma and Hetty, however confusingly, the narrator makes the reader remember their common ground as employees of Adeline. This prepares the reader to contrast Emma and Hetty's fate at the end of the story, when Emma, who had once lived more luxuriously than Hetty, now lives much less comfortably than the former maid does. Unlike Emma, Hetty never aspires to become a Tate. Hetty saves her earnings, then puts them into educating her own nieces and nephews. After Adeline dies, Hetty inherits her small bequest from Adeline and moves in with her brother, as happily ensconced in her own family as Adeline had long been among the Tates.

Observing Adeline's Edenic garden from her study window, the narrator again draws attention to the similarities and differences between the three old ladies. When Adeline pours tea for Hetty — though the servant drinks it standing — the narrator feels she is observing a peaceful community of women. The exotic imagery the narrator uses to describe Adeline's garden evokes its utopian, magical aura: 'Viewed from my study window, indeed, the whole of Miss Tate's garden looked as unreal but as entrancing as the miniature Japanese gardens that children used to construct long ago in shallow saucers, which, when finished, tantalized them with a longing to be small enough themselves to wander within.'[38] The narrator here compares Adeline as the garden's designer to a child, but in a more attractive way than when she compared Adeline to a child focused on choosing a funeral wreath rather than on the death it commemorates. Yet when Adeline eventually takes her final shot at Emma by withholding her inheritance, the reader realizes the dark potential in childishness: Adeline's smallness of mind is like that of a bonsai tree, stunted by decades of training in snobbery. One can speculate perhaps that had Emma cultivated her Blodgett style that is as exotic in the Tate world as a Japanese shrub, her mistress would have liked her better.

In Adeline's garden, 'there were bowls of water of all shapes and sizes, wide and narrow, deep and shallow, to facilitate the different needs of bird, beast and butterfly'.[39] Adeline's Eden seems to demonstrate her philanthropic nature, including her ability to appreciate diverse objects of charity. That Adeline is kind to her pets may bolster Emma's faith in Adeline's good intent towards her. Months after Adeline dies, though, the narrator notices that stray animals and half-tame pigeons still forlornly wait for food in Adeline's now empty garden; somewhat ludicrously, the narrator is reminded of a disappointed pigeon when she runs into Emma. Again, as when the narrator noticed Emma eating the treats Adeline's relatives brought to their aunt, she conjures an image of Emma as her employer's deserted pet, not her employee or friend.

Though Emma believes the Tates 'think of me as one of themselves', she is proven wrong by their unwillingness to settle her claim on their aunt's estate out of their own well-filled pockets.[40] Emma's illusions about the Tate heirs are as generous and mistaken as they are about Adeline herself. Is Lavin suggesting that Emma is as stupid as the narrator thinks her, or that Emma is noble in her unshakeable faith in the Tates?[41] The latter, I think, for Emma appears to be susceptible to the utopian dream that the narrator conjures on seeing Adeline's garden at night: 'And in the middle of this misty moonlit sea [of light] the small white-painted glasshouse with its pointed roof seemed to float through the night like a silver barque of romance.'[42] This is not the kind of 'romance' that involves heterosexual passion, for this garden belongs to an elderly woman. However, the moon and the sea are often linked with women. Emma's impossible 'romance' is that in Adeline's cloistered garden she might escape the seedy capitalism Yeats associates with the Irish middle class. Caitriona Clear explains that after 1945, the proportion of women in domestic service in Ireland dramatically declined as women emigrated, or, by 1961, often became factory workers or typists.[43] As elderly women serving an even older employer in the 1940s, Emma and Hetty are dinosaurs, examples of a dying tradition of lifetime domestic service. Emma's self-abnegation in spending her salary on the Tates fits the womanly ideal of her time as described in publications such as the Catholic Church's *Irish Messenger*.

Emma embodies the other-directedness latent in the word 'companion' through following the feminine ideals she had been taught.

It may be that the Tates secretly share Adeline's resentment of Emma, and that is why they do not rectify the problem in Adeline's will. The narrator provides a clue about the likelihood of the Tates' irritation with Emma when she comments that 'when one heard Miss Blodgett familiarly chaffing with judges and peers, and scolding a bishop for having snuff on his cuff, it was a little surprising to recollect that she had originally joined the Tate household in a most humble capacity'.[44] The narrator uses gardening metaphors throughout the story to emphasize that the Tates regard themselves as a result of careful breeding, implying that they share Adeline's prejudices along with her delicate ankles. The Tates may be as willing as Adeline to open their garden to outsiders and to provide their pets — animal or human — with special diets suitable to their tastes, but they will never accept a member of another class — which to the Tates means almost another species — as one of themselves. It is ironic that the story's gardening imagery contains both Edenic promise and the cruel distinctions between so-called species that spoil Adeline's artificial paradise.

While 'The Small Bequest' is told by a first-person narrator, 'The Mock Auction' is narrated in the third person from the point of view of the protagonist Miss Lomas. Hence, the reader doesn't fully realize that Miss Lomas' employers, the Garret brothers, are not as nice as she thinks they are until well into the story. Nevertheless, a hint of George Garret's ruthlessness appears: 'George was so pleased that he slapped his thigh the way he did when he'd tell her he'd bought a herd of cattle for next to nothing.'[45] Here readers see that George gloats over defrauding cattle owners of the payment they deserve. These are the cattlemen George entertained with Miss Lomas at Brook Farm to lower their defences and thus reduce their ability to bargain with him. Miss Lomas had regarded these cattlemen as 'almost ... one large happy family' that included her and the Garret brothers.[46]

With an inflated sense of self, Miss Lomas deludes herself that she is 'above money'.[47] The definition of 'loma' in Spanish is hill, suggesting that Miss Lomas' perspective may be warped. Miss Lomas does not see herself as exploited even though the Garrets pay her no wages, until after both brothers die and their lawyer, Mr Parr, tells her that she will have to leave the house for which she has cared for decades. Perhaps the reason she agrees to work for room, board and clothing is that she grew up in an era when in Ireland 'the landlord's patriarchal authority is both maintained and enhanced by the strategic employment of benevolence'.[48]

It seems likely that Parr knew Miss Lomas was never paid, though he pretends he doesn't, for Parr is the one who had suggested that George Garret make up a list of Brook Farm expenditures as a way to defraud George's nephew, Christy. Even so, after George's death, Parr threatens to prosecute Miss Lomas for perjury for having confirmed the false salary figure for her as caretaker that George invented, if she attempts to get her decades of unpaid wages out of the Garret estate.

Later in the story, Parr resembles Jason Quirk from Maria Edgeworth's *Castle Rackrent* (1800). Miss Lomas hears that George Garret's elderly sister, a semi-invalid, has been sent to a public nursing home, a come-down for a once-wealthy lady. Yet when she offers to care for Miss Garret at Brook Farm, Parr demurs, saying neither she nor Miss Garret has a right to the farm and that Miss Garret has no money, only debts. Miss Lomas learns that Miss Garret has willed her jewels to Mr Parr, but he claims they merely have sentimental value. How has Mr Parr gotten Miss Garret to make him her beneficiary? Is it through courtship? Blackmail? Or is Miss Garret repaying a private loan? Not only does Mr Parr echo the deviousness of Jason Quirk in manipulating Protestant landowners but in eventually buying some of their property himself. What enables Parr to do this is that Miss Lomas shifts her alliance to him, her old enemy, advising him to buy Brook Farm 'for a song' when she realizes he's the only one left who might give her a home there.[49] That she sees Parr as 'a fox' and 'a leathery little bat' suggests she recognizes his ability to prosper by figuratively devouring the Garrets.[50]

Still, once Miss Lomas has decided Parr is the only one who will let her stay at Brook Farm, she casts him in a newly positive light, conveniently transferring her faithfulness from the Garrets to him. She recalls that the Garrets had once made fun of Parr for being thin and pale, then reminds Parr that he has managed to outlive the plump Garrets whose hearty looks were deceiving. Miss Lomas flatters Parr too by suggesting that owning Brook Farm will raise his status, benefitting his nieces and nephews. Parr can use the farmhouse as a weekend retreat that will show his nieces' suitors that they come from an established family. Instead of being a setting for the Garret brothers to entertain cattlemen, Brook Farm will become a place of relaxation and genteel entertainment for the Parrs when they want to escape the rush of town life.

Parr agrees to keep Miss Lomas as caretaker because she legitimizes his purchase of Brook Farm. Parr states his anxiety that the neighbours will resent him, but how can they resent Miss Lomas, whom they have known for so long? If she forgives Parr, so will the neighbours. Miss Lomas requests no salary from Parr, seeming to remain as trusting of her new employer as she was of her old one.

She speaks of Parr's nieces and nephews with an enthusiasm she once reserved for the Garrets; the Parrs replace the Garrets as her adopted family.

Parr and Miss Lomas are not the only characters in the story whose class positions are slippery. Christy, George and Joss Garret's nephew, becomes their charge after his mother, a Garret, dies. Instead of keeping Christy with them and Miss Garret in the main house, though, they have Christy live with Miss Lomas at Brook Farm. Their lodging choice suggests that the Garrets don't regard Christy as one of their family. Also, the Garrets assign Christy humble chores and laugh at his awkward manners, treating him as a poor relation.

After George's brother Joss dies without leaving a will, George and Parr use a mock auction to keep Christy from inheriting the one-third of the money from the sale of Brook Farm that the young man has coming. However, a few months later, George's unexpected death leads Christy to become the nominal owner of Brook Farm, though without the funds he needs to keep it up, and with the Garret estate holding a heavy mortgage on it. Parr tells Miss Lomas that he will 'starve [Christy] out'.[51] It is at this point that she joins Christy in hating Parr, for he intends to drive her out of Brook Farm along with Christy, regarding them as '[t]wo leeches' on the Garret estate.[52]

When Christy and Miss Lomas burn their letters from Parr without reading them, they become allies, after having lived in the same house in enmity for years. Richard F. Peterson calls this part of Lavin's novella 'an unyielding study of the bitter symbiotic relationship between Miss Lomas and Christy'.[53] Even though they continue to detest each other, Christy supports Miss Lomas when her funds run out. He does so by selling the furniture of Brook Farm, its stock, farm implements and even its gates. When Christy finally leaves the farm as he fears Parr will prosecute him for despoiling it, Christy gives Miss Lomas his last ten-shilling note. This implies that he cares about her, despite his never-changing rudeness to her.

The depredations of Christy make Brook Farm look as poor as the surrounding farms, which use broken bedsteads as gates. Gothic imagery shows the sad state of the farm after Christy starts neglecting and figuratively consuming it. Miss Lomas had always felt contempt for Christy because his father's family was as poor as Brook Farm's neighbours. Ironically, she fails to see that while she is just a caretaker, Christy is a member of the same Garret family that she idolizes. However, as with her initial disparagement of Parr as weak and weedy, she learned to belittle Christy from the Garret brothers. Yet because the story is told through Miss Lomas' perspective, the reader does not disagree with her low estimate of Christy, nor begin to blame the Garrets for mistreating him until late in the story. It is, surprisingly, Parr who says, 'I thought George should be given a chance to die without having his shabby treatment of Christy on his conscience.'[54] Parr informs Miss Lomas that the Garret brothers sabotaged Christy's future by refusing to leave him enough money for him to be able to keep up Brook Farm. In fact, the lawyer takes Christy's part not due to a sense of justice but because Parr thinks that buying Christy out of the estate by giving him Brook Farm would be best for Miss Garret, her brothers' principal heir, and his employer.

Julia Kristeva's notion of abjection can be used to explain the Garrets' contempt for Christy. Kristeva defines the abject as 'the not-I'; its recognition causes loathing for certain foods, corpses, and even classes of people whom one associates with death.[55] Abjection occurs when we counter our dread of death with negative projections onto marginalized groups. Ostracized groups are viewed as sources of contamination as well as exemplars of one's own hidden corruption. Kristeva observes that 'the in-between, the ambiguous, the composite' tend to stimulate repulsion because they disturb our sense of order.[56] To his Garret uncles, Christy is a 'composite' of their own respected Protestant blood and his lowly Catholic father's. That the Garret brothers refuse to make proper arrangements for Christy to inherit suggests that they deny the inevitability of their own death. At least in part, they despise Christy because as their heir, he reminds them of their mortality.

What Vera Kreilkamp says of patriarchs in Irish Big House novels and stories applies to the Garret brothers: 'Often the landlord is simply too old, too much the product of worn-out and in-bred stock to perform; the persistent trope of his decaying house becomes a metaphor for his sexually inadequate body.'[57] At one time Miss Lomas had thought one of the Garrets might marry her, but instead the brothers create the household of aging, unwed siblings that was common in rural Ireland after the Famine. That Brook Farm decays after the Garret brothers' death due to their unwillingness to treat Christy properly in their wills fits Kreilkamp's observation that a Big House's decline symbolizes the dwindling of a family due to its patriarchs' sterility.

As in Synge's *Playboy of the Western World* (1907), Lavin's patriarchs resent their heir. The Garret brothers resemble Old Mahon in disparaging their heir for an awkwardness that is normal in youth. Treated disrespectfully by older male relatives, both Synge and Lavin's Christies behave rather brutishly in turn. Lavin's Christy carries an unloaded rifle to scare off anyone who might dispute his ownership of Brook Farm. Though Parr hears gossip about Christy and Miss Lomas living at the farm without chaperones, when he sees the aging lady he realizes such tales are absurd; Lavin's Christy is no playboy, and Miss Lomas, no Widow Quinn. Christy learns that he does not truly belong to the Garret family even though he is a close relative, while Miss Lomas refuses to accept that she cannot join the family through decades of unpaid labour. It is no accident that like Christy, Miss Lomas is a Catholic, following the tradition of Catholic Irish serving Anglo-Irish Protestants; maybe the Garrets would have respected a Protestant caretaker enough to pay her. Lavin's portrayal of the Garrets as exploitative confirms Ruth-Ann Harris' observation that 'Literary accounts have notoriously stripped the veneer of paternalism from the Irish landlord, exposing him as feckless, greedy, and predatory.'[58]

Miss Lomas presents Christy as a male Cinderella whom she looks down upon. 'Poor Christy had a yellow face, weedy yellow hair and even the whites of his eyes were yellow … It was a thorn in [Miss Lomas'] flesh that he was sometimes taken to be a relative of hers.'[59] In fact, the Garret brothers treat Miss Lomas with greater respect than their own nephew: 'In spite of [Christy's] spinelessness he would hardly put up forever with the humiliations that were heaped on him by his uncles in their disappointment at how he had turned out.'[60] Even after signing the loan papers at the mock auction, Christy is given menial tasks by his uncle: 'It was the sort of job Christy always got, but Miss Lomas was surprised at his being given such a menial job today of all days.'[61] Of Christy's 'old straw suitcase', Miss Lomas observes: 'Only an orphan would have had luggage like it'. When Miss Lomas travels to George's deathbed, her driver asks if Christy is coming, and she replies: 'He'd be the last one I'd want to see if I was ill, and I'm sure his uncle would feel the same.'[62]

Ironically, the supposed miser Parr might be a better uncle to his sister's fatherless children than the Garrets were to Christy. Parr employs his pimply nephew as his clerk, though Miss Lomas regards the young man as even thinner and more unpromising than Christy. The reader never finds out whether Parr has continued to lodge his sister, nephews and nieces in one of the 'dismal cottages' Miss Lomas knew they once lived in.[63] If so, Parr's choice might be similar to the Garrets' lodging of Christy at Brook Farm, at a distance befitting poor relations. If that is the case, Miss Lomas' idea about Brook Farm being a setting in which Parr might display his nieces for genteel suitors might be a mere dream.

As with 'The Small Bequest', the story's ambiguity raises questions. Who is the villain and who the victim? Are the Garrets villains for undermining Christy and exploiting Miss Lomas? Is Parr a villain for manipulating the Garret brothers, their sister and their nephew until he ends up as the owner of Brook Farm? Or is Parr the saviour of his impoverished nieces and nephews, as well as of Miss Lomas, who would have had nowhere to live had he not bought Brook Farm? Are Miss Lomas and Christy justified in despoiling Brook Farm to feed themselves after George dies, or are they thieves and vandals? If Christy and Miss Lomas have been indirectly robbed by the Garrets, don't they have a right to pay themselves back indirectly? The right of ownership is the issue the story and its title portray.

Like Emma Blodgett, Miss Lomas at the start of her story 'was as plump as a goose'.[64] Both are cosseted by their employers. Like Emma, Miss Lomas is snobbish towards maids — 'there had not been [a maid] who would have appreciated the quality of such clothes, neither the superior fabric nor the elegant cut'. In her knowledge of clothes, Miss Lomas contrasts with Emma, who is content with imitation silk; perhaps Miss Lomas grew up in a genteel background and Emma didn't. Like Emma, Miss Lomas 'regarded herself as one of the family'. The Garrets 'did not make a display of their wealth, but one had only to look at their sister to see the stock from which they had been bred'.[65] Miss Lomas here uses metaphors from animal husbandry to draw class distinctions in which Emma and Adeline also believe.

Like 'The Small Bequest', 'The Mock Auction' includes disturbing humour that augments Lavin's questioning of class dichotomies. It is comical that Miss Lomas is loyal to whoever will let her remain at Brook Farm, no matter how she feels about that person, as we see when her allegiances shift to Christy and finally Parr. She and Christy manage to keep hating each other even while they are allies living alone together. It is also ironic that elderly Miss Lomas has lost so much weight during her years of hardscrabble living with Christy that she is able to fit into the barely worn dress in which she arrived at Brook Farm as a young woman. Since the dress has a hobble skirt, we can guess it may be from about 1910, more than fifty years before Lavin's story was published, and thirty or forty years before it ends.

Irony also appears when George accuses Christy's paternal relatives of a desire to rob Christy: 'I wouldn't put it past them to rig the bidding.'[66] But George, guided by Parr, is the one who rigged the bidding at the mock auction. Parr sends what Miss Lomas thinks are 'stooges' to view Brook Farm. George has Miss Lomas invent a list of expenses for Brook Farm, since 'Parr will see that you get away with anything you put down'.[67] Further, it is ironic that as she travels to George's deathbed 'the neighbouring farms were an eyesore to Miss Lomas, the gaps in their mearings stopped with dead branches, and between the fields instead of gates discarded bedheads. Oh, how she despised the mean and petty economies by which the local farmers, not having the broadness of the Garrets eked out their scanty profits.'[68] Later, Christy's neglect of Brook Farm makes it fit into the local squalor: 'It was no worse, of course, than the small farmhouses around about, but if Christy was satisfied with this comparison, she was not.'[69]

Some of the story's humour is savage. In a cruel taunt, Parr plays with Miss Lomas when he says '"I didn't think we'd get away with that item [her invented salary on the list for the mock auction]. You must have a nice little nest egg stashed away." That ought to fix her, he thought.'[70] When Christy goes off on an old bike to buy food for them, Miss Lomas invests him with 'manliness', until 'She saw with disgust he had not taken the trouble to pump the tyres. It was not to be wondered he was a long time away, and that he came back on foot.'[71] It is also sadly comical that Miss Lomas' efforts to clean Brook Farm's house accelerate its decay, as when she scrubs a grease stain off the wallpaper only to have 'a long triangular piece of paper [give] way under her finger', or finding a toadstool on the kitchen ceiling, 'she hit at it as if it was a living creature. When it splattered all over the floor, she felt like a murderer.'[72]

Such black humour shows both Miss Lomas' flaws and her virtues. When Miss Lomas looks at the ten-shilling piece that Christy left her when he emigrated, she again thinks, 'Had she not always been above money?'[73] Such a thought, given her poverty, seems ludicrous, at a nearly insane level of denial, like Emma's belief that Adeline really meant to leave her a bequest. Yet Miss Lomas, unlike Emma, through force of will makes others do what she wants — first Christy, who stays at Brook Farm at her urging as the so-called owner though he has no money to run it, and then Parr, who buys the wrecked property at her behest. Miss Lomas' epiphany is that 'Parr and Miss Garret and Christy ... had all thought it was money she wanted. Oh, what a dreadful mistake!' She proves Parr mistaken when she offers to care for Miss Garret at Brook Farm without pay and, later, to work for Parr, again without pay. She convinces Parr that he is the one who is 'blind' to the opportunity Brook Farm offers, not she. In a hyperbolic image, she 'manacled [Parr's] hands in a warm moist clasp'.[74] The word 'manacled' suggests Miss Lomas uses her unstinting devotion to Brook Farm to trap its successive owners into letting her remain its caretaker, no matter whether they like her or not.

Noting that Miss Lomas is 'the least likeliest of Mary Lavin's heroines to overcome personal misfortune', Richard F. Peterson argues that her success at staying at Brook Farm 'stands out as a tribute to the enduring strength of the human heart'.[75] This is the somewhat comical triumph of the eternally hopeful dependent, a Candide who fares better in this later story than in Lavin's earlier

'The Small Bequest'. Perhaps in the 1960s the gradual loosening of class strictures in Ireland allowed Lavin to envision a happier future for Miss Lomas than she had for Emma Blodgett in a story written eighteen years before. Peterson believes that Miss Lomas' persistent optimism in 'The Mock Auction' is a precursor to the resilient philosophy seen in 'Happiness', the title story of Lavin's next collection.

Or readers may look backward to 'The Will' (1944), which more clearly endorses blind faith and loyalty than does either 'The Mock Auction' or 'The Small Bequest' — loyalty of daughter to mother, not of employee to employer, whose links are usually much weaker. Lavin's stories show an idealist who contrasts with a sceptic. In 'The Small Bequest', the sceptical narrator keeps her identity private beyond the fact that she is a single writer living next door to Adeline. In 'The Mock Auction', Parr is a successful, ruthless social climber, so his view of the idealist character is more suspect than that of the seemingly disinterested narrator of 'The Small Bequest'. Though the narrator regards Emma's blind faith in Adeline as proof of her stupidity, and Parr wonders more than once if Miss Lomas is mad in her devotion to Brook Farm, readers see that both women's self-deceived optimism supports their survival. Thus, Lavin celebrates the communal values of her women protagonists. As Elizabeth Abel has argued, 'Historically, only the masculine experience of separation and autonomy has been awarded the stamp of maturity; feminist theory suggests that the insistence on relationship reveals not a failed adulthood, but the desire for a different one.'[76] Looked at in this light, Emma and Miss Lomas become unlikely proto-feminist rebels. James W. Cahalan has claimed that Irish male authors usually write novels of development that valorise individualism, while Irish female authors value community; Lavin clearly fits this pattern.[77]

Though the *bildungsroman* traditionally focuses upon young protagonists who grow when confronted with challenges, Lavin writes about elderly women facing disasters that demand coping strategies. According to Susan Fraiman, *bildungsromane* by women often violate the conventional marriage plot.[78] Lavin does this on a dramatic scale by focusing upon aged women who have never married. Adeline punishes Emma Blodgett's communalism through leaving her out of her will. Yet since the reader does not approve of Adeline's vengefulness that is the opposite of Emma's generosity, 'The Small Bequest' confirms Emma's values. Miss Lomas clings as blindly to her communalism as Emma does, but is rewarded for doing so. Uncertain endings in narratives by women like Lavin enable avoidance of the marriages that often close works by men: 'The world turned upside down can prove that the world has no rightful position at all.'[79] So Lavin shows us in 'The Small Bequest' and 'The Mock Auction.'

Endnotes

1   Richard F. Peterson observes that 'The Small Bequest' resembles the first part of 'The Mock Auction' due to the similarity of their protagonists 'in occupation and dilemma'. He also claims that Lavin's notes single out 'Posy' (1947) and 'The Small Bequest' as stories she dislikes because of their reliance on plot twists. Nevertheless, Lavin included 'The Small Bequest' not only in her three-volume collection by Constable cited here, but also in her *Selected Stories* (New York: Macmillan, 1959) and her *Collected Stories* (Boston: Houghton Mifflin, 1971). R.F. Peterson, *Mary Lavin* (Boston: Twayne Publishers, 1978), pp.119, 86.

2   M. Lavin, 'The Mock Auction', in *The Stories of Mary Lavin, Volume 3* (London: Constable, 1985), p.173.

3   See R. Caswell, 'Irish Political Reality and Mary Lavin's *Tales from Bective Bridge*', *Éire-Ireland*, 3, (1968), p.59; and A. Martin, 'A Skeleton Key to the Stories of Mary Lavin', *Studies*, 52, 208, (Winter 1963), p.393.

4   E. D'hoker, 'Beyond the stereotypes: Mary Lavin's Irish women', *Irish Studies Review*, 16, 4 (2008), p.415. With regard to the feminist dimension, Sarah Briggs argues that Lavin uses spinsters in 'The Long Ago' (1944) and 'Heart of Gold' (1964) to critique the overvaluing of male-dominated marriage in Ireland. If we connect Emma and Adeline in 'The Small Bequest' to the marriage theme, it might be through Adeline's overvaluing of the familial bonds that are created via marriage to which Emma seems to have no access except through her unofficial adoption of the Tates. S. Briggs, 'A Man in the House: Mary Lavin and the Narrative of the Spinster', in A. Marshall and N. Sammells (eds), *Irish Encounters: Poetry, Politics and Prose since 1880* (Bath: Sulis Press, 1998).

5   J. Fulmer, *Folk Women and Indirection in Morrison, Ní Dhuibhne, Hurston and Lavin* (Burlington, VT: Ashgate, 2007), p.170. Fulmer also argues that Lavin uses folk elements in her fiction to approach controversial issues indirectly, thus avoiding censorship.

6   G. Smyth, *The Novel and the Nation: Studies in the New Irish Fiction* (London: Pluto, 1997), p.43.

7   L. Levenson, *The Four Seasons of Mary Lavin* (Dublin: Marino Books, 1998), p.41.

8   R. Girard, *Deceit, Desire and the Novel*, trans. Y. Freccero (Baltimore: Johns Hopkins University Press, 1965), p.7.

9   M. Lavin, 'The Small Bequest', in *The Stories of Mary Lavin, Volume 2* (London: Constable, 1974), pp.153–175, 168.

10 Girard, *Deceit*, p.10.

11 According to Leah Levenson's biography, Mary Lavin purchased only high-quality clothing for herself and her daughters, though she wore her tweeds and cashmeres carelessly. See Levenson, *The Four Seasons*, p.139.

12 Along these lines, Zack Bowen observes, 'Still another story of servants overstepping their prerogatives ['The Small Bequest'] has exactly the same outcome'. Z. Bowen, *Mary Lavin* (Lewisburg, PA: Bucknell University Press, 1975), p.26.

13 Lavin, 'The Small Bequest', p.173.

14 Nevertheless, Emma repeatedly asserts her superiority over Hetty, Adeline's maid. This implies that Emma believes in class distinctions except when they apply to herself.

15 Girard, *Deceit*, p.51.

16 Lavin, 'The Small Bequest', p.174.

17 Ibid., p.154.

18 Girard, *Deceit*, p.10.

19 Lavin, 'The Small Bequest', p.162.

20 Girard, *Deceit*, p.100.

21 Ibid., p.185.

22 Ibid., p.10.

23 Ibid., p.178.

24 Ibid., p.83.

25 Lavin, 'The Small Bequest', p.167.

26 Ibid., p.168.

27 As opposites, Adeline and Emma may to an extent fit Angeline Kelly's observation that Lavin often creates a Martha character who is hard-headed and harsh, contrasted with a Mary character who is kind and sensitive; though Emma is not sensitive, she does have a warm heart. A.A. Kelly, *Mary Lavin, Quiet Rebel: A Study of Her Short Stories* (Dublin: Wolfhound Press, 1980), p.30.

28 Ibid., p.156.

29 Martin, 'A Skeleton Key', p.393; T. J. Murray, 'Mary Lavin's World: Lovers and Strangers', *Éire-Ireland*, 7 (Summer 1972), p.125.

30 P. Stallybrass and A. White, *The Politics and Poetics of Transgression* (Ithaca NY: Cornell University Press, 1986), p.191.

31 Lavin, 'The Small Bequest', p.153. If we follow some contemporary critics in reading Shakespeare's *The Tempest* as an allegory about the Irish and the English, Caliban plays a role similar to Emma's in representing the Irish underling as bestial. Patrician Prospero is echoed by the Anglo-Irish Adeline, who proves herself a kind of twisted magician when she exercises strange powers through punishing Emma from beyond death. Of

course, Prospero eschews his vengefulness when he breaks his magician's staff, while Adeline glories in hers.

32 Ibid., p.156.

33 Ibid., p.157.

34 Ibid., p.155.

35 Ibid., p.175.

36 Ibid., p.155.

37 Ibid., p.156.

38 Ibid., p.159.

39 Ibid., p.158.

40 Ibid., p.175. Marie Arndt's argument about the outsider in Lavin stories could be applied to Emma Blodgett as well: 'The constrictive religious and social morality of Ireland in the stories causes suffering and turns those forced to live by these conventions into internal exiles.' Somewhat similarly, David Norris writes about Lavin's stories in terms of 'A central character whose joyful accord with nature is mirrored in the imagery of freshness and organic growth, comes into conflict with the unyielding structure of conventional social attitudes, yet manages to keep the flag ... defiantly flying.' Ironically, Emma doesn't care for gardening while Adeline does, but Emma is the warmer, more sincere woman of the two. M. Arndt, 'Narratives of Internal Exile in Mary Lavin's Short Stories', *International Journal of English Studies* 2, 2, (2002), p.110; D. Norris, 'Imaginative Responses versus Authority Structures: a Theme of the Anglo-Irish Short Story', in P. Rafroidi and T. Brown (eds), *The Irish Short Story* (Buckinghamshire, UK: Colin Smyth, 1979), p.58.

41 Richard J. Thompson suggests that 'Emma Blodgett comes to suggest a facetious version of bovine, unconsciously vulgar Emma Bovary ... Blodgett's refusal to admit disappointment after she is rejected in the will becomes her source of secret mirth and a proof to us of her pride and unwillingness to be subjugated, and so of her ultimate victory.' Though I am not convinced by Thompson's argument, he reads against the grain of Lavin's story in an original, provocative way. R. Thompson, *Everlasting Voices: Aspects of the Modern Irish Short Story* (Troy, NY: Whitston, 1989), p.89.

42 Lavin, 'The Small Bequest', p.159.

43 C. Clear, *Women of the House: Women's Household Work in Ireland 1926–61* (Portland, OR and Dublin: Irish Academic Press, 2000), p.18.

44 Lavin, 'The Small Bequest', p.154.

45 Lavin, 'The Mock Auction', p.167.

46 Ibid., p.159.

47 Ibid., p.173.

48 R.M. Harris, 'Negotiating Patriarchy: Irish Women and the Landlord', in M. Cohen and N. Curtin (eds), *Reclaiming Gender: Transgressive Identities in Modern Ireland* (New York: St. Martin's Press, 1999), p.209.

49 Lavin, 'The Mock Auction', p.197.

50 Ibid., pp.162, 195.

51 Ibid., p.176.

52 Ibid., p.179.

53 Peterson, *Lavin*, p.120.

54 Lavin, 'The Mock Auction', p.174.

55 J. Kristeva, *Powers of Horror: An Essay on Abjection*, L.S. Roudiez (trans.) (New York: Columbia University Press, 1982), p.2.

56 Ibid., p.4.

57 V. Kreilkamp, 'Losing It All: The Unmanned Irish Landlord', in Cohen and Curtin, *Reclaiming Gender*, p.112.

58 Harris, 'Negotiating Patriarchy', p.209.

59 Lavin, 'The Mock Auction', p.139.

60 Ibid., p.140.

61 Ibid., p.169.

62 Ibid., pp.192, 171.

63 Ibid., p.195.

64 Ibid., p.156.

65 Ibid., p.138.

66 Ibid., p.162.

67 Ibid., p.166.

68 Ibid., p.172.

69 Ibid., p.189.

70 Ibid., p.179.

71 Ibid., p.182.

72 Ibid., pp.181, 189.

73 Ibid., p.194.

74 Ibid., p.199.

75 Peterson, *Lavin*, p.121.

76 E. Abel, M. Hirsch, and E. Langland, *The Voyage In: Fictions of Female Development* (Hanover: University Press of New England, 1983), p.10.

77 J.W. Cahalan, *Double Visions: Women and Men in Modern and Contemporary Irish Fiction* (Syracuse: Syracuse University Press, 1999), p.108.

78 S. Fraiman, *Unbecoming Women: British Women Writers and the Novel of Development* (New York: Columbia University Press, 1993), p.ix.

79 R. Barreca, *'Untamed and Unabashed': Essays on Women and Humor in British Literature* (Detroit: Wayne State University Press, 1994), p.33.

8 | 'I had always despised him a little': Plumbing the Depths of Feeling in Mary's Lavin's Two Irish Novels

Derek Hand

Mary Lavin's two novels, *The House in Clewe Street* (1945) and *Mary O'Grady* (1950), have received little attention from literary critics. One reason for this is her celebrated reputation as a short story writer. Indeed, the influential critical template put forward by her contemporaries Frank O'Connor and Seán O'Faoláin[1] that argued for the short story being considered as *the* literary mode in Ireland, rather than the novel form, appears to define Lavin's writing career almost perfectly. Their argument is that the novel form's rage for order, its perceived link to a notion of coherence and stability in modern society, could never fully flourish in an Ireland that was provisional and makeshift, in the process of continual becoming rather than being. A consequence of this first theorising of the novel form in Ireland, and its relationship, if any, to the codes of nationhood then prevalent, is a palpable self-consciousness on the part of many authors.

Mary Lavin herself concentrated on the aesthetic possibilities of both forms, emphasising that there were differences in intensity between the short story and the novel and suggesting that the short story form was superior to the novel for her artistic needs.[2] Her own bluntly dismissive assessment of the literary worth of both of her novels, that they were both 'bad' and that she wished they could be 'torn down like houses'[3], points to a literary trajectory that positions these novels as early experiments in the form which are abandoned as the short story is fully embraced and exploited. Lavin herself, then, reads her novels as if they were disappointed short stories:

> I even wished that I could break up the two long novels I have published into the few short stories they ought to have been in the first place. For in spite of these two novels and in spite of the fact that I may write other novels, I feel that it is in the short story that a writer distils the essence of his thought.[4]

Contemporary reviewers of both certainly considered them failures. Kate O'Brien, a novelist of distinction, recognises the ambition underpinning *The House in Clewe Street* but argues that this 'big awkward book' possesses 'no one coherent reason for the whole theme' and blames a lack of technical skill in the novel form on the part of Lavin in expressing what she detects as the world of real human feeling within the work.[5] *Mary O'Grady* was simply said not to be 'a success' and that Lavin, 'though a competent short story writer, [is] yet to find her length as a novelist'.[6] Critic Augustine Martin in the late 1980s, in his 'Afterword' to the republished *Mary O'Grady*, continued to argue that the proper means of approaching the work is as a series of set pieces that might be akin to notes towards a collection of short stories: 'The excellence of *Mary O'Grady* resides in its episodes, its single unique moments plucked out of time, and its tyrannies of cause and effect.'[7]

Interpreting Lavin's novels through this prism of the short story alone ensures that they are always already failures, interesting for their manifestation (albeit clumsily) of the themes which underpin her successful writing in the short story genre. I have argued elsewhere that this type of Manichean thinking, viewing the novel and the short story in Ireland as diametrically in opposition with one another, is based on a serious misconception of what a novel does and can do and is bound up very closely with a postcolonial notion of a metropolitan and novelistic literary canon that has its high point in the nineteenth century.[8]

The Irish novel of this period reflects the cultural currents of an Ireland isolated from the great historical upheaval of the Second World War, and still drained from shaking off the yoke of British imperialism. Certainly, the writers of this period are self-consciously casting about for a reason to exist in this New Ireland, trying to discover, or create, a role that might allow them to be. The theorization of the novel by the likes of O'Connor and O'Faoláin is a part of this manoeuvring;

their argument makes them as much social commentators as it does artists, as they grapple with the nature of Irish society rather than the aesthetic value and worth of the novel form itself. In this context what might be more useful is to read both of Mary Lavin's novels within the tradition of the novel form in Ireland generally and specifically the form as it stood in post-independent Ireland in the 1940s and 1950s when they were written. Doing so acknowledges their limitations, undoubtedly, but also re-establishes a sense of significance to these novels that manifest clearly a struggle toward the expression of a complicated and complicating view of Irish life. For that is one important feature of so much writing of this moment, endeavouring to depict an Irish reality that is alive to the subtleties and nuances of character in the post-heroic moment of the revival.

Both *The House in Clewe Street* and *Mary O'Grady* capture perfectly the difficulty that Mary Lavin and her generation had with the novel form in mid-twentieth century Ireland. The opening section of *The House in Clewe Street* reads like the opening of so many great nineteenth century novels, locating the town of Castlerampart — a fictional rendering of Athenry in Galway — within the surrounding landscape and locating the family within that wider topographical space. As with the work of Jane Austen and George Eliot, a knowing narrator is deployed to present Theodore Coniffe as a man of means who surveys with pleasure the numerous properties he owns on Clewe Street:

> Theodore stood for a few minutes upon the bridge … and then he began to walk back slowly towards the centre of town. [He] kept turning his head continually and looking from one side of the road to the other. At some houses he stared with particularly keen attention. Others he treated with equally great indifference. From this alone it might perhaps be possible to guess the source of his income …[9]

One effect of this type of opening is to both present the world as immediate — that is, as known and relevant — but also to suggest a kind of cultural timelessness wherein reader, author/narrator and characters can imaginatively, and uncomplicatedly, share these ideas as a hoped for connection between historical past and present is made. At the outset then, with this narrator appealing to the reader's mutual sense of bourgeois pieties, the reader is being offered a story of generations, focusing on the Coniffe family and the passing on, of not just material inheritance, but an awareness of social position and expectation. The picture drawn of the town and of the family, of the structures of society and of family, indicates that Lavin desires to expose an Irish small-town mentality to prolonged critique in her novel. The trusted techniques of the nineteenth-century novel come into play. A Mrs Molloy is allowed to speak, for instance, giving voice to the village, and offering up the minutiae of the comings and goings of everyday life, as well as presenting a glimpse of the provincial mind at work, just as Austen does with her brilliant Miss Bates in *Emma*.[10] This overall picture, then, is one of a leisurely, slow world, of order and calm, and this is echoed formally and reinforced in the unhurried nineteenth century authorial style chosen.

However, there are many problems with any easy engagement with the novel in this way. First of all, not only does Lavin make use of the conventions of the nineteenth-century novel but she sets the action of the story in the late nineteenth and early twentieth centuries, though that fact is never actually made plain to the reader. The unfolding narrative, as a family story, hints at progression from that past into the contemporary moment, and certainly the later scenes set in Dublin do seem to be more aware of the modern moment. Still, her image of Dublin on the frayed edges of Bohemia possesses no echoes of Joyce's urban world in either *Dubliners* (1914) or *Ulysses* (1922), though there are echoes of Liam O'Flaherty's Dublin in *Mr Gilhooley* (1926) and *The Puritan* (1931). Nonetheless, a studied vagueness concerning time marks off the action in the novel, as it does in *Mary O'Grady* also, as if Lavin is wary of having to justify an observable or even verifiable reality. In *Mary O'Grady*, the tumultuous events of Ireland's independence struggle of the early twentieth century and the national questions of post-independence are studiously ignored in the intense focus on Mary's life and her family. Both novels, therefore, fail to fully embrace the possibilities that a historical novel would afford, failing to tell us of the past as it was and, following on from that, undermining the connection and relevance that the past might have to the present, or telling us how history is written or mediated to us in the present. In *The House in Clewe Street*, Lavin's use of the historical form cannot be sustained and with the shift of focus toward the story of Gabriel Galloway, Theodore's grandson, the narrative moves into the realm of the *bildungsroman* and history is abandoned altogether.

One consequence is that there is no effort to make this world 'exceptional' or strange in an Irish manner, as the detailing of the bourgeois codes takes precedence over everything else in the opening sections of the novel. Ironically, then, Lavin's 'history' novel actually manages to exist outside history, specifically Irish history, with no reference at all being made to the upheavals of nineteenth- or twentieth-century Ireland. So complete is the mimicking of the nineteenth-

century metropolitan form that there is absolutely nothing to alert the reader to
the fact that this might be an 'Irish' story at all, with no effort made to capture the
energies of Irish speech, or any overt signalling to the possibilities that an Irish
rendering of life might possess a unique vision, or indeed a vision at all, of the
codes and manners of bourgeois life. Perhaps this deliberate avoidance of any
Irish markers by Lavin is best understood as her not wanting to wallow in the
usual stereotypes attached to Ireland and the Irish. Thus, her West of Ireland has
absolutely nothing to say of the sturdy or spiritual Irish peasant perpetuated by
the Revivalists. Indeed, her intent is to complicate that rather fixed view of the
Irish by offering a story of 'provincial life' that might actually rival that of George
Eliot's *Middlemarch* (1871–72) in its detailing of the mundane.

Marianne Koenig perceptively suggests that, at one level, *The House in Clewe
Street* is pastiche, meandering lazily between different novelistic genres and
never finally fixing on one.[11] While this argument correctly acknowledges an
obvious anxiety with the novel form, it does not offer any reasoning as to why
this might be occurring. A cursory glance at a typical Irish novel from the early
nineteenth century onward would suggest that the Irish novel is burdened with
the need to tell not only individual stories but also the story of Ireland itself. In
other words, history and Irish history specifically, is a major problem for the
would-be Irish novelist, obscuring a human dimension that will always already
be predetermined by the national story and the national question. Thus, what
the reader is witness to in Lavin's work is a Herculean effort to render a version
of everyday ordinary Irish middle-class life as just that, ordinary and everyday.
For Lavin, in *The House in Clewe Street*, the medium of the novel *is* the message.
The form's link to modernity, its basic retelling again and again of the story of
lived life and pressures of the middle classes, becomes, then, the story of this
particular novel. At an unconscious level perhaps, what *The House in Clewe Street*
charts formally is the progression of the novel form in Ireland, from the potential
of the grand sweep of the nineteenth-century novel toward the more intimate
and personal sphere of the *bildungsroman*, from a national to a personal story. In
Mary O'Grady, the conscious disregard of Irish history is also to be understood as
a reorientation toward the individual life as it is lived. Thus, both novels not only
tell that story but also enact it. Of course, what is interesting is how Lavin refuses
to engage with the modernist lessons and techniques that Joyce, Flann O'Brien
and others engendered and made use of, preferring instead the conventionalities
of straightforward non-experimental forms. The real story being told here is the
forced reorientation of the reader's focus toward the more intimate human world

of interaction, breaking away from any preordained or reductive sense of the Irish personality that might be defined, and confined, by being viewed through the filter of Irish history or any stereotypical account of Irish character.

On their escape to Dublin, Onny is brought sightseeing by Gabriel. She is thoroughly bored by this exercise, being more interested in the people of the city rather than its buildings: 'People, people, people. Faces, faces, faces. Walking along the streets she looked from side to side. Over her head the city soared into the sky unheeded.'[12] Onny, self-reflexively, gives a clue as to what this particular novel is struggling toward: a picture of people, complicated and nuanced, as they are and not as they have been endlessly (mis)represented. Gabriel brings her to College Green and points out Trinity College, and the Bank of Ireland, hinting at an Irish historical narrative. However, Onny's indifference produces in Gabriel a curious reflection on an apocalyptic future when the buildings will all be destroyed and tourists will 'try to imagine the life that was led by the unimaginable people who inhabited it in its time!'[13] It is clear that Onny's 'here and now' interests should be Gabriel's, and indeed, the novel's itself.

Gabriel, as the main focus of the deployment of the *bildungsroman* form, should, of course, be the locus of moral and intellectual development within the novel. Rachel Sealy Lynch discerns, through this characterization of Gabriel, a decidedly subtler and more nuanced engagement with the theme of middle-class values than some earlier critics had given Lavin credit for.[14] To be sure, once it is accepted that he is no conventional hero, that his problems will largely remain unresolved, then Gabriel's low-key confrontations with family and society can be understood as a quiet working through of everyday issues and concerns. In his conversations with Sylvester's fellow artist Helen especially, his anxieties find expression. On looking out on the city streets he muses: 'So many people; and all, all unknown to him. He was overcome by a sudden feeling of his own temerity in having come among them; come to swell the already swollen, overwhelming number of human beings.'[15] But he is calmed in a chance view of Helen returning from Mass with a prayer book in her hand. Later, she says to him: '"I think you are like myself and that however strongly you may revolt against the superstitious growths that spring up around the codes of religion and morality, you would still respect those codes"'.[16]

In other words, Gabriel's dilemma is something more than the usual and simplifying revolt against all things traditional: nationality, language and religion. He is trying to discover a means, perhaps, of being more complicatedly Irish than straightforward either/or choices might allow. In this reading, Onny's wildishness in comparison to the staidness of almost every other character in Castlerampart and Dublin is representative of an extreme that Gabriel, in the end, is unable to embrace. Certainly, the dilemma for Gabriel is one of trying to come to terms with his position in society, and his relationship with Onny can be read as an act of rebellion against his background and the imposed limits of a bourgeois future. Reinforcing this is how she is presented in a visual manner, as being seen and gazed at by others, usually men. Much is made of her appearance and when she comes to Dublin pages are given over to her being dressed in city clothes and the transformation that this brings about in how she looks and is seen. However, the consequence is that she remains merely a talisman, a muse, rather than a person. Being seen always from the outside means that the reader is never permitted to penetrate beyond that surface, her thoughts and story remaining unplumbed.

Another consequence of this reading of Gabriel as the unlikely hero, in that his desires are prosaic rather than romantic, is that the other characters around which he whirls need also to be reassessed beyond the stereotypical either/or templates then fashionable. While not an artist himself, his friend Sylvester is a painter and possessed of an artistic vision, so that, vicariously at least, the novel is located in the wake of George Moore and James Joyce's aesthetic understanding of imaginative, if not actual, liberation seen in work such as *A Drama in Muslin* (1886), *The Lake* (1905) and *A Portrait of the Artist as a Young Man* (1916). However, unlike Patrick Kavanagh's contemporaneous novel, *Tarry Flynn* (1948), for instance, which celebrates this type of liberating artistic imagination unquestioningly, Lavin in a thoroughly ruthless manner, dismisses the pretensions of Ireland's underground artistic community, a community that would later be popularized and celebrated in books such as Anthony Cronin's *Dead as Doornails* (1976), his novel *The Life of Riley* (1964) and J.P. Donleavy's *The Ginger Man* (1955). She indicates how myopic this artistic vision is and how limited the range of poses it offers for the would-be-artist of Ireland in the 1940s and 1950s. As with the other characters that populate Dublin's bohemia, there is an air of playacting and pretence about the whole Dublin affair. Gabriel casts about for a role of what he thinks a modern life ought to be rather than what it actually could be in reality. Part of his difficulty, as it is for the other characters, perhaps as it is for Lavin herself as an author, is the paucity of genuine role models to emulate other than those associated with the Literary Revival of a generation earlier. Sylvester, for example, is not unlike Lord Henry Wotton in Oscar Wilde's *The Picture of Dorian Gray* (1890), in that he is no true destroyer of middle-class values; rather, his mocking of them is simply one more pose to be taken up and played out. Even Gabriel recognises this, 'that stupid

145

sneering at everything' and wonders about his friendship with the artist.[17] One of the major drawbacks of the novel therefore is that most, if not all, of the characters are hateful in their own imitable ways.

Throughout this story there are moments of disruption, hints of these other narratives, challenging the restrictive formal impositions of the conventional novel. Onny, of course, is a consciously disruptive figure within the narrative, though this too, as has been argued, is dissipated somewhat by her being presented in an either/or template that positions her as wildly beyond Gabriel's bourgeois sensibility. That she is from the lower classes of Castlerampart merely confirms this. The incident of her slip in the river, as a strange man chased her, possesses a brooding ambience, intimating a realm of hidden desire and frustrated passion. Gabriel, while out looking for her, believing that she has gone off to a dance, thinks it might be a good idea to hide until her return so that 'he might enjoy the spectacle of her punishment at her mother's hands, which he longed at that moment to have the pleasure of inflicting himself'.[18] Of course, Gabriel's fear of real action means that this will remain but a thought. Nonetheless, it does suggest that beneath the veneer of respectability there is a well of potentially destructive violence that might explode into public view at any moment.

The end of the novel sees the death of Onny and Gabriel's uneasy contemplation of his future. At first he seems to desire a return to Castlerampart to 'face whatever punishment it would be decreed he deserved'.[19] Yet, he is offered a fresh vision of the city that he now acknowledges he had never really seen, 'never for one hour been a part of' and he chooses to confidently stride forward to embrace this new reality. As with his grandfather, perhaps, at the opening of the novel, an element of Gabriel's vision is one of economic possibility and possession. It is therefore a somewhat uneasy ending. Gabriel does not repudiate his inherited middle-class value system; rather, it is suggested that he can alter those values accordingly to a new situation. In this image of Gabriel turning to the city as if for the first time, Lavin realizes that the form of the novel she has deployed has been singularly unable to capture the story she had wanted to tell. The demands that the conformities of the nineteenth-century novel, and the conformities of the artistic *bildungsroman*, have in the Irish setting restricted the story that could be told and the type of characters that might inhabit that story. The ending suggests that perhaps Gabriel will now attempt to be a part of a narrative outside these restrictive boundaries.

Mary O'Grady, with its very localized static setting in the Dublin suburb of Ranelagh, might be that new story. Certainly, in its presentation of Mary, as a mother figure, Lavin once again confronts the stereotypes of Irish life and culture, challenging readers' expectations of what an Irish novel might be and the narratives it might convey. Near the close of the novel Mary is offered a vision of her life as a mother: 'Mother! The name that signified her own being for so long suddenly took on the meaning it had in the distant golden past, and before he eyes she seemed to see her own mother.'[20] Earlier she had tried to articulate her notion of motherhood to her children:

> Do you know the lines of the Gospel: Not a sparrow shall fall — Well, I often thought to myself that it was like as if Almighty God was looking into a mother's heart when He said those words, because I always used to think that not a hair could fall from your heads, any of you, but I'd feel something in my own heart fall with it'.[21]

The use of Marian imagery and of Mary's resemblance to the Cathleen Ní Houlihan figure has been noted by critics, and certainly this emphasis feeds into the pervading stasis that underpins the narrative.[22] Mary is the focus of the narrative and the centre around which all the other characters rotate. All movement is either away from Mary and the home or back again toward her and the orbit of the home. Lavin carefully presents the realm of the home as the only site of important action. When her daughter Ellie walks out with her boyfriend Bart, they move through 'the city streets, which seemed, even late at night, to be always populated'.[23] They look longingly at houses as they go for their walks along suburban roads, the house being the object of desire, the place of possible private intimacies away from public scrutiny.

While undoubtedly such imagery allows for a concentration on the limitations of traditional female Irish roles, it is surprising how Lavin brilliantly deconstructs those very images even as she presents them. Directly after her panegyric to motherhood, she says to her son Larry: '"Oh, it's all very well for you," she said, "you and Rosie. What is he to you but a brother? A brother!" She sneered. "What is a brother?" … Brother — What did the word mean: nothing!'[24] Motherhood is superior to brotherhood; even the words signify in their meaning and meaninglessness the real nature of family life. Many historians and literary critics point to Éamon de Valera's 1937 constitutions as enshrining the family as the proper basis of Irish society. Lavin, in this novel, demonstrates how utterly aspirational de Valera's vision actually was. Rather than the family unit being the site of nurture and benevolence, it is presented here as a place of confrontation and battle where power is wielded and authority imposed.

Thus, Mary's 'sneer' is strange and seemingly out of place. Certainly it disturbs any easy appreciation of Mary and the novel. As a battleground, then, the family home begins to take on a different, less sentimental, hue. Larry wants to respond to his mother but 'when he raised his own eyes he felt his face redden because she was looking at him with contempt'. The presence of such extreme emotion in the world of the novel obviously upends and challenges the readers' understanding of Irish life and its representations. Indeed, it can be argued, that the presence of such extreme emotion is registered at the level of form as well as narrative. As was the case with *The House in Clewe Street*, *Mary O'Grady* also ignores the great events of Irish history in the twentieth century. The turning away from public narrative, inward to the private world of the family and home, once again indicates the scope of Lavin's art of the everyday. The absence of the intensity of the 1916 Easter Rising, the War of Independence and the Civil War from the novel refocus the reader's view to the devastating violence of quotidian interaction between individuals. In other words, violence is not something distant or solely connected with communal and national concerns; rather, its reverberations have a much more intimate sphere of consequence. Thus, these moments of intense feeling, that underscore Mary's relationship with all her children, startle the attentive reader who might be expecting the foibles of class and family to be revealed through the polite form that is the modern novel. Instead of enjoying verbal jousting between characters, the reader is presented with feelings that range from contempt to anger.

In an early interaction with her eldest son Patrick, we see the nature of this power struggle for Mary. After the death of her husband, Patrick becomes the 'head' of the family as the eldest son. This new dispensation in Mary's eyes humiliates her. Patrick's decision to emigrate to America forces Mary to reconsider her love for her son and again, it is only through her conception of the role of a mother that she can articulate this position: '"Oh, Patrick! What have I ever done that you should treat my love like this? Did you think that, whoever else might impede you in your ambitions, I, your mother, would have set obstacles before you? My son, I love you; but I love you less".'[25] Despite her own protestations, it would appear that development and growth and maturity seriously undermine her position of authority: 'Was this her son, who, only the other day it seemed was a helpless little bundle of pink flesh lying in the laundry basket looking up at her?'[26] Vindictiveness, spleen, and anger mark out these exchanges between Mary and her children. At one stage, she contemplates her son Larry: 'Sometimes when he was a boy she had complained that Larry at times could look so stupid he was like a half-wit. Well, that was how he looked now: half-witted.'[27] Again and again throughout this novel, Mary's mother love is presented as domineering and stifling, the very opposite of the stereotypical Irish mother who nurtures and cares.

As a novel, *Mary O'Grady* is more successful than its predecessor: its scope is more manageable and the development of character, especially Mary, is more subtle and nuanced. She is complicated in that she is not rendered as one thing but as possibly many things. Other characters remain shadowy and their motivations unplumbed, but this only serves to keep Mary as flawed heroine to the fore. All action and reaction, all feeling and emotion revolve round her and the form of the novel reflects that. The strain within her use of the form is actually its strength in one way. The novel form's tendency to render modern experience as unexceptional is continually undermined here with the bursting into view of the various passions and violent emotions that have been noted. It is as if a game is being played between author and reader: each knows what ought to be happening, what ought to be presented and revealed, but rather than the banalities of Irish life being offered, the narrative is punctuated, and perhaps punctured, with these glimpses of sentiment that if given full vent might destroy the fabric of social interaction.

Hedda Friberg argues that Mary's home place of Tullamore, while never actually returned to in reality, looms large in her imagination through her life in the urban and suburban world of Dublin.[28] Hers, then, is a life of exile and her lot is to be caught between traditional values and modernity, between an atavistic image of home and the reality of Ranelagh. Her sense of motherhood is also bound up with this discourse and her 'charged rhetoric of a golden, rural Tullamore'.[29] What is significant about this reading that prioritizes Mary's experience as one based on exile is how it reflects, as do all those disturbing moments discussed, the out of place nature of her existence. In many ways, Mary's dilemma, in living in the city, is that she possesses no tradition (or has no ready access to it in any real or meaningful way) and thus is forced to create a world and a set of values out of nothing. As John McGahern argued, each Irish family, as mini-republic, creates its own set of codes and manners, and Lavin, it would seem, concurs with that estimation of Irish life.[30] The 'newness' of this world is therefore registered in a novel that might be read as a series of set pieces, as a series of short stories strung together. This anxiety, then, has everything to do with Lavin's ambition to tell a new story in a new way.

Mary Lavin's achievement as a writer of novels is that she challenges her contemporary readers' expectations of what an Irish novel can and could do. The prevailing sense of the impossibility of the form's usefulness in 1940s and 1950s Ireland imbues her efforts and her ultimate abandonment of the form. *The House in Clewe Street*, in its narrative permutations, charts that course from traditional to something new and strange and *Mary O'Grady* is that new story from the outset. Perhaps part of the negative reception that met these novels has everything to do with the templates by which literary critics have approached and continue to approach Irish writing: if a thing does not fit, well then it is to be rejected and dismissed. Part of any novelist's ambition is not only to comfort us with stories we already know but also to challenge us with stories that we do not know and, perhaps, do not want to know.

Endnotes

1   F. O'Connor, *The Lonely Voice: a Study of the Short Story*, (London: Macmillan, 1965), p.17, and S. O'Faoláin, 'Fifty Years of Irish Writing', *Studies* 51, 201 (Spring 1962), pp. 93–105.

2   L. Robert and S. Stevens, 'An Interview with Mary Lavin', *Studies*, 86, 341, (Spring 1997), pp.43–50; C. Murphy, 'Mary Lavin: An Interview', *Irish University Review* 9, 2 (Autumn 1979), pp.207–224.

3   Quoted in M. Koenig, 'Mary Lavin: The Novels and the Stories', *Irish University Review*, 9, 2, (Autumn 1979), p.244.

4   Quoted in P. Rafroidi, 'A Question of Inheritance: The Anglo-Irish Tradition', in P. Rafroidi and M. Harmon (eds), *The Irish Novel in Our Time* (Publications de l'Université de Lille, 1975–76), p.27.

5   K. O'Brien, 'Short Stories: In and Out of Place', *The Irish Times*, 5 January 1946, p.4.

6   Anon. 'Recent Fiction', *The Irish Times*, 30 September 1950, p.6.

7   A. Martin, 'Afterword', in M. Lavin, *Mary O'Grady* (London: Virago Press, 1986), p.390.

8   See D. Hand, *A History of the Irish Novel* (Cambridge: Cambridge University Press, 2011), pp.1–13.

9   M. Lavin, *The House in Clewe Street*, (London: Faber and Faber, 2009), p.9.

10 Ibid., pp.71–74.

11 Koenig, 'Mary Lavin', pp.244–261.

12 Lavin, *The House in Clewe Street*, p.332.

13 Ibid., p.334.

14 R. Sealy Lynch, '"The Fabulous Female Form": The Deadly Erotics of the Male Gaze', in Mary Lavin's *The House in Clewe Street*', *Twentieth Century Literature*, 43, 3, (Autumn

1997), pp.326–38.

15 Lavin, *The House in Clewe Street*, p.357.

16 Ibid., p.375.

17 Ibid., p.358.

18 Ibid., p.278.

19 Ibid., p.460.

20 M. Lavin, *Mary O'Grady*, p.350.

21 Ibid., p.264.

22 A. Fogarty, '"The Horror of the Unlived Life": Mother Daughter Relationships in Contemporary Irish Fiction', in A. Giorgio (ed.), *Writing Mothers and Daughters: Renegotiating the Mother in Western European Narratives by Women* (Oxford: Berghahn Books, 2002), pp.85–118 and J. Fulmer, *Folk Women and Indirection in Morrison, Ní Dhuibhne, Hurston, and Lavin* (Aldershot: Ashgate, 2007).

23 Lavin, *Mary O'Grady*, p.107.

24 Ibid., p.265.

25 Ibid., p.97.

26 Ibid., p.87.

27 Ibid., p.268.

28 H. Friberg, 'Managing Exile: A "Tullamore Discourse"', in Mary Lavin's *Mary O'Grady*', *Nordic Irish Studies*, 4, (2005), pp.99–108.

29 Ibid., p.103.

30 Fintan O'Toole, 'The Family as Independent Republic', *The Irish Times*, 13 October 1990: Weekend, p.2.

9 | Family and Community in Mary Lavin's Grimes Stories

Elke D'hoker

In the 1950s, in what is known as 'the middle period' of her career, Mary Lavin published a sequence of stories about the Grimes family.[1] 'A Visit to the Cemetery' first appeared in the 1951 collection *A Single Lady*. Three more stories — 'An Old Boot', 'Frail Vessel' and 'The Little Prince' — were published in *The Patriot Son* (1956), and the final Grimes story, 'Loving Memory' (1960), appeared in *The New Yorker* in 1960 and was subsequently included in *The Great Wave* (1961).[2] The stories all deal with the members of the middle-class Grimes family, shopkeepers in a small Irish town. In the first story, Alice and Liddy Grimes visit their mother's four-month-old grave in the old cemetery of the town and their dismay at the overgrown and gloomy cemetery gives way to happy dreams of their own futures as married wives and mothers. In the next three stories, Alice disappears from view and attention shifts to Bedelia Grimes and her relations with her younger siblings, Liddy and Tom.[3] The events related in 'The Little Prince' move far beyond the initial time setting — the first months after their mother's death — to the old age of Bedelia and Tom. Yet the final story returns again to the setting of 'A Visit to the Cemetery' as it relates the courtship and marriage of Matthias and Alicia up until the latter's death. This story thus literally ends where the first one started — at the cemetery — where Alice is again paying a visit to her mother's recent grave. This circular structure and the obvious links between the stories invite the reader to integrate the stories into a larger plot. The stories then add up to a short story cycle or short story sequence[4] and can be read as an extended family 'saga', or as Lavin's 'most sustained effort to capture the atmosphere of the Irish middle class'.[5]

At the same time, as A.A. Kelly remarks, there are also many 'non-sequiturs in events between one Grimes tale and another'.[6] Kelly notes, for instance, that 'in "Loving Memory" Alice, not Bedelia, is the eldest of the four children' and that 'in "The Little Prince", the child Bedelia is expecting in "Frail Vessel" is never mentioned'. Neither are Alice, Liddy and the latter's husband and child mentioned in 'The Little Prince', even though this story gives an overview of the lives of Bedelia and her husband, Daniel, in the family shop. Disruptions in chronology also occur between the first four stories, which are — rather improbably — all set within a year after the mother's death and in 'Loving Memory', the father is called Matthias rather than Matthew. Given Lavin's usual extensive and careful editing of her stories, these inconsistences are likely to be deliberate.[7] They effectively frustrate the reader's attempt to provide closure to the stories or to unify them into an overarching plot.

In an article tellingly entitled 'Resisting the Pull of Plot', Suzanne Ferguson describes a similar resistance to novelistic coherence in the 'Faith' stories of the American short story writer Grace Paley.[8] Expanding her observations in a later essay, she applies the term 'anti-sequences' to groups of stories 'that obviously do fit together, or could fit together in a sequential pattern, but whose authors have refused to put them together or even allow them to be put together'.[9] For Ferguson, the main function of these anti-sequences lies in their resistance to the novel's sense of coherence and closure, effectively keeping 'the reader from any comfortable sense of unity or resolution'.[10] A similar concern may well have been Lavin's when she was writing and publishing these stories in the 1950s. By that time indeed, she had already published two novels which she was not entirely satisfied with. 'Two bad novels' is how she famously referred to them in an interview[11] and in a preface to her 1959 Selected Stories, she wrote that she wished she 'could break up the two long novels ... into the few short stories they ought to have been in the first place'.[12] Given these misgivings, Lavin's failure to harmonize the chronology of the Grimes sequence, to account for all the characters, and to fully integrate the stories in a novel or unified collection could indeed be read as a form of resistance against the contrivances of a unified plot providing closure and coherence.

Another explanation for the lack of complete accord between the stories, however, might be the sense that individual details such as names and dates do not really matter; that the Grimes family is but a variation on a theme, a concrete instantiation of a more archetypal structure in Lavin's fiction: the small-town middle-class family primarily concerned with social status and material wealth. Variants of this archetypal family can be found in the Coniffes of *The House in Clewe Street* (1945), the Conroys of 'The Will' (1944), the shopkeeping families of 'Lemonade' (1961) and 'Posy' (1947), and even the more prosperous merchants of 'The Becker Wives'(1946). As several critics have observed, all of these families are modelled to some extent on the family of Lavin's mother in Athenry, with whom Lavin lived for some time after her return from the US.[13] Lavin herself has noted that her move to Athenry did have a formative impact on her work:

> An abrupt change of continent such as I had when I came to Ireland from America, could awaken one's awareness. The first eight or nine months in Athenry made a profound visual impression on me. For many years I almost always placed my characters in Athenry. When I thought of a human situation, I seemed to see it enacted in the streets of that little town and often in my grandmother's house, where I had lived.[14]

As Lavin indicates, the setting and the characters are of secondary importance to the more general 'human situation' she seeks to address. If the Grimes sequence is thus, on one level, very much the story of a middle-class shopkeeping family in a small Irish town, the stories also go beyond that specific social context and attempt to shed light on the way any individual is inevitably enmeshed in the intricate networks of family, community, and the larger society.

The very mention of family and community in an Irish context already evokes the classic work of Conrad M. Arensberg and Solon T. Kimball, *Family and Community in Ireland* (1968). In their introduction, the authors explain that the title of their work reflects the two central pillars of life in Ireland in the 1930s. While the structure of community life in Ireland 'could not be understood apart from the kind of relations among persons bound by blood and marriage', the dynamics of marriage and family relations themselves, they argue, are to be considered as part of a larger social and economic network rather than as private concerns.[15] Arensberg and Kimball in fact demonstrate the interweaving of family and community in their detailed descriptions of social and familial practices in both a rural village and a small town in County Clare. In their discussion of the town, they single out for special attention the 'vast army' of 'shopkeepers and their assistants', and their subsequent discussion of marriage, family and upward mobility focuses on this social group.[16] Life in Ennis in the early 1930s cannot have differed very much from the life Lavin experienced in Athenry in the 1920s. Indeed, many of the observations made by Arensberg and Kimball appear highly familiar to a reader of Lavin. About the issue of class, the 'master key to the structure of the town', they write:

> The people of Ennis know their 'places.' They are for the most part keenly aware of social standing, position, and class. As in any community, 'appearances' must be kept up. Class does not make for aloofness as it does in metropolitan regions, for everyone lives more or less in sight of everyone else. Nor do the folkways demand as in America that a pretense of social democracy be kept up. Each man knows fairly well what to expect of the other and respects the difference. Superiority and inferiority are relative matters. There are infinite gradations. But there are broad outlines none the less, and a man knows the 'station' that is his.[17]

In this essay, I propose to examine Lavin's representation of family and community in the Grimes stories against the background of her larger fictional oeuvre on the one hand, and Arensberg and Kimball's sociological account of an Irish market town on the other. Although *Family and Community* came under attack in the 1970s and 1980s for painting an all too harmonious and static picture of Irish communities, a recent reappraisal has shown these criticisms to be only partially justified.[18] Very much like Lavin's short fiction in fact, their work remains highly valuable for its study of human relations in the context of family and community, not just in Ireland but in Western societies at large.

In an overview of Lavin's work, Seamus Deane identifies Lavin as a social writer, focusing not on 'singular individual relationships with the mediocre world', but on 'the closely meshed nexus of feelings in which the protagonists are bound'. Love is her subject, Deane argues and 'love demands relation'.[19] Following on from Deane's argument, Ann Owen Weekes even claims, 'life demands relation in a Lavin story'.[20] Connections and connecting are indeed the primary concerns of Lavin's fiction and many of her stories specifically explore the nature of family relations. The Grimes stories in particular can be seen as Lavin's most extended 'consideration of love in the family framework'.[21] Yet, love does not fare well in these stories and the first four of the Grimes stories can be read as a chronicle of how the 'bonds of blood' are broken.[22]

In 'A Visit to the Cemetery', the tensions and small jealousies between Alice and Liddy are still largely a matter of the 'drama of opposed sensibilities', which Peterson has detected in several of Lavin's stories.[23] While the older and more practical Alice remembers the humiliation she suffered at her mother's funeral in the overgrown old friary cemetery, the sensitive Liddy is concerned about her mother's soul in this dark and gloomy place. Still, both sisters experience 'a great feeling of sisterly affection', when considering their futures as married wives and mothers and they impulsively decide to go for a walk at the much nicer new cemetery at the edge of the town, first making 'doubly sure' that the iron gate of the old cemetery is 'locked all right'.[24]

From the second Grimes story onwards, attention shifts to Bedelia. The most practical (and ugliest) of the three sisters, she takes on the care of the shop and the family after their mother's death and their father's subsequent illness. Under her conniving command, however, the Grimes family disintegrates entirely. In 'An Old Boot', Bedelia decides to marry the shopboy, Daniel, to secure her own position in the business. In 'Frail Vessel', after Alice has left, Bedelia's largely practical arrangement with Daniel is contrasted with Liddy's romance with the solicitor O'Brien. Jealous of her sister's happiness and always seeking to advance her own position, Bedelia causes the break-up of Liddy's socially inconvenient marriage. Yet her manipulations backfire and although Bedelia has Liddy at her side again, the relations between the sisters are severed rather than restored. 'The Little Prince', finally, focuses on Bedelia's relation with her youngest sibling, Tom. Although Bedelia had lovingly cared for him as a child, she now sees his cavalier and spendthrift behaviour as a threat to the business and decides to send him to America, for 'a fresh start'.[25] Yet the proud Tom breaks with his family more radically than she had anticipated and they do not hear from him again. When, forty years later, they hear of a man called Tom Grimes dying in a hospice in Boston, Bedelia and Daniel make the long voyage to the States. Bedelia anticipates a happy reunion and briefly experiences again the love she felt for him when he was her 'little prince'. Yet when she is faced with the dead body of Tom Grimes and its 'implications of poverty and illness', she fails to recognise him: 'But if it was her brother, something had sundered them, something had severed the bonds of blood, and she knew him not.'[26] As an extended exploration of relations within a family, the Grimes stories are a clear testimony to the lack of lasting love between siblings and to the fact that even blood-ties can be broken by selfish and materialistic concerns.

In the three Grimes stories published in *The Patriot Son*, it is Bedelia who is chiefly to blame for the disintegration of the family. On the one hand, Bedelia's connivance — a term often repeated in these three stories — is simply a part of her character. Like Alice in 'A Visit to the Cemetry', Bedelia is an example of the practical, materialistic and manipulative female type which often occurs in Lavin's fiction. Bedelia and Liddy — like Alice and Liddy — are thus a representation of what Angeline Kelly has called 'the Mary/Martha female types who so often confront each other in Mary Lavin's work and who also each symbolize preponderant leanings towards the external or internal worlds'.[27] Overly concerned with money, social status and personal advancement, Bedelia lets her manipulative side triumph over moments of sisterly affection or sympathy until there is no love left in her heart. With a clear reference to the preceding story, 'A Frail Vessel', the end of 'The Little Prince' reads: 'But it [her heart] was too old and cracked a vessel to hold any emotion at all, however precious, however small a drop.'[28] According to this explanation, in other words, it is Bedelia who is personally responsible for the disintegration of the family.

On the other hand, the stories also repeatedly hint at the social context as an explanation for Bedelia's behaviour. In 'An Old Boot' in particular, Bedelia's difficult position is referred to. Although she is effectively managing the family shop, as a woman Bedelia has no real claim on it. With her father forsaking his family responsibilities after her mother's death, she cannot count on him to secure a good match for her. Her only brother too fails to take on responsibilities as head of the shop and the family. Since she is not beautiful like her sisters, moreover, she cannot hope to get married on the basis of looks alone. The opening paragraphs of the story show her reflecting on these less than rosy prospects:

> No wonder the customers were falling away one by one. It wouldn't be long until the business went to the bottom of the hill. For of course, Tom, their brother, was as good as useless and it was only a matter of time until Alice and Liddy shook the dust of the place from their feet. If, like them, she could be sure there was a chance of her getting married, the state of the business would have troubled her as little as anyone in the family. But she had no illusions about her dumpy person, and now, up to her neck in mourning clothes, she knew she

looked as plain as the black minorca hens that pecked and scratched in the backyard.[29]

Faced with these bleak prospects, Bedelia takes the matter into her own hands and decides to marry Daniel, the meek but capable and faithful 'shop-boy': 'Dispassionately she examined him, like something she had got by chance in a lottery. And she was satisfied enough with what she saw. He might not be all that Liddy or Alice would demand in a suitor, but she knew instinctively that her choice was wise according to her standards.'[30]

Arensberg and Kimball's description of the Ennis shopkeepers confirms the difficulty of Bedelia's position. In a familistic society where marriage was as much a social and economic transaction as a personal affair, daughters would be condemned to lifelong spinsterhood if they were not provided for by their father.[31] Only 'runaway matches', like that of Alice, or 'marrying beneath' one, like Liddy, could offer a way out.[32] Women's position in the patriarchal system was necessarily a subordinate one: only as wives could they carve out a position for themselves in the community and only widows could autonomously run a business before passing it over to the next male heir.[33] Bedelia is shown to chafe under the restrictions of her sex. Expected to devote herself to the role of wife and mother, 'she did her best to keep her thoughts engaged on domestic matters' and necessarily lays her ambitions for the family business into her husband's more humble hands. Yet she comes to resent his limited ambitions: 'the ability he had shown in those days seemed to her to have been only the ability of a servant. Why else had they not prospered and advanced? … it occurred to her that it was not the business he loved, but the shop itself, the tangible thing upon which he could lavish his care and attention'.[34] Seen in this light, Bedelia's petty manipulations acquire a more tragic dimension as the consequence of ambition and ability stifled by a restrictive social context and its gendered norms.

This reading of the story too is in tune with the rest of Lavin's oeuvre, since the lives of her protagonists inevitably unfold within the normative framework of both the local town and the larger society. 'Mary Lavin is always acutely aware of the social framework in which her characters move', Kelly argues, 'For small shopkeepers and farmers of her youth, society was very hierarchic, to the modern mind unpleasantly so. This framework then provided a solid social structure against which the surface of life could be painted in.'[35] While the social embeddedness of her fiction is generally acknowledged, critics disagree about Lavin's attitude towards this social dimension. Some argue that her stories offer a critique of the restrictions that social norms and hierarchies impose on individuals and that they side with those characters who manage to escape from these restrictions. For Zack Bowen, for instance:

> ... her vision of reality is harsh and closely circumscribed by an acute awareness of social class and society's sanctions and rules .... In the tightly controlled, sometimes fatalistic sphere in which her characters live, many of them succumb to a life of quiet frustration or desperation, while others try to escape, to rationalize, to hide, or to seek freedom through love, nature, insanity or death'.[36]

David Norris and James Heaney also read in Lavin's fiction a criticism of the restrictive social context of post-Independence Ireland.[37] For critics like Seamus Deane and Ann Weekes, on the other hand, the social context in Lavin is simply the backdrop against which ordinary lives are played out, the outline within which characters can — and have to — take responsibility for their own lives. Far from favouring the outsider, the one who escaped from the impositions and restrictions of the community, they argue, Lavin considers it rather 'a mistake to think that one can isolate and separate oneself and a chosen one from the web of life'.[38] Comparing Lavin to Kate O'Brien, Weekes comments: 'although focusing on the community, O'Brien emphasizes the sacrifice of the individual for the community, whereas Lavin emphasizes the value of the community'.[39]

Returning to the Grimes stories, it is interesting to note that the final story offers yet another explanation for the disintegration of the family, precisely by looking at its position within the local community. That this position is not as it should be is already realized by Alice, the focalizer of much of the story, at an early age. The opening lines of 'Loving Memory' read: '"The child of a ghost — who'd marry me?" Alice said bitterly. She was fifteen then, but even before that she knew she'd never marry. Years before her mother died she knew it'.[40] The Grimes children are mockingly referred to as 'the love-birds' children' in the community, because of the excessive and obsessive love of their parents. From Alice's awareness of their family being considered an oddity, the story shifts to an explanation of the community's verdict. Matthias, it seems, has violated the rules and customs of love and marriage in the town. Courtship in the town is described as 'a sort of co-operative effort', the subject of endless banter and the recognised road to a public proposal: 'In a way that nook behind the door was a symbol of love as understood by the town. The nearer a couple got to marriage the more they were given cover, till finally marriage itself came down like a snuffer over their flame'.[41] Matthias refuses to partake in these courtship patterns. Instead, he searches for a bride outside of the town and marries her within six weeks. Disregarding social custom and propriety, he keeps the courtship and the marriage private: 'Matthias announced that he was not bringing Alicia home until after the wedding, which — for sentiment sake — was being held in Lisdoonvarna, Alicia having no real home or family connections'.[42] The town reacts with consternation: 'Not a cuddle, not a squeeze would anyone have seen. Cold fish that he was, no better might have been expected from Matthias.' Consternation turns to outrage when they learn that the newly married couple will not go on the traditional honeymoon, but want to spend their wedding night in their own house. The story dwells at length on the general 'embarrassment' that ensues: 'Before the couple were home ten minutes, everyone in the town had stolen a glance at that oblong window [of their bedroom]' and the whole town watches how 'Together they contemplated the night for all the world as if they were on a balcony in some Italian resort'.[43] The narrator explains the town's upset: 'Now, this was not what the town had been let to expect. They'd been told there would be no honeymoon — not that it was to be spent brazenly before their eyes in their own town. After all, it is not only the couple concerned that a honeymoon safeguards. Friends, relations and acquaintances are entitled to a like protection.'[44] And the married couple continues to give offense by blatantly displaying their love on their church visits and daily walks, with their hands invariably linked together in Matthias' coat pocket or in Alicia's muff — a clear sexual symbol which is dwelt on at length in the story.[45]

Arensberg and Kimball's detailed description of the customs and conventions surrounding courtship and matchmaking in *Family and Community in Ireland* help explain the transgressions of the couple. The anthropologists emphasize time and again the social nature of such seemingly private affairs as courtship and marriage in rural and small town Irish communities. Devoting three entire chapters to the proceedings of 'matchmaking' both in town and country, they demonstrate very clearly that marriage and sexuality are primarily thought of in social terms, as a way of maintaining one's family and its status in the community: 'Sexual behaviour is merely one aspect, not of individual personality, but of sociological role.'[46] As a result, the process leading up to a match is also a largely public one, governed by the customs of the community:

Although premarital virginity and complete abstinence from any kind of sexual activity is the ideal for the young, local custom emphasizes marriage all the while. Local dances and other festivities are the chief times of meeting and play for the young men and women of the rural communities. The customs and conventions which surround them are constant reminders of marriage and its hopes and privileges. Yet as soon as any intimacy of acquaintanceship builds up between a particular pair, they are matched together in local gossip. They are forced to take a position which is only a single step from betrothal.[47]

Although this description applies to the rural areas, the parallels with Lavin's evocation of courtship rituals in the town are striking. They help to explain the extent of Matthias' transgressions of social customs and conventions. In marrying a girl in secret in another town, he flouts the social dimension of courtship and does not allow the local community to sanction the match. In the public display of their married love, on the other hand, the couple contravenes the convention that married (sexual) relations are a private matter, where the only thing that counts is offspring.

Of course, the town's disapproval of the Grimes' behaviour need not be Lavin's. After all, in many of her stories characters are condemned for shying away from love or for putting social status before personal happiness. The first part of the story could indeed be read as a critique of the town's hostility to all that is different, rather than as an indictment of the couple's behaviour itself. Yet, as the second part of the story dwells at length on the negative consequences of this behaviour for the Grimes children, who are not given their share of this love, it becomes clear that the implied author disapproves: 'Their house wasn't littered with love … Love didn't thunder like a cataract down their staircase. It was all kept stored in their mother's room, and only their father had the key.'[48] The excessive and self-centred love of the parents clearly prevents the children from joining in this love. After Alicia's death, moreover, Matthias completely neglects his children and is only concerned with how he can create a fitting memorial for his wife. As the final story of the Grimes sequence, in other words, 'Loving Memory' offers the fundamental absence of sharing and love within the family as a final explanation for the heartless behaviour of Bedelia and the subsequent disintegration of the family.

Although Peterson argues that 'it is the mother … who is the root cause for the tragic events that shape the Grimes family'[49], I would argue that Matthias is at least as much to blame for jealously keeping his wife away from the family and the larger community. Matthias refuses to have his wife 'set foot in the shop' and insists that 'she keep to her room and rest for most of the day'.[50] While this prevents her from creating a bond with her children, it also sets her apart from the community, which comments spitefully, 'Who did he think she was? — the Queen of Sheba?' As a result, she remains an elusive figure in the community, 'like a lady in a tower', or even 'a ghost', as Alice realizes early on. And this spectral, liminal status is confirmed at the end of the story when after her death, and her father's obsessive mourning, Alice overhears the mothers of the town call out to their children: '"Stay out, so —" the woman said, "and see what'll happen! Have you forgotten Alicia Grimes? Oh-ho, you haven't! Alicia Grimes will get you! Alicia Grimes will get you!"'[51]

I would argue then that the origin of the Grimes tragedies lies in Matthias' obstinate flouting of the community's customs about courtship, love and marriage. In extricating himself — and later, his wife — from the necessary networks of family and community, he upsets the social equilibrium and causes his family's downfall. The lack of love in the family, Bedelia and Alice's excessive regard for social decorum and Tom's self-destructive desire to play popular fellow can, in retrospect, be linked to the selfishness and social mistakes of their parents. In 'Loving Memory', in other words, a more positive perspective on social norms and codes can be found. The story reveals the communal wisdom that lies behind apparently idle habits and traditions and shows these to be necessary in regulating individual behaviour and facilitating social relations. In going against these codes and customs, Matthias does not just incur the censure of the community, he also brings about the downfall of his family.

Community is not often present in such an overt way in Lavin's short fiction. Mostly its customs and sanctions remain implicit, present only in the characters' — often excessive — concern over what 'the people will say'.[52] Thus, even though the title of Lavin's first collection, *Tales from Bective Bridge* (1942), raises expectations of a collection grounded in a local community (of the kind of Jane Barlow's *Irish Idylls* [1892] or Sarah Orne Jewett's *The Country of the Pointed Firs* [1896]), the stories focus on individual characters in a variety of locales and situations.[53] Yet there is a shared sense of social context in the collection as a whole and community is given a more important role in two of the stories: 'Sarah' and 'A Fable'.

Very much like 'Loving Memory', 'Sarah' opens with an account of the convictions and customs of the community:

> Sarah had a bit of a bad name. That was the worst the villagers said of her, although Sarah had three children, and was unmarried, and although, moreover, there was a certain fortuity in her choice of fathers for them. She was a great worker, tireless and strong, and several people in the village got her in by day to scrub. Women with sons, and young brides, took care to not to hire her, but oftentimes they were the very people who were kindest to her.[54]

This narratorial account is then supported by a conversation among some of the matrons of the village who praise her for her industry and healthy children and put her 'tendency to evil' down to her bad upbringing. In short, the community accepts Sarah in spite of her social transgressions and even defends her against outsiders.

The social equilibrium is disturbed, however, when Kathleen Kedrigan, 'a newly married woman who had recently come to the village', hires Sarah to mind the house while she goes to Dublin, disregarding the cautionary remarks of the village women.[55] When Sarah is pregnant again, her brothers and the villagers have their suspicions yet collude in ignoring the question of the child's paternity just as they did with her other children. However, the studied ignorance of the community is disturbed by Kathleen who goes to inform Sarah's brothers of an anonymous letter she received, which names her husband as the child's father. Now the matter is brought into the open, the eldest brother feels compelled to publicly defend the family name and he roughly throws Sarah out of the house, causing her death and that of her child. As in 'Loving Memory', this story sees the social equilibrium disturbed by a character who violates the unwritten conventions and sanctions of the community out of a sense of pride and superiority. In the starkly rendered opposition between the sickly, hysterical Kathleen and the healthy, sensual Sarah, the implied author clearly sides with Sarah and blames Kathleen for the latter's death.

A rather different account of a community's attitude to an outsider can be found in another story from Lavin's debut collection, 'A Fable'. Here it is not so much the outsider who places herself above the customs of the village, but rather the men and women of the village who ostracize the outsider for being different, in this case, so beautiful as to be quite perfect. Couched in the language of legend, the story describes how the villagers only come to accept the beautiful woman when her face is scarred in a hunting accident. Only when she is revealed to be human like them can they love and admire her. Once she has become a valued member of the community, the villagers are unconditional in their support, even when a skin graft hides the scars again. The ironic narrator clearly mocks the villagers' behaviour, yet the mock-epic language and the absence of any names also serve to suggest that this village's attitudes and gossip are somehow universal, part and parcel of the social dynamics of any human community.

The explicit treatment of village life in these early stories serves to deepen our understanding of Lavin's attitude towards community, as a complex, structured, yet surprisingly flexible system of rules and norms that governs social relations. Although individuals may chafe under or suffer from these norms, they also make human interaction possible, enabling a community to deal with difference and deviation rather than reject it. Moreover, as 'Sarah' and 'Loving Memory' suggests, individuals who are too proud or self-centred to obey these rules and place themselves above the community, do so at their own peril. Interestingly, it is not the community's disapproval in itself that finally brings down these protagonists, but rather the disruptive consequences their anti-social behaviour has within their own families. In 'Sarah', Kathleen's cruel actions lead to a — probably permanent — estrangement from her husband. In the Grimes saga, as we have seen, Matthias' breach of social codes leads to the ostracising of his wife and the breakdown of his family.

In conclusion, by chronicling the fate of the Grimes family through a not entirely coherent sequence of stories, Lavin highlights the complex nature of the family and its embeddedness within the equally complex structures of community and society. Rather than offering one explanation for the family's disintegration, the different stories foreground distinct causes and look at the family from multiple perspectives. On the one hand, as we have seen, the stories can be read as criticising the restrictive patriarchal context of mid-century Ireland for curbing individual freedom and self-realization. This is the reading favoured by critics such as Bowen, Heaney and Norris, who liken Lavin's critique of de Valera's Ireland to that of her contemporaries Frank O'Connor and Séan O'Faoláin. Yet the stories also invite being read as a more neutral evocation of the social context as a network of conventions and relations in which any individual life is enmeshed and from which it is a mistake to try to extricate oneself. The different Grimes stories show how this holds true for relations of family — with Bedelia's misguided attempt to free herself from the siblings which seem to hold her down — as well as for the larger communal network in which Matthias refuses to participate. The narrator's detailed rendering of Bedelia's conflicting thoughts and emotions in 'A Frail Vessel' shows, further, that even within these networks individuals have enough leeway to shape their own personal destinies. After all, none of the Grimes family members is presented as simply a victim of a restrictive social milieu; instead, their lives are shaped as much by their choices and personalities as by their circumstances. Moreover, as the sad final fate of Bedelia and Matthias serves to demonstrate, for Lavin, personal happiness and self-fulfilment are to be found within rather than outside of the particular familial, communal and social context in which the characters find themselves. This is not 'fatalistic' as Zack Bowen has argued, but rather an appreciation of connection and community as fundamental principles of human life.[56]

As an extended and multi-layered treatment of the family, therefore, the Grimes sequence is crucial for a better understanding of Lavin's overall social vision, which gives her work resonance and meaning beyond the immediate Irish context to which critics have sometimes sought to confine it. As my reading of the Grimes stories has tried to argue, the ever-present social context of Lavin's fiction functions not just — or not primarily — as an element of critique addressed at a historically-defined Irish society, but rather as an expression of a fundamentally social world-view, which sees individual lives as necessarily enmeshed within larger networks of family, community and society. Although this social vision is expressed through Irish characters in an Irish setting in her stories, it easily transcends that particular milieu and extends to an encompassing vision of human life as shaped and defined by relation and interaction. Again, the structure of the Grimes sequence itself compellingly enacts this social world-view, as the interaction between individuals within the larger frames of family and community is mirrored in the formal interplay of the individual stories within the larger sequence — or anti-sequence, as Ferguson would have it. While the links and non sequiturs between the different stories highlight the fraught relations between the Grimes siblings, the individual stories, like the individual characters, can only properly be understood within the context of the larger whole. Precisely because this 'whole' of the Grimes stories is as imperfect as it is indispensable, I would argue, the sequence can be read as the most comprehensive expression of Lavin's fundamentally social vision.

Endnotes

1 R.F. Peterson, *Mary Lavin* (Boston: Twayne Publishers, 1978), pp.76–99.

2 Prior to its appearance in the collection, 'Frail Vessel' had been published in *Irish Writing* in 1955 and *Cosmopolitan* in 1956. See H. Kosok, 'Mary Lavin: A Bibliography', *Irish University Review*, 9, 2, (Autumn 1979), pp.279–312.

3 'Frail Vessel' refers to Alice's disappearance in rather cryptic terms: 'She [Bedelia] was glad to be able to give her little sister a home; a real family life again. It might prevent a repetition of what happened with Alice'. M. Lavin, 'Frail Vessel', in *The Patriot Son and Other Stories* (London: Michael Joseph, 1956), p.149.

4 'Short story cycle' and 'short story sequence' are critical terms used to denote a series of linked stories. Prototypical examples of this literary form are Joyce's *Dubliners* (1914) and Anderson's *Winesburg, Ohio* (1919). For theoretical approaches to the short story cycle, see for instance S. Mann, *The Short Story Cycle: A Genre Companion and Reference Guide* (New York: Greenwood, 1989).

5 Peterson, p.95.

6 A.A. Kelly, *Mary Lavin, Quiet Rebel: A Study of Her Short Stories* (Dublin: Wolfhound Press, 1980), p.56.

7 Ibid.

8 S. Ferguson, 'Resisting the pull of plot: Paley's anti-sequence in the "Faith" stories', *Journal of the Short Story in English*, 32 (Spring 1999). Online: http://jsse.revues.org/index180.html.

9 S. Ferguson, 'Sequences, Anti-Sequences, Cycles, and Composite Novels: The Short Story in Genre Criticism', *Journal of the Short Story in English*, 41 (Autumn 2003). Online: http://jsse.revues.org/index312.html, p.6. In yet another essay, Ferguson also applies the term 'anti-sequence' to Katherine Mansfield's New Zealand stories about the Burnell family. It is precisely these stories that are singled out for special praise by Lavin in an interview with Maurice Harmon: 'Other favourites are Racine, George Sand's pastoral novels, Sarah Orne Jewett, and I like the stories by Katherine Mansfield in which she is homesick for New Zealand.' S. Ferguson, 'Genre and the Work of Reading in Mansfield's "Prelude" and "At the Bay"', in F. Iftekharrudin et.al. (eds), *Postmodern Approaches to the Short Story* (Westport: Praeger, 2003), pp.25–38; M. Harmon, 'From Conversations with Mary Lavin', *Irish University Review*, 27, 2, (1997), p.289.

10 Ferguson, 'Sequences', p.7.

11 M. Kennedy, 'The Saturday Interview: Maev Kennedy talked to Mary Lavin', *The Irish Times*, 13 March 1976.

12 M. Lavin, 'Preface', in *Selected Stories* (New York: Macmillan, 1959), p.vii.

13 See, for example, the contribution of Maurice Harmon in this collection.

14 Harmon, 'Conversations', p.287.

15 C.M. Arensberg and S.T. Kimball, *Family and Community in Ireland*, 2nd edition (Cambridge, Harvard University Press, 1968), p.xxxviii.

16 Ibid., p.318.

17 Ibid., pp.322–23.

18 A. Byrne, R. Edmondson and T. Varley, 'Introduction to the Third Edition', in C.M. Arensberg and S.T. Kimball, *Family and Community in Ireland*, 3rd edition (Ennis: CLASP Press, 2003), pp.1–101.

19 S. Deane, 'Mary Lavin', in P. Rafroidi and T. Brown (eds), *The Irish Short Story* (Publications de l'Université de Lille, 1979), pp.245–246.

20 A. O. Weekes, *Irish Women Writers: An Uncharted Tradition* (Lexington KY: University Press of Kentucky, 1990), p.142.

21 Kelly, p.53.

22 M. Lavin, 'The Little Prince', in *The Patriot Son*, p.251.

23 Peterson, pp.25–43; see also Kelly, *Mary Lavin*, p.30.

24 M. Lavin, 'A Visit to the Cemetery', in *The Stories of Mary Lavin, Volume 1* (London: Constable, 1970), p.119.

25 Lavin, 'The Little Prince', p.207.

26 Ibid., pp.250–51.

27 Kelly, *Mary Lavin*, p.30.

28 Ibid., p.252.

29 Lavin, 'An Old Boot', in *The Patriot Son*, p.66.

30 Ibid., p.71.

31 Arensberg and Kimball, *Family and Community*, p.197.

32 Ibid., p.114.

33 Ibid., pp.372–73.

34 Lavin, 'The Little Prince', p.221.

35 Kelly, *Mary Lavin*, p.39.

36 Zack Bowen, *Mary Lavin* (Lewisburg, PA: Bucknell University Press, 1975), p.23.

37 D. Norris, 'Imaginative Response vs. Authority Structures. A Theme of the Anglo-Irish Short Story', in P. Rafroidi and T. Brown (eds), *The Irish Short Story* (Publications de l'Université de Lille III, 1979), pp.39–40; James Heaney, '"No Sanctuary From Hatred": A Re-Appraisal of Mary Lavin's Outsiders', *Irish University Review*, 28, 2, (1998), p.296.

38 Weekes, *Irish Women Writers*, p.142.

39 Ibid., p.154.

40 M. Lavin, 'Loving Memory, in *The Stories of Mary Lavin, Volume 2* (London: Constable, 1974), p.264.

41 Ibid., p.266.

42 Ibid., p.268.

43 Ibid., p.271.

44 Ibid., p.272.

45 It is certainly symbolic that they take their walks outside or on the outskirts of town: 'Those walks! Linked like lovers, every afternoon they set off out of the town and round the rampart-walls, seemingly aware of none but themselves'; ibid., p.273.

46 Arensberg and Kimball, *Family and Community*, p.197

47 Ibid., p.206.

48 Lavin, 'Loving Memory', p.265.

49 Peterson, *Mary Lavin*, p.99.

50 Lavin, 'Loving Memory', pp.272–73.

51 Ibid., p.281.

52 The early story 'Lilacs', for instance, clearly condemns an all too great concern for public opinion as when Phelim's wife and daughters are shown to be ashamed of their father dealing in 'dung' even as they enjoy the material profits it gives them.

53 Lavin herself identified Sarah Orne Jewett as a 'favourite' (see Note 9). Zagarell has called these works 'narratives of community' because of the way they 'take as their subject the life of a community (life in its "everyday aspects") and portray the minute and quite ordinary processes through which the community maintains itself as an entity'. S. Zagarell, 'Narrative of Community. The Identification of a Genre', *Signs*, 13, 3 (1988), p.499.

54 M. Lavin, 'Sarah', in *Tales from Bective Bridge* (London: Michael Joseph, 1945), p.48

55 Ibid., p.49.

56 Bowen, *Mary Lavin*, p.23.

10 | The Mystery of 'The Yellow Beret': Mary Lavin and the Art of Short Fiction

Julie Anne Stevens

To look at a star by glances — to view it in a side-long way, by turning toward it the exterior portions of the retina (more susceptible of feeble impressions of light than the interior), is to behold the star distinctly — is to have the best appreciation of its lustre — a lustre which grows dim just in proportion as we turn our vision fully upon it.[1]

The yellow beret in Mary Lavin's 1960 *New Yorker* story about a double murder in Dublin acts in a somewhat similar way to that of a star in the heavens as described by Monsieur Dupin in 'The Murders in the Rue Morgue' (1841). Like the star's gleaming lustre that only shows its fullness within the compass of the sidelong glance, so too does the beret only reveal its meaning by indirect means. Lavin's story about the murders of a younger and an older woman in the anonymous city streets directly recalls Edgar Allan Poe's earlier tale about a mysterious double murder of two women in Paris. Through his detective, Dupin, Poe introduces discourse on visual perception. The Frenchman claims that looking is not the same as seeing and sometimes half-looking allows one to see more. He argues that 'there is such a thing as being too profound. Truth is not always in a well.'[2] Dupin's observations not only prove to be useful when considering the elusive beret in Lavin's twentieth-century story but also when discussing more generally the form itself. The short story can also resist the direct gaze, especially the kind of story that emerged during what one might describe as the yellow period of the *fin de siècle*, the modern short story.[3]

In 'The Yellow Beret' (1960), visual perception becomes the focus. However, despite its central focus, the story's content constantly shifts meaning as it goes about reflecting multiple sources: the mystery story as found in Poe's work and a later French novel set during the 1890s called *The Mystery of the Yellow Room* (1907); Irish reality of the 1950s and a notorious murder case where the central evidence was a yellow beret; the modernization of vision; and discussion of the retinal yellow spot in optics. In this chapter on Mary Lavin's artful approach to the short story genre, I will explore a range of material that the central object of the story — the beret — suggests by providing glints of meaning through swift snatches and indirect glimpses.

When considering this story, we might note that even though Mary Lavin had established herself as an important short story writer by the early 1950s, the ensuing decade saw significant changes in her life. Her husband, William Walsh, died in May 1954, and her supporter, the fantasy and short story writer, Edward Plunkett, Lord Dunsany, followed soon afterward in 1957. Somewhat adrift as a widow with three daughters, she eventually located her family in Dublin and by the end of the decade lived near her friend, Frank O'Connor, in the Mespil Flats on Baggot Street.[4] Like O'Connor, she had secured a contract with *The New Yorker* magazine and eventually published some of her most compelling fiction in the American publication. 'The Yellow Beret' was the seventh of her sixteen *New Yorker* stories and it might be seen as a midpoint story in Lavin's career.

Like much of Lavin's earlier fiction 'The Yellow Beret' reveals the dual nature of reality. Typically in such writing, opposing characters' viewpoints are juxtaposed to show a double perspective; for example, Annie and Manny in 'At Sallygap' (1941) and Kate and Stacy in 'Lilacs' (1942). At times, the more imaginative character perceives a disturbing hidden version of reality (see, for example, the carter in 'The Cemetery in the Demesne' of 1944). In 'The Yellow Beret', the main character, Mag, confronts not just the complex nature of her darling son but the limits of knowledge itself and a disturbing intimation of the darker undercurrents of life. The story opens with Mag and her husband, Don, arguing about a double murder reported in the Dublin papers. Their disagreement arises from their differing reactions to the women's deaths. They also remark on the central missing evidence: a yellow beret. When the couple discover their son,

Donny, absent from bed, their argument becomes more personal as underlying resentments regarding their different relationships to the young man emerge. But where is Donny? And what a night he has chosen to go missing from home. When Donny finally appears, he explains that he wanted to walk away his nerves before his big university exam that day. He tells his parents he walked so far — across the city and nearly up into the Dublin hills — that when his blistered foot was beginning to pain him, he was delighted to find a beret which he tore up to use as a bandage. He still has the yellow hat — in his pocket.

The story recalls writing by Lavin about domestic tensions and life's underlying complexities, but its setting and content differ. The fiction of Lavin's middle years of writing, the late 1940s, 1950s and early 1960s, is her most conservative and forms the backbone of her work. Many of the stories delineate the environment, social mores, and religious hypocrisy of a place, usually a small town called Castlerampart based on Mary Lavin's mother's hometown of Athenry, County Galway. Grouped together, they give an impressive, if pessimistic, panorama of a place that breeds a 'half-way people, belonging in neither city nor country but affecting the mean or boorish airs of both ways of living'.[5] The middle-class Coniffes of Lavin's novel *The House in Clewe Street* (1945) demonstrate a quality frequently shown in the characters of these works, their inability to develop or to change having 'been bred too long in a servile position'.[6] Such characters often belong to the merchant class and a central conflict of their situation resides in how they might reconcile their dreams and passions to the stultifying confines of place. 'The Yellow Beret', however, locates itself in the city and although its characters express middle-class concerns, the subject of murder is unusual. I would argue that although the story reflects the decade in which it is set — Ireland in the 1950s — it might be considered alongside the writer's fiction that self-consciously comments on the art of the form. The choice of setting and subject matter has been determined by artful intents.

Mary Lavin's self-conscious and ironic treatment of form, her evident interest in what she described as the 'mystery of creativity', is revealed in the stories themselves: 'anything [she] learned about [her] craft has gone into the making of the stories'.[7] Some early fiction of the 1940s, 'A Story With a Pattern' (1945), 'A Fable' (1940), 'The Bunch of Grape' (1944) and 'The Widow's Son' (1946), comments on the art of fiction. Fiction is but an artistic arrangement controlled and determined by the author ('The Widow's Son'); indeed, can fiction ever be true and who might judge whether or not human lives shape a pattern ('A Story With a Pattern')? In fact, can we ever really appreciate or even see an idyllic order — a perfect beauty

— in the way things occur ('A Fable')? And if we do perceive absolute beauty/ truth, can we endure its ephemeral quality ('The Bunch of Grape')?[8]

These artful, even contrived, stories with their self-conscious commentary on the nature of art and fiction never assume realistic contours. Instead, they have a 'narrative cleverness' which Richard Peterson sees as providing a 'less interesting study of human nature' than the stories that rely on less overt means of resolving action.[9] In a 1958 letter to her editors, Mary Lavin herself regretted 'a certain contrivance ... [that she] failed to eradicate from some of [her] stories like Posy and A Gentle Soul [sic]',[10] and both she and Seán O'Faoláin distinguished this kind of story from that which 'comments on human nature'.[11]

Lavin's regretful awareness of plot contrivance in the late 1950s directs itself at her realistic stories. She does not mention self-consciously contrived fiction that comments on form or art. Her 1960 story, 'The Yellow Beret', continues to employ device and contrivance. Given Lavin's awareness of plot contrivance, this short story might be considered as writing that continues to draw attention to the art of short fiction. Various clues suggest that the story concerns itself with more than a married couple's early morning kitchen conversation about two murders and the subsequent discovery that their only son is missing. The biggest clue is the yellow beret. Its bright hue and simple shape suggest symbolic possibilities. Yet the tendency to study Mary Lavin's writing as a reflection of Irish social conditions may lead readers to neglect its artful intentions. Mary Lavin was an avid reader of art history and collected paintings; she knew a number of visual artists and corresponded with Jack B. Yeats.[12] She also seemed to have enjoyed mystery writing, as she once told me that she read criticism as though it were detective fiction.[13] Reading 'The Yellow Beret', I wonder if she also read detective fiction as though it were criticism. Certainly, consideration of Visual Studies or attention to popular discourse, as found in newspapers, film or detective fiction, reveals writing that is much more than social document.

The item at the heart of the story, the yellow beret, might be considered as a means of plot contrivance. The object serves to twist the plot around, and its vivid colour makes it stand out. Because of Lavin's careful and self-conscious handling of her stories, her inclusion of the yellow object at this stage of her career deserves careful consideration. In addition, placing a story about Dublin murders in an American magazine raises further questions regarding Lavin's purpose. 'The Yellow Beret' presents an urban mystery by a writer better known for works about the small towns and fields of the Irish countryside. Why did Lavin select this story for *The New Yorker*?

Lavin's concentration on the metropolis and a middle-class couple's domestic squabble could be considered as a response to *The New Yorker*'s trends at the time of publication. In a study of the Irish and Irish-American life and writings of Lavin's exact contemporary, Maeve Brennan (1917–1993 as compared to Lavin's 1912–1996), Angela Bourke notes that Brennan's work for *The New Yorker* may have been directed in part by the magazine's female readership.[14] Maeve Brennan joined the American magazine in 1949 and was best known for her sketches from 1953–1968 about the 'ordinary ways' of New York life in 'The Talk of the Town' section and under the sobriquet, 'the long-winded lady'.[15] Mary Lavin published her stories for the magazine during a similar period, from 1958–1976, most appearing during the years 1958–1961. During these years, over half of the magazine's readership was female and Angela Bourke argues that such readers responded to a kind of coded discourse. Thus, Maeve Brennan's arch and rather coy chat as the 'long-winded lady' could mask what Bourke describes as 'subversive messages' discernible to those who enjoyed Brennan's send-up of female chatter.[16] Mary Lavin's Irish story in *The New Yorker* published during this time also offers more than it initially suggests. Its central clue and main material evidence is the yellow beret. I will investigate the mystery of the yellow beret.

Lavin's interest in the colour yellow had already been declared with the publication of her 1946 collection of stories, *The Becker Wives and Other Stories*. Bookending the collection are stories that feature female characters described in terms of bright yellow. In the opening story, 'The Becker Wives', new wife, Flora, appears like a bird, a lark or a chaffinch with 'yellowy golden hair', amidst a family very like the Coniffes of *Clewe Street*, the stolid middle-class Beckers.[17] Flora's artistry is made evident in part by her theatrical turns and imaginary abilities which include a pretend green dragon. In the final story, 'Magenta', the country servant girl's aspirations when she moves to Dublin are indicated by her borrowed finery that is topped off by an elaborate, canary yellow hat. Four long stories make up the 1946 collection and the colour yellow continues to appear in various ways (a yellow tie and yellow shoes in 'The Joy Ride', yellow hair in 'A Happy Death'). Lavin emphasized further the dominating colour of her stories by selecting a vivid yellow cover sleeve for the book; horizontal grey-brown stripes across the yellow emphasize the colour's hue and Lavin's black and white portrait on the back cover is outlined in the same deep yellow shade.

This same year, Tennessee Williams published his short story, 'The Yellow Bird'. The story provides a useful, first clue in the unravelling of the mystery of the yellow beret because it suggests with its title a possible source for Lavin's early interest in yellow. The American story responds in part to Albert Lewin's film version of Oscar Wilde's *The Picture of Dorian Gray* that appeared the previous year. A star turn by Angela Lansbury playing Sybil Vane included her singing on stage the vaudeville song, 'Little Yellow Bird'.[18] In the movie, Lansbury as Sybil Vane trills the song as she stands alongside a backdrop scene with a picture of a caged canary. The stage frames and confines the actress who sings about the yellow bird in its cage. The original source of the song was the vaudeville comedy, *Easy Dawson*, produced in 1905, in which the well-known vaudeville star, Flora Zabelle, sang 'Little Yellow Bird'. In the song, a common sparrow flies into a mansion where a pet canary in a gilded cage asks her to share his comfortable home. She loves him, but she loves her liberty more:

> Goodbye, little Yellow-bird, I'd gladly mate with you;
> I love you, little Yellow-bird,
> But I love my freedom too;
> So, goodbye, little Yellow-bird, I'd rather brave the cold
> On a leafless tree
> Than a prisoner be
> In a cage of gold.[19]

In the film version of *Dorian Gray*, Angela Lansbury/Sybil Vane wears a hat with sparrow feathers and sings about the yellow bird to an audience that includes Dorian Gray. Towards the conclusion of the song, she turns and sings to him as though he were the canary of the vaudeville song. Some viewers may have noted the underlying significance of the yellow bird in this scene. In the United States, the abiding memory of Oscar Wilde's visit may well have been his venture into the mines of Colorado. In later years, some may have compared his fate to that of the doomed canary lowered into the mines to test for poisoned air.[20]

With her artist, Flora, in an Irish 'cage of gold' in 'The Becker Wives', Mary Lavin recalls popular theatricals, thus suggesting her artful intent and cautioning against too literal a reading of the fiction. Recently, Theresa Wray has wondered about the origins of Flora in 'The Quest for Flora: Who is She?' and suggests the story's grounding in social and economic Irish realities as they impacted upon women's lives in post-1937 constitution Ireland.[21] Yet even more important than the social backdrop might be the story's reflection on art in Ireland. Flora does not really belong with the Beckers and her descent into madness suggests a rather grim fate for a gay songster like her in a place called Castlerampart. The stifling of Flora reminds us of other silenced voices in Ireland, while the story's context in a collection that gives the colour yellow precedence demands consideration of a visual discourse. Lavin's interest in the significance of the colour yellow might be examined more fully if we turn to the later story, 'The Yellow Beret', which the author placed alongside 'The Becker Wives' in her 1974 collection of short stories, *The Stories of Mary Lavin, Volume 2*.

Yellow evokes the decadent 1890s and the 'French lubricity' of *The Yellow Book* magazine.[22] In a search for clues as to the origin of the yellow beret in Lavin's 1960 story, works such as Charlotte Perkins Gilman's 'The Yellow Wallpaper' (1892) come to mind. However, as already noted, Lavin's story recalls more directly the murder mystery genre as demonstrated in Poe's early tale, 'The Murders in the Rue Morgue'. In Poe's story, a mysterious double murder of a younger and older woman invites the astute detecting abilities of Monsieur Dupin who says he can read an individual as though he could see right through him or her. Dupin professes that 'most men, in respect to himself, wore windows in their bosoms'.[23] Dupin's powers of ratiocination include both wildly creative mental leaps and painstakingly careful deduction, a kind of double ability so that he seems to be two people instead of one: 'Observing him', says his friend, 'I often dwelt meditatively upon the old philosophy of the Bi-Part Soul, and amused myself with the fancy of a double Dupin — creative and resolvant'.[24] The characters in Mary Lavin's story also believe they know each other through and through, but they discover that they actually lack the ability to discern the inner thoughts of the other. As Donny says to his mother, 'Nobody's made of glass, anyway. Nobody!' In fact, because of his sudden change, Donny seems like two people to his mother, and when the young man takes the torn beret from his father and 'almost absently ... fitted the two pieces together for a minute till they made a whole' we know that Donny also possesses a kind of double nature like that of Monsieur Dupin in Poe's early murder mystery.[25]

A popular French mystery of the early twentieth century and set in the 1890s helps to unravel even further the mysterious origins of the yellow beret. *Le Mystère de la Chambre Jaune* or *The Mystery of the Yellow Room* by Gaston Leroux includes a beret as evidence in its puzzle about a woman who is attacked in a locked room. Leroux continues to investigate the nature of perception as introduced in Poe's 'The Murders in the Rue Morgue'. He transports Poe's discourse on perception and optics into the twentieth century and provides a connecting linchpin between early short fiction and modern works such as Mary Lavin's story. But before considering the French murder mystery, the decadent period and visual discourse as they impact on the writing of Mary Lavin, I want to investigate the Irish side of this story and to consider more closely the murders upon which the story revolves.

The first murder in Lavin's story, a strangled girl of seventeen, occurs 'down at the docks'.[26] The newspaper reports that a Dutch sailor is wanted for questioning. More specifically, the murder happened at the Pigeon House near the Alexandra Basin of Dublin's north side. Mag imagines the spot alongside the water. She repeatedly 'pictures' in her mind the scene of the crime and in her imagination she sees how the wharf narrows to become a 'promenade for birds, with bollards here and there splattered with glaring white droppings; and where in places steps led down into the water they seemed senseless, more than half of them under water, wobbly-looking and pale, and when a wash of water went over the top steps it lay on them as thin as ice'.[27] Mag vividly pictures the crime scene and even imagines the Dutch sailor standing on Butt Bridge. She thinks she sees the murderer, a man with carroty red hair and a blue shirt. How foolish she feels when she realizes that her seeming vision or premonition turns out to be her memory of a self-portrait by Vincent Van Gogh. Mag sees things that are not there and looks too hard in trying to see to the heart of things, to the heart of her son in particular. Significantly, as noted at the beginning of the story, Mag has hypermetropia, long-sightedness.

The second murder, of a fifty-four year old schoolteacher, happens on the Sandford Road on the other side of the city. The double murder provokes the couple's troubled conversation about assault and possible rape, unusual talk in this household because up until now, Mag has been careful to avoid unpleasant topics; she has attempted 'to draw a circle ... around their home, and keep out all talk of violence and crime'.[28] The killings crack open Mag's circling embrace.

How incongruous that the yellow beret, mentioned as missing evidence in the newspaper, should be sported by the grey-haired schoolteacher rather than the young woman murdered down by the docks where sailors and prostitutes roam. Odder still is the fact that the missing son who eventually returns from his all-night walking expedition pulls the same article from his pocket and admits to having used a small section of it, 'a bit of sweat-stained, blood-soaked felt' as a bandage for his blister.[29] The beret abruptly introduces evil into the seemingly innocent life of the Irish family. Its introduction, however, may strike some readers as too coincidental in what appears to be a realistic study of suburban living. In any case, Donny's possession of the hat raises a practical problem: will he return the evidence to the police or will he hurry to his exams and neglect his duty. Pragmatic Don encourages Donny's decision to take the latter course. Donny does so and abruptly the close connection between the mother and son is broken. Mag wonders at her son's change — nobody's made of glass, he tells her, nobody.

Richard Peterson claims that 'the impact of the last insight into Mag's isolation is marred by the intrusiveness of the yellow beret in shaping the crisis'.[30] The beret's appearance creates a conflict that must be resolved and the critic implies that the unrealistic use of the device jars in this realistic story. But does the beret have other purposes than that of directing the turn of events? Is the narrative more artful than it initially appears to be?

Close consideration of the story reveals a pattern of inconsistencies disturbing the seemingly normal surface of family life. The couple demonstrate markedly different reactions to the murders: Don shows sympathy for the young girl and what seems to Mag to be indifference about the older woman's death. Mag views the younger woman's death — what she assumes to be a sexual crime — with distaste and feels compassion for the schoolteacher. Equally opposing are their attitudes toward their son, Donny, whose name reflects back to that of his father, Don. The father feels impatience for his son's consistent obedience while the mother encourages it. Yet, contrarily, the doting mother connects her son's disappearance with the murders — doubts come rushing in at the first opportunity. Don is horrified by his wife's suspicions yet when the beret is produced he believes the worst might happen and his son will be incriminated by the article.

The unexpected reactions of characters parallel the incongruities to which the situation gives rise: a spinster's gay hat, Donny's blood on the yellow beret. And as the narrative proceeds, it becomes apparent that most of these contradictions depend upon the perception of reality, so that Mag's need for corrective lenses begins to have greater significance. What seems like innocence to Don — the young girl who is possibly a prostitute — suggests evil to Mag. Or Donny's innocence becomes the opposite depending on how he is perceived. In fact, innocence and evil are not as easily distinguished as they initially may appear to be, and the story shows that people and their actions reveal incongruities. The revelation of character complexity through the study of differing perceptions occurs because of the situation's oddity and the hat's sudden appearance in Donny's hand. The yellow beret conjoins innocence and evil while also operating as an activator of the turn of events.

The beret's meaning becomes even more potent if we examine the Irish scene of the 1950s and note that certain details of Lavin's story suggest a notorious murder case that took place in Limerick six years earlier in 1953.[31] First, the main evidence of the murder of the 'elderly spinster' in Lavin's story,[32] the yellow beret, is also central to the case of Catherine Cooper from Clare, a sixty-four year old senior nurse attacked and murdered on a dark autumn evening along the Dublin road in Limerick. Cooper's dress consisted of yellow garments: a yellow polo neck, a yellow scarf and a yellow beret.[33] Second, Don's throwaway remark when he sees his son arriving home after his night's walking expedition — 'They didn't hang him yet anyway: he's coming down the road!' — also recalls the well publicized Cooper case.[34] In fact, the brutal sexual attack and murder by young married man, Michael Manning, resulted in the final hanging that occurred in the Irish state. The 1953 murder and subsequent trial deserve further consideration for their impact on Lavin's later Dublin murder story. The facts of the Limerick case reflect interestingly on the fiction of Lavin's work and throw some light on the mystery of the yellow beret.

The murder of Nurse Cooper and the subsequent trial and hanging of Michael Manning involved important Irish figures in its enactment and was recorded assiduously in the *Limerick Leader*, *The Clare Champion* and the Dublin papers. The future bishop of Galway, a man who would be notorious in his own right, Father Eamonn Casey, assisted in the last rites of the victim; the barrister heading the case for the defence in the trial, Sir John Esmonde, had stood twice as Fine Gael Dáil deputy for Wexford.[35] Indeed, the heads of government held a special cabinet meeting in April 1954 to decide on an appeal for clemency from the Bishop of Limerick.[36] Mary Lavin's lawyer husband, William Walsh, who had stood for the Dáil as a Fine Gael candidate before his sudden illness and death in May 1954, must have been very familiar with the case. One imagines that the execution of Manning on 20 April 1954, and all the absorbing details of the case as it was tried in Dublin the previous February, would have preoccupied the young politician and his writer wife as they stood on the threshold of political life in Ireland before the abrupt and sudden death of Mr Walsh.

A detail of grisly significance lay with the nurse's brightly coloured beret and the head gear of the murderer, a kind of Mountie hat. These hats were central in the case as both the man's hat and the beret had been discovered on the night of the event by two passing young men. A study of the case describes how the men picked up the items from the trampled grass on the verge of the roadside and pranced along down the road and into the local garage with hats on their heads. One of the men eventually headed home with the hats, the yellow beret 'dangling ... on a stick' as he walked along, and then put the hats in an outhouse before going to bed.[37]

The innocent young man going home with the incriminating yellow beret after a night's gadding about clearly resonated with Mary Lavin, as we see in her later story that concentrates on a similar action as central to the plot. But what may have struck Lavin even more forcibly was a further detail of the case that recalled a more literary backdrop to this tragic affair. The victim came from the Killimer parish in Clare and she was buried in the family plot in Burrane cemetery. In the same place lie the bones of a murder victim whose story Gerald Griffin retold in his 1829 novel, *The Collegians*: Eileen Hanly, murdered at sixteen by the son of 'one of the leading county families', John Scanlon, who despite a strong defence by Daniel O'Connell, was found guilty and hanged in March 1820.[38] In the Clare burial plot, then, lie two victims of murder, one an 'elderly spinster' and one a young woman, like the two victims in Lavin's 1960 story.

Murder will out, they say, but fiction can resist straightforward interpretation. Various elements of Lavin's *New Yorker* story seem to have little to do with the Limerick background of the Cooper case, and we need to look further to plumb the mystery of the yellow beret. Already mentioned is the allusion to Van Gogh whom Mag sees in her imagination when she and Don discuss the newspaper account of the murders. A portrait of the artist springs into her mind when she hears that the police are looking for a sailor in connection to the murder of the young girl. Clearly, seeing something may have little to do with what actually exists. As Mag says when doubts about Donny suffuse her frightened mind: 'What comes into one's mind at a time like this has nothing at all to do with the other person. ... It's as if all the badness of the world — all the badness in oneself — rushes into one's mind.'[39] Then, the Dublin setting, emphasized by the careful recording of places across the city, also leads us away from Limerick and suggests other significances in relation to the yellow beret.

The visual discourse that the mention of Van Gogh raises becomes more important when we examine the pattern suggested by the Dublin topography. The initial movement across 1950's Dublin that the two murders invoke, from the docks of the north side to the suburban edges of Sandyford, traces one straight vertical line. Mention of Butt Bridge and Jervis Street Hospital, then, provides a horizontal line moving into the city centre. A third movement is provided by the careful record of Donny's night walk as he relates how he starts off from somewhere close to the city centre, the family home, and strikes out past Milltown and Goatstown of the south side toward the Dublin hills to meet the end point of Sandyford. A second vertical line is thus marked and this one meets the end of the first vertical line. The lines make a kind of triangle or a zigzag that takes in much of the cityscape. The triangular-like shape traced through the story's careful listing of Dublin sites repeats itself in the relationship of the three characters — mother, father and son — and the pattern that the females of the story make up: mother, virgin and whore. Then, in addition to the triangle shape, we note references to an image that Mag uses to express her determination to protect her small family from unpleasant reality: 'She had made a point to draw a circle, as it were, around their home, and keep out all talk of violence and crime'. Mag's circle recalls the beret itself and draws attention to yet another basic geometric shape.

The possible significance of these shapes might be ascertained if we look again at Lavin's interest in colour and art. Interestingly, the story writer sent the great Irish colourist, Jack B. Yeats, some of her writing, and he especially enjoyed 'The Becker Wives'. Mary Lavin owned his oil paintings, *The Old Ale House*, *The Man in the Shooting Gallery*, *Secret Eyes*, and *The Hard Sailor Man*.[40] Her introduction of a visual artist in 'The Yellow Beret', then, one who initially appears as a 'hard sailor man' in the main character's imagination, deliberately draws attention to visual discourse and, in particular, the colour yellow: the artist mentioned is Vincent van Gogh who celebrated yellow during his time in the Yellow House in Arles, France when he included large glorious circles of the bright pigment in his paintings of the sower in his field.

Of the primary colours, yellow seems to demand most attention. As a warm colour it advances towards the viewer, but, as the abstract artist Vasily Kandinsky observed, it can also distract because if 'steadily gazed at in any geometrical form, [it] has a disturbing influence, and reveals in the colour an insistent, aggressive character'.[41] Kandinsky's non-objective paintings, with their strong colours in circles and triangles often positioned alongside jagged lines, may already have dazzled New Yorkers' eyes in 1960 when Lavin's story appeared. The year before on 21 October, the Guggenheim museum opened its doors for the first time and, of course, Kandinsky's works would have been amply displayed in Solomon Guggenheim's substantial collection.

Mary Lavin's story makes prominent the yellow circle that we find displayed in both objective and non-objective art. In so doing, the fiction appears to be responding to developments in the visual arts. Lavin's interest in perception and consciousness in 'The Yellow Beret' would corroborate this supposition. In fact, Lavin's sense of the pictorial and her attention to perception in this story recall arguments regarding visualization and its changing nature as explored throughout the nineteenth century. The story reminds us that vision is located in the body and in the processes of perception. The art historian, Jonathan Crary, argues in *Techniques of the Observer* and *Suspensions of Perception* that vision is an historical construction subject to change, and he explores the modernization of vision and the transformation of the observer throughout the nineteenth and into the early twentieth centuries. His particular interest in the science of optics draws attention to the physiology of the eye: 'retinal afterimages, peripheral vision, binocular vision, and thresholds of attention'.[42]

At the end of the nineteenth century, 'attention becomes a fundamentally new object within the modernization of subjectivity'.[43] Crary points to studies by scientists and physiologists absorbed by the concept of attention — a means of selecting and isolating 'certain contents of the sensory field', an automatic sorting through and selecting from the wide range of sensory input that the individual faces in the modern world.[44] This process of selection 'implied an inevitable fragmentation of a visual field in which the unified and homogenous coherence of classical models of vision was impossible'. Ultimately, the modern study of vision showed that 'perception was an activity of exclusion, rendering parts of a perceptual field unperceived'.[45] This sense of modernized perception reflects upon the new kind of short fiction appearing at the same time. We might speculate that the form of the modern short story conveyed especially well developing notions about perception and consciousness. Thus, Mary Lavin's later twentieth-century story, with its emphasis upon perception and perspective, recalls an important aspect of the modern form, and it offers with its central point — the yellow beret — a possible key to understanding the direction of the author's intent.

To explore further the suggestive possibilities of Lavin's yellow beret in relation to visual discourse, we might turn to one final source, a murder mystery of the *fin de siècle* by Gaston Leroux, author of *Phantom of the Opera*, whose locked-room detective novel, *The Mystery of the Yellow Room*, was recognized as one of the most successful of its kind.[46] The novel's plot revolves around a room where the assault of a woman takes place, and on the yellow carpet of this yellow-papered room lies a central piece of evidence, a beret.

The Mystery of the Yellow Room concentrates on the unreliability of eyewitness testimony and — ultimately — vision's susceptibility in the perception of reality. So puzzling is the attack that some believe that its mystery outdoes the strange fancies of Edgar Allan Poe himself:

> And that [locked room] is just what makes this mystery the most puzzling I have known, even in the realms of the imagination. Even Edgar Allan Poe invented nothing to compare with this in *The Murders in the Rue Morgue*. There the scene of the crime was secure

enough to prevent the escape of a man, but there was a window through which a monkey — the perpetrator of the murders — could slip away; but here there can be no question of an opening of any sort. With the door and the shutter fastened and the windows closed, as they were, not even a fly could either enter or escape.[47]

The young journalist/detective of the story argues that logic must prevail in the search for the truth. Reason will supply the answer, and he describes a 'circle drawn by [his] reason' within which the evidence he finds must fit: 'that event must fit — you know it! ... remember that when you traced that circle — drawing a geometrical figure upon your brain, as on a sheet of paper — you began to apply your reason'.[48]

This mental circle becomes central in the reporter's reasoning that the only possible culprit must be one within the orbit of people surrounding him. As he tells the court room during the sensational trial at the end of the novel: 'I had within the circle one person who was really two, that is to say, a being who, in addition to being himself was also the attacker'. The puzzle of the case could not be worked out until reason had 'brought together those two people, or, rather, *the two halves* of that one person'.[49]

I am interested not only in Leroux's repeated use of the geometric shape and the colour yellow as it might be reflected in Lavin's later story, nor merely in how Leroux recalls Poe's reflections on the double nature of man — his Bi-Part Soul as described in the earlier story — in a work that studies the workings of logic as it relates to vision. Of course, these things reflect intriguingly on Lavin's fiction, as when at the end of the story Donny picks up the two halves of the torn beret and fits them together to make a whole. The gesture gains much in significance if considered in the context of the mystery genre. Or, indeed, we could argue that all these works show the unreliability of eyewitness testimony. But I am even more interested in considering Leroux's yellow room and Lavin's yellow beret as objects that reflect upon studies in visual discourse on the workings of the eye and, in particular, the function of the retinal yellow spot.

The French literary critic, Andrea Goulet, studies the impact of nineteenth-century scientific debate in optics on popular fiction of the *fin de siècle*, and pays close attention to discussion on the retinal yellow spot in relation to Leroux's novel. She argues that the popular novel responds to 'contemporary scientific debate in optical physiology'[50] and she explores how the work reacts to the discovery of the retinal yellow spot by providing Felix Giraud-Teulon's definition of the phenomenon in his 1861 work on vision: the 'punctum centrale, ou tache jaune de la rétine'.[51] Goulet argues that the enclosed yellow room of Leroux's novel serves to demonstrate the physiological workings of the human eye. She maintains that the locked yellow room recalls the eye's central point of fixation in the eye, the yellow spot:

> The optical Yellow Spot and the literary Yellow Room share a ... shifting value according to the perspective from which observation takes place. Both can be understood as 'blind spots': the 'tache obscure' in the optical chamber mars the transparency of the eye, while the Yellow Room fulfils the classic function as the site of mystery, as that which cannot be seen.[52]

The yellow spot or the *macula lutea* is the most sensitive part of the retina. It allows for the retina's perception of the most vivid colour. The tiny yellow spot is both the site of utmost acuity for the observer looking out, but also, as Goulet points out, appears opaque (the 'tache obscure') to the observer looking in.

In a work about perception and its unreliability set during the 1890s, a study of the visual significance of the popular mystery such as that advanced by Goulet is convincing. Moreover, discussion on optics and visual discourse in relation to mystery fiction such as Leroux's novel provide an intriguing backdrop to Mary Lavin's short fiction and, in particular, her mystery story, 'The Yellow Beret'. Throughout her career, Lavin was preoccupied with point of view and 'double vision' and critics frequently describe her as possessing an ironic vision.[53] Many of her stories revolve around the fact that reality might be seen in absolutely different ways, and so it is no surprise that in 1960 she produced a work that devoted itself to the nature of consciousness and perception. The story's subject matter deliberately recalls an early study of perception by Edgar Allan Poe. However, by situating her study within the period of the impressionists and drawing attention to a visual discourse, the reader is indirectly reminded of the development of the form.

In this essay I have touched on various possible sources of the yellow beret in an attempt to plumb its mystery. In the end, however, I would maintain that the work merely reflects these various influences: the Irish murder of Nurse Cooper in 1953; the opening, in 1959, of the Guggenheim with Kandinsky's celebration of geometric shapes and colour; and the backdrop of mystery fiction and the short story genre as it developed into a modern form. If one were to press any harder

for meaning on the surface of the yellow beret, I maintain that it would disappear
— much like the glimmering star in the firmament that Poe's detective describes
in the earlier story, 'The Murders in the Rue Morgue'.

Endnotes

1 E.A. Poe, 'The Murders in the Rue Morgue', *The Fall of the House of Usher and Other Writings* (1841; London: Penguin, 2003), p.157.

2 Ibid., pp.156–7.

3 C.E. May argues that impressionism heralded the modern short story at the end of the nineteenth century in *The Short Story: The Reality of Artifice* (New York: Routledge, 2002), p.12.

4 See H. O'Donovan Sheehy, 'Memories', in H. Lennon (ed.), *Frank O'Connor* (Dublin: Four Courts, 2007), p.161.

5 T.J. Murray, 'Mary Lavin's World: Lovers and Strangers', *Éire-Ireland*, 7, (Summer 1972), p.125.

6 M. Lavin, *The House in Clewe Street* (London: Penguin, 1949), p.98.

7 M. Lavin, 'Afterword', in C. Murphy 'Mary Lavin: An Interview' *Irish University Review*, 9, 2, (Autumn 1979), p.224.

8 For further discussion of these stories, see J. A. Stevens, *Plot Patterns and Plotting Techniques in Mary Lavin's Fiction*, MA Thesis, University College Galway, 1989. Research based on the Mugar Memorial collection of Mary Lavin material in Boston University and accompanied by interviews with the writer.

9 R.F. Peterson, *Mary Lavin* (New York: Twayne Publishers, 1978), p.106.

10 Mary Lavin, letter to Patience (presumably working for publishers Michael Joseph), 18 March 1958, Mary Lavin Collection, Mugar Memorial Library, Boston, MA, USA, Box 23, Folder 2.

11 S. O'Faoláin, *The Short Story* (Cork: Mercier Press, 1972), p.200. Lavin's discussion of contrivance is found in Murphy, 'Mary Lavin: An Interview', pp.215–9.

12 L. Levenson, *The Four Seasons of Mary Lavin* (Dublin: Marino Books, 1998), p.205. Although Lavin's daughters disliked Levenson's critical biography, it remains the only work including valuable biographical material gleaned from Lavin's personal correspondence. For a report on the book's controversy, see J. Burns, 'Mary Lavin book stalled by daughter', *The Sunday Times*, May 1998.

13 Interview with Mary Lavin, Westbury Hotel, Dublin, 8 June 1989.

14 A. Bourke, *Maeve Brennan, Homesick at The New Yorker* (London: Jonathan Cape, 2004), pp.189–91.

15 M. Brennan, 'Author's Note', 1969, *The Long-Winded Lady, Notes from The New Yorker* (Berkeley, CA: Counterpoint, 1997), pp.1–3.

16 Bourke, *Maeve Brennan*, p.189.

17 M. Lavin, 'The Becker Wives', in *The Becker Wives and Other Stories* (London: Michael Joseph, 1946), p.33.

18 *The Picture of Dorian Gray*, dir. Albert Lewin, perf. George Sanders, Hurd Hatfield, Donna Reed, Angela Lansbury. Metro-Goldwyn-Mayer Studios, 1945.

19 C.W. Murphy and W. Hargreaves, 'Little Yellow Bird' (New York: Sol-Bloom, MDCCCIII). Performed by Flora Zabelle in Raymond Hitchcock's *Easy Dawson*, 1905.

20 Members of a research seminar held in Umeå University, Sweden, in February 2012 noted how canaries were commonly used in mining. I am grateful to Professor Heidi Hansson for the opportunity to give my paper to the research seminar.

21 T. Wray, 'The Quest for Flora: Who is She? Establishing One Woman's Place in Mary Lavin's "The Becker Wives"', in K. Jenčová et al. (eds), *The Politics of Irish Writing* (Prague: Centre for Irish Studies, Charles University, 2010), pp.118–28.

22 *The Times* on the first appearance of *The Yellow Book* in 1894. Quoted in F. Harrison, 'Introduction', in *The Yellow Book: An Anthology* (1914; Woodbridge, Suffolk: Boydell Press, 1982), p.9.

23 Poe, 'The Murders in the Rue Morgue', p.146.

24 Ibid.

25 M. Lavin, 'The Yellow Beret', in *The Stories of Mary Lavin, Volume 2* (London: Constable, 1974), p.298.

26 Ibid., p.282.

27 Ibid., p.283.

28 Ibid.

29 Ibid., p.295.

30 Peterson, *Mary Lavin*, p.106.

31 Mary Lavin suggested that two murders on 20 July 1959 reported in the *Dublin Evening Press* gave her the idea for 'The Yellow Beret'. I have been unable to locate any reports of Irish murders on that date. In any case, the evidence of the yellow beret indicates clearly the earlier Limerick murder. Mary Lavin Collection, Mugar Memorial Library, Box 18, folder IV, 'Memorabilia'.

32 Lavin, 'The Yellow Beret', p.285.

33 D. Walsh, *Beneath Cannock's Clock: The Last Man Hanged in Ireland* (Cork: Mercier Press, 2009), p.29.

34 Lavin, 'The Yellow Beret', p.292.

35 Bishop Eamonn Casey's fathering of a son with American, Ms Annie Murphy, became a national scandal in Ireland in the early 1990s.

36 Walsh, *Beneath Cannock's Clock*, pp.56, 112 and 134.

37 Ibid., pp.44–7.

38 J. Cronin, 'Introduction', in G. Griffin *The Collegians*, (1829; Belfast: Appletree Press, 1992), pp.vii–x.

39 Lavin, 'The Yellow Beret', p.290.

40 Levenson, *The Four Seasons*, pp.82, 89, and 203.

41 W. Kandinsky, *Concerning the Spiritual in Art* (1911), translated by M.T.H. Sadler, ebook from Project Gutenberg, March 2004. Online: http://www.gutenberg.org/cache/epub/5321/pg5321.html; See also T. Bashkoff, C. Derouet, and A. Hoberg, Exhibition Guide for Vasily Kandinsky's works celebrating the fiftieth anniversary of the Guggenheim Museum, September 18, 2009–January 13, 2010.

42 J. Crary, *Techniques of the Observer: On Vision and Modernity in the Nineteenth Century* (Cambridge, MA: Massachusetts Institute of Technology, 1992), p.16.

43 J. Crary, *Suspensions of Perception: Attention, Spectacle, and Modern Culture* (Cambridge, MA: Massachusetts Institute of Technology, 1999), p.17.

44 Ibid.

45 Ibid., pp.24–5.

46 T. Hale, 'Afterword', in G. Leroux, *The Mystery of the Yellow Room* (1907; Sawtry, Cambridgeshire: Dedalus, 2008), pp.232–6.

47 Leroux, *The Mystery*, p.52.

48 Ibid., p.137.

49 Ibid., pp.204–5.

50 A. Goulet, 'Retinal Fictions: Villiers, Leroux, and Optics at the Fin-de-siècle', *Nineteenth-Century French Studies*, 34, 1&2, (Fall–Winter 2005–2006), p.108.

51 Ibid., p.114.

52 Ibid., p.115.

53 V.S. Pritchett refers to Lavin's 'double vision' in his introduction to Mary Lavin's *Collected Stories* (Boston: Houghton Mifflin, 1971), p.ix. See also Marianne Koenig, 'Mary Lavin: The Novels and the Stories', *Irish University Review*, 9, 2, (Autumn 1979), p.257.

11 | 'Stranded Objects': Topographies of Loss in Mary Lavin's Widow Stories

Sinéad Mooney

This essay aims to consider Mary Lavin's 'widow stories' in terms of their narrative representations of death, loss and bereavement, and the Freudian 'work of mourning' (*die Trauerarbeit*) which is their frequent preoccupation. Lavin's early widowhood looms large in the way in which she herself is remembered and commemorated. A centenary *Paris Review* essay notes how she 'wrote as a young widow, and she wrote as the mother of three young girls; she wrote longhand early every morning, sitting up in bed before her daughters rose, the pages set down on a wooden breadboard; she wrote at night, at the kitchen table'.[1] An *Irish Times* account of a recent New York showing of *An Arrow Still in Flight*, a 1992 film tribute to Lavin, leads off by describing her as 'the twice-widowed Irish writer', and concludes with the claim that her well-known story 'Happiness' (1968) is Lavin's 'autobiographical account of her widowhood', written, moreover, in the voice of her daughter Caroline Walsh.[2] The widow stories are viewed as constituting some of her finest work, and yet, compared to the rest of her oeuvre, they are frequently read in a reductively autobiographical way, thereby simultaneously praising Lavin and relegating her to the position of astute memoirist, denying her work the full status of an art disengaged from its autobiographical sources. I want, while acknowledging the stories' sources in Lavin's lived experience, to propose a reading of the widow stories' rehearsals of grieving, remembering, exorcising, forgetting and survival in relation to Freudian mourning theory, and of Lavin as an elegist in prose.

For a writer who has at times been damningly associated with what Seamus Deane calls a 'nefarious sweetness' of tone, her work, from its earliest appearances in print — a decade and a half before she was first widowed — is death-haunted.[3] Augustine Martin writes of Lavin's 'virtual obsession with the theme of death', while Marianne Koenig, in her survey of Lavin's novels and stories, notes that 'burials, cemeteries, wills, all the paraphernalia of death, figure largely'.[4] A glance at the titles of her short stories amply demonstrates this preoccupation: 'The Small Bequest' (1944), 'The Green Grave and the Black Grave' (1940), 'Grief' (1944), 'Loving Memory' (1960), 'A Happy Death' (1946), 'A Visit to the Cemetery' (1951), 'The Will' (1944), 'The Cemetery in the Demesne' (1944), and 'Tomb of an Ancestor' (1972), among others.

V.S. Pritchett's 1971 introduction to the first volume of her *Collected Stories* begins his list of Lavin themes with 'country deaths and widowhood', while a 1986 review of *A Family Likeness and Other Stories* (1985) dubs the collection a 'series of bleak vignettes [whose] recurring themes are death and widowhood'.[5] In Lavin's work as a whole, small town Ireland is strongly death-dominated, her stories crammed with deathbeds, wakes, funerals, and wills; graveyards litter her fictional landscapes.

It could be argued that this is simply a factor in Lavin's realism — that any account of life in mid-twentieth-century rural Ireland would need to accommodate itself to the frequent depiction of Irish mourning rituals — but in an oeuvre that makes its moral arguments via innuendo and implication, Lavin's representations of death tend to go beyond the requirements of verisimilitude. In fact, it is difficult not to regard the centrality of death to Lavin's earlier work — as distinct from the later widow stories of her mid-period — as arising less from a personal thematics of bereavement, than as a pointed, cumulative symbol of the stultification of the Irish society which is her fictional milieu.

As Terence Brown points out, in the earlier work of Lavin, as in that of Frank O'Connor and Seán O'Faoláin, 'we see an Irish provincial world … where inhibition is disguised as economic prudence, land hunger and stolid conservatism as patriotic duty, subservience to Church authority as piety'.[6] Lavin's early stories, moreover, were written in an Ireland still formed by a nationalist rhetoric of sacrifice, remembrance and commemoration which, for David Lloyd, make post-independence Ireland a state founded on a reiterated 'injunction to mourn'.[7] The extent to which in Lavin's writing the memory of the dead 'acts to impair the actions of, or paralyse the living', as Augustine Martin phrases it, suggests a form of political allegory.[8]

My topic in this essay, however, is the strand of short stories generally dubbed Lavin's 'widow stories', which are quite distinct in tone and preoccupation. Written over a period of some twelve years in the wake of the death of her first husband, William Walsh, in 1954, they are generally acknowledged to include some of her most outstanding work. This loose group begins with 'In a Café' (1960), continues with 'In the Middle of the Fields' (1961), 'The Cuckoo-Spit' (1964), and 'Happiness' (1968), and concludes with the two Italian stories, 'Trastevere' (1971) and 'Villa Violetta' (1972); several were initially published in *The New Yorker*, when Lavin began to be a regular contributor from 1958 onward. The widow stories bear a certain family resemblance to one another, featuring the recurrent figure of Vera Traske (though an obviously similar figure is nameless in 'In the Middle of the Fields' and is called Mary in 'In a Café'), and, taken together, offer an extended meditation on bereavement and loss.[9]

There are certainly unabashed autobiographical resonances, large and small: a young widow left, like Lavin, with three daughters, is a recurring figure; Lavin's daughter Elizabeth Walsh Peavoy identifies the Italian trip in 'Villa Violetta' as strongly rooted in the family European trips of her mother's early widowed years, and the café of 'In a Café' as a short-lived Dublin establishment frequented by her mother; Leah Leveson suggests that the location of Abbey Farm, the house Lavin and her husband built with her inheritance from her father and the royalties from *Tales from Bective Bridge* (1942), is reflected accurately in the topography of the house and farm in 'In the Middle of the Fields' and 'The Cuckoo-Spit'.[10] Ann Owens Weekes sees as significant the fact that Lavin kills Vera Traske off in 'Happiness', 'the year the widow Mary Lavin metaphorically died through Lavin's marriage to her long-term friend Michael MacDonald Scott'.[11] The stories constitute less anything approaching the 'purely' autobiographical, however, than they suggest an apparently irresistible pull towards the thematics of mourning and recovery which Lavin is compelled to revisit again and again. I want to suggest that Lavin's widow stories operate as a form of intermittent narrative elegy, engaging in a version of the Freudian work of mourning by their repeated conjuration of the relationship between the living and the dead, and the psychology of survival, as well as an acknowledgement of the stigmatized position of the widow on the margins of her society,

Before turning to the stories themselves in more detail, let me sketch briefly the chief arguments of Freudian mourning theory, as outlined in 'Mourning and Melancholia' (1917) and revised in *The Ego and the Id* (1923). Freud famously distinguished between two responses to loss: 'normal' mourning and 'pathological' melancholy. Mourning (*Trauer*), for Freud, occurs when an object that one had loved for its intrinsic selfhood, as distinct from one's self, is lost. This form of love, as Eric Santner says, depends on a capacity to tolerate the 'potential awareness that "I" and "you" have edges', and that inscribed within the space of this interval are the possibilities of misunderstanding, disappointment, and even betrayal:

> Reality-testing has shown that the loved object no longer exists, and it proceeds to demand that all libido shall be withdrawn from its attachments to that object ... Normally, respect for reality gains the day. Nevertheless its orders cannot be obeyed at once. They are carried out but by bit, at great expense of time and cathectic energy, and in the meantime the existence of the lost object is psychically prolonged. Each single one of the memories and expectations in which the libido is bound to the object is brought up and hyper-cathected, and detachment of the libido is accomplished in respect of it.[12]

Mourning ends when the subject severs its emotional ties to the dead, and reinvests the now-liberated libido in a new object.

A more 'primitive' melancholic response to loss, on the other hand, takes place in a grieving subject with weaker or no boundaries between self and beloved object, i.e. when the object was loved not as separate and distinct from oneself, but rather as a mirror of one's own sense of self and power. As Freud says, 'In mourning it is the world which has become poor and empty; in melancholia it is the ego itself.'[13] In reality, as Freud came to acknowledge in *The Ego and the Id*, pure forms of either mode of grieving are rare.[14] As love inevitably seems to include an element of narcissism — in the most general sense a residual resistance to the perception of the separateness of self and other — it might make more sense to speak of a continuum of mourning and melancholic modes of mourning in any specific experience of loss. In either case, as Freud came to recognize, the trauma of mortal loss, which is the shock of separateness, necessarily involves the more fundamental task of re-establishing the boundaries of the self; hence his later recognition of the endlessness of 'normal' mourning, and that the work of mourning may be an interminable labour.

Lavin's widow stories, as I will argue, both engage with and problematize the earlier Freudian model of mourning as a matter of severance and redemptive replacement. They, like her other work, take as their great theme the examination of the nature of love in restricted lives within a society much given to social and psychological repression. Her oeuvre as a whole features an undue number of celibates, religious and other, which testifies to the sexual puritanism and sublimations of mid-twentieth-century Irish society, but which further, in Lavin's work, bespeaks 'forms of fidelity to a lost love, whether it be lost in the past or lost in the sense that it was never attained'.[15] The widow stories by definition deal with the strength of married love regarded, with tenderness or bitterness, retrospectively; as Seamus Deane notes, marriage in Lavin is 'rarely inhabited in the present tense by a living soul ... Marriage is the past tense of love.'[16] Lavin's widows permanently inhabit this 'past tense', continually looking backward; they are, to use Santner's term, 'stranded objects', aftermaths, bodies dealing with the existential conundrum of phantom limbs which continue to cause pain after their amputation.[17] Such strandings make the familiar strange, amplifying a melancholic out-of-placeness in the prose of these stories. The paradox is that it is absence which is thus rendered palpable, echoing the Russian formalist Viktor Shklovsky's statement on art, that it serves to undo habituation such that we might again feel the sensation of life as a heightened phenomenological encounter.[18] As the Vera Traske of 'The Cuckoo-Spit' notes, unnerved by moonlight on the first occasion she has left the house at night since she was widowed, 'the unreal alone ha[s] shape'.[19]

This *Verfremdungseffekt* institutes Lavin's widow stories' subtle skewings of Irish pastoral. 'In the Middle of the Fields' is set entirely within the protagonist's farmhouse, surrounded by her land, and its opening sentence suggests an Irish pastoral of the kind to which Lavin's work is often assimilated, as well as the traditional woman-as-land trope of much Irish literature: 'Like a rock in the sea, she was islanded by fields, the heavy grass washing about the house, and the cattle wading in it as in water.'[20] The incongruous image of being 'islanded' by dry land, however, foreshadows the way in which this 'woman of the house', far from securely inhabiting her domestic hearth and lands, lives only a half-life within her own home, going upstairs before nightfall, and locking herself into her room off the children's bedroom, dreading a 'knock after dark'.[21] The rural hearth, moral talisman of de Valera's Ireland, has been rendered dangerously *unheimlich* by the experience of bereavement, and the resultant vulnerability of the lone woman on a farm. Similarly, 'The Cuckoo-Spit' begins with a nocturnal doorstep encounter between the protagonist and the nephew of an elderly neighbour on the first night she has dared to set foot outside the house after dark since her husband's death four years earlier. The defamiliarizing effect of the displaced water imagery of 'In the Middle of the Fields' is repeated: the Traske fields are 'drenched' with moonlight, hedges 'dissolved in mist', thorn bushes 'floated loose like severed branches … trees in the middle of the fields streamed on the air'.[22] As if to underline the fact that the home is no longer a secure place for Lavin's widows, who have become amphibian half-creatures moving between opposed elements, when the unnerved Vera turns back to the house, it too has 'an insubstantial air'.[23] Sites of dwelling seem to have become dangerously penetrable or porous, as if the widows' ownership and inhabitation of house and land is rendered tentative or provisional by their widowhood.

Part of the cause of this sociological and psychological alienation effect is, of course, that Lavin's widows have, in some sense, virtual internal exile status by virtue of being on the margins of the patriarchal social order. James Heaney identifies '[u]nexpected widowhood' as the cause of many of Lavin's women's perplexed relation to their world; despite their isolation, they retain the trappings — children, land, jobs — that tie them to their particular patch of the landscape, but are nonetheless left in an incongruous situation, 'straddling its borders, half in and half out', with 'no positive sense of place', knowing that 'they are at home, but not where they belong'.[24] Lavin's widows resemble the 'submerged population groups' Frank O'Connor identifies as the true inhabitants of the short story, albeit they do not possess the romantic individualism of his 'tramps, artists, lonely idealists, dreamers, and spoiled priests'.[25] Unlike the alienated male figures who flee into exile in the work of Lavin's male modernist contemporaries, Lavin's widows remain generally too entrammelled in their communities to detach themselves, but are set apart within their society, no longer sanctioned by being defined relationally to a husband or father. As Edward Relph formulates it, following Heidegger, if 'To be human is to live in a world that is filled with significant places. To be human is to have and know *your* place', then Lavin's work charts her widows' insecure emplacement.[26]

The fact is that widows have lost caste, even when they retain land; they stand somewhat outside the rural class structure Lavin's work examines with such savage irony. It is explicitly because of her widowhood that Mary in 'In a Café' has taken to frequenting the nameless café, a makeshift, bohemian place with 'the peculiarly functional look you get in the snuggery of a public-house or in the confessional of a small and poor parish church' on all of her visits to Dublin.[27] The comparison with the cramped, transient, non-domestic spaces associated in mid-twentieth-century Irish life with sin and vice is significant. Mary now frequents the café precisely because the status their Meath farm conferred on her and her husband meant that they 'would have been out of place here': 'It was a different matter to come here alone. There could be nothing — oh, nothing — snobby about being a widow. Just by being one, she fitted into this kind of café.'[28]

The disorientation of the tourist or foreigner further becomes an oblique metaphor for widowhood in Lavin's work. 'In a Café' explicitly compares the stigmatized figures of the widow and the foreigner as anomalous, other, at a loss, separated by a barrier from the rest of society, and it is not accidental that the café is both the haunt of the widowed Mary and the foreign artist Johann von Stiegler, with whom she strikes up a conversation. Maudie, Mary's companion, pities him as a lonely foreigner: 'I always think it's sad for them; they don't have many friends, and even when they do, there is always a barrier, don't you agree?'[29] Mary, on the other hand, is powerfully drawn to him as to a fellow anomaly: 'His face took on a look of despair that could come upon a foreigner, it seemed, at the slightest provocation, as if suddenly everything was obscure to him — everything.'[30] Similarly, in 'Villa Violetta', Vera, in Florence for the first time since she visited with her dead husband, and attempting to seek a temporary home for herself and her children in a series of glacial *pensioni*, cannot read the map the tourist office gives her 'in order to establish her new position', and unable to manage the currency or the language, is unable to communicate.[31] Later she explicitly links her panicked status as foreigner to her widowhood — explicitly characterising herself as a 'freak' to an unfriendly tourist office clerk — and wonders whether the foreign trip had 'in some way duplicated the circumstances that had followed immediately upon Richard's sudden death'.[32]

The widow stories, thus, chart an elliptically-described terrain in which mourning women move towards some epiphanic realization in relation to death and survival which is only obliquely conveyed to the reader via indirection and implication. The territory of grieving in Lavin is extensive, ranging geographically from rural Ireland and Dublin ('In the Middle of the Fields', 'The Cuckoo-Spit', 'In a Café', 'Happiness') to New York, Rome and Florence ('Trastevere' and 'Villa Violetta'). The stories are tentatively held together as a group by the recurring figure of the widowed Vera Traske. A possible first version of this character appears in the story 'What's Wrong with Aubretia?' (first published in 1959 as 'The Villas'), as an unmarried woman in her mid-thirties engaged in a tentative romantic relationship with a younger man, the inhabitant of one of the vulgar new villas built on her squireen father's demesne.[33] It would be inaccurate to say that the character unproblematically unites the widow stories, however, as details shift and are not consistent throughout the texts. Vera Traske is a novelist in 'Trastevere' but appears to be a librarian in 'Happiness', while in 'In the Middle of the Fields', 'The Cuckoo-Spit' and 'In a Café', she remains on, and works, her dead husband's farm, identified as being located in Meath in the two latter texts. Traske in 'The Cuckoo-Spit' is childless, but in all the other stories has children; in 'Happiness' and 'Villa Violetta', the children are three daughters. Neither does Traske's character remain constant, bar her condition of bereavement: the panic-stricken traveller of 'Villa Violetta' bears little obvious resemblance to the self-contained protagonist of 'The Cuckoo-Spit' or the whimsical mother figure of 'Happiness'.

Some of these mismatched details can be reconciled — the Vera of 'Happiness' could conceivably be the same woman as that of 'Villa Violetta' twenty years later; others cannot and are mutually exclusive. Other echoes reverberate across the stories: several of the protagonists dread the posthumous falsification of the dead spouse and ponder the issue of happiness; the dead husband is a politician in 'The Cuckoo-Spit' and 'Happiness'; both the protagonists of 'In the Middle of the Fields' and 'The Cuckoo-Spit' are afraid in their homes at night; Mary in 'In a Café' and Vera in 'The Cuckoo-Spit' both think of how their happy marriages held them apart from any unmediated experience of nature; images of impeded resurrection repeat themselves — Vera in 'Happiness' refers to her determination to recover from her bereavement as an 'effort to push back the stone from the mouth of the tomb and walk out', while the heroine of 'In the Middle of the Fields' thinks of the farming anxieties and night terrors which distract her from 'dry love and barren longing' as 'the stones across the mouth of the tomb'.[34]

Reading the widow stories as a group, the effect gives rise to uneasiness in the reader; the similarities are too marked to ignore, while the details do not reconcile, creating a form of readerly *déjà-vu*. It is as if the stories, while purporting to 'fit' in the same unified fictional universe — as Lavin did with other recurrent characters such as the Grimes family — deliberately fail to do so, neglecting to reconcile separate and disparate elements into the accustomed narrative coherence. This is unexpected from a writer generally accepted, as Seamus Deane writes, as not 'in any technical sense an innovator', but a writer so thoroughly immersed in the domestic, practical world as to be 'committed by that involvement to the demands of verisimilitude'.[35] The marked but inexact repetitions of the widow stories recall the repetition-compulsion Freud first outlined in 'Remembering, Repeating and Working-Through' (1914), and later in *Beyond the Pleasure Principle* (1920), in which a trauma is repeatedly re-experienced, and which he would eventually come to associate with the death drive. In the context of repetition, it is worth mentioning how many drafts of each Lavin story there typically are: Janet Egleson Dunleavy's account of the genesis of 'Happiness' notes the existence of twenty-seven dated heavily-edited typescript and manuscript versions from between 1965 and 1967, as well as over a hundred undated manuscript pages.[36] Lavin also expended an enormous amount of energy on rewriting and re-editing old stories when they were republished, claiming in an interview that she disagreed with Seán O'Faoláin's assertion 'that an author has no right to re-edit his published stories, that the work should stand as it was when it was written'.[37]

One is reminded of Julia Kristeva's association between loss and a compensatory creativity, in relation to *Beyond the Pleasure Principle*'s account of the *fort/da* ('gone'/'there') game Freud observed in the play of his grandson. In this game, the child masters his grief over separation from his mother by repeatedly staging his own performance of disappearance and return using a toy prop. Disturbed by the mother's absence, and more generally by the dawning realization that there is a potentially disturbing interval between him and the mother, he re-enacts this first experience of absence within the controlled space of a ritual; absence becomes represented by substitutive figures, and a lost omnipotence becomes an ability to function within the symbolic and a capacity for creative play. Kristeva links this to literary creation: 'Literary creation is that adventure of body and signs that bears witness to the affect: to sadness as the mark of separation and the beginnings of the dimension of the symbol ... the affect being transposed into rhythms, signs, forms.'[38] The traditional literary elegist, thus, reflects an essentially Freudian economy, where a consolatory substitution is the primary aim. Peter M. Sacks argues that the aims of the elegy, from Spenser to Yeats, has explicit parallels with the aims of mourning, both repairing the mourner's 'damaged narcissism' by finding consolatory cultural fictions about the transcendence of death (*Lycidas*, *In Memoriam*), but also — and more importantly for a consideration of Lavin as narrative elegist — from the way in which the elegy itself emerges as consoling substitute for the dead. The very act of writing, for Sacks, moves the poet from bereavement to resolution, as the act of figuring the loss linguistically, rather than simply mourning, 'brings about the reluctant submission to language itself'. The elegy consoles because the elegist has accepted, in some sense, the literary artefact and the use of language as a compensation for loss.[39] I will return to the issue of whether this works in a reading of Lavin's widow stories as a form of cumulative narrative elegy.

For the Freud of 'Mourning and Melancholia', as stated earlier, it is incumbent upon the survivor of loss — literal or symbolic — to consciously proceed by *working-through* (*durcharbeiten*) the libidinal wreckage that the loss of the love object results in, and during which the mourner relinquishes emotional ties to the lost object. Such a process of working through is expected to be painful, energy-consuming and long or short depending mainly on the mourner's *will* to attain mastery over a situation to which he or she was forced to submit.[40] 'In a Café' offers a particularly telling epiphany at the telos of *durcharbeiten* in Mary's encounter with the painter Johann von Stiegler. Freud suggested that this detachment of libido takes place through a 'testing of reality', maintaining that the mourner severs attachments primarily through a labour of memory: 'Each single one of the memories and expectations in which the libido is bound to the object is brought up and hypercathected … When the work of mourning is completed the ego becomes free and uninhibited again.'[41] Mary's sharpest grief, two years after her husband's death, is that she retains only nightmarishly partial visions of him. In accordance with Freud's account of the work of mourning, she works at literally 're-membering' him from individual parts:

> In her mind she would see a part of him, his hand — his arm, his
> foot perhaps, in the finely worked leather shoes he always wore —
> and from it, frantically, she would try to build up the whole man.
> Sometimes she succeeded better than others, built him up from foot
> to shoulder, seeing his hands, his grey suit, his tie, knotted always in
> a slightly special way, his neck, even his chin that was rather sharp,
> a little less attractive than his other features.[42]

Mary is attempting to engage in the work of mourning, which entails a kind of hyper-remembering, a process of obsessive recollection during which the mourner resuscitates the existence of the lost other in the space of the psyche, replacing an actual absence with an imaginary presence. Yet, she is defeated each time: 'Never once voluntarily since the day he died had she been able to see his face again. And if she could not remember him, at will, what meaning had time at all? What use was it to have lived the past, if behind us it fell away so sheer?'[43] It is in relation to this repeated failure to remember fully (suffered by several of Lavin's widows, and often linked to their horror of retrospectively falsifying or 'whitewashing' the dead) that the tentative encounter with von Stiegler is crucial.

Ironically, Mary's companion, the more newly-widowed, young and beautiful Maudie — who 'didn't even look like a widow. There was nothing about her to suggest that she was in any way bereft or maimed' — seems, at least to Mary, to have concluded her 'work of mourning' to the extent that she meditates remarriage, and to have relinquished her psychological ties to her dead husband to the extent that she feels their baby is 'illegitimate', thereby retrospectively eliminating her marriage.[44] Partly in irritation at Maudie's assumption that she, an older woman, will never remarry, Mary departs from convention and decides to take up von Stiegler's irregular invitation to visit him at his apartment to see his paintings. Her walk down the alley towards the painter's 'mysteriously sealed' yellow door both reiterates the claustrophobia of the confessional and the snug through which widowhood is metaphorized in this story, and yet also the tantalising possibility of new vistas and spaces of selfhood: 'It was like the mystifying doors in the trunks of trees that beguiled her as a child in fairytales and fantasies. Did this door, too, like those fairy doors, lead into rooms of impossible amplitude, or would it be a cramped and poky place?'[45] Her panicked rush away from the door, having glimpsed the painter's naked ankles and his belongings through the gaping letterbox, realising that all she could have said to him was an admission of loneliness, ends in a valedictory address to her dead husband, and, finally, in a vision of his face for the first time since his death, during which she realizes there is now 'no urgency in the search'.[46] The story ends with Mary, for once, getting into the driver's side of the car first time: 'Not till then did she realise what she had achieved. Yet she had no more than got back her rights. No more. It was not a subject for amazement. By what means exactly had she got them back though — in that little cafe? That was the wonder.'[47]

The Freudian *Trauerarbeit* is successfully achieved; the magical restoration of the lost object enables the mourner to assess the value of the relationship, comprehend what he or she has lost in losing the other, and acknowledge that the lost object no longer exists. With a very specific task to perform, the Freudian grief work seeks, then, to 'convert loving remembrances into a futureless memory'.[48] Mary has ceased to mourn Richard and has been given back to herself as agent and libido, as symbolized by her unconsciously taking the wheel of the car in which she has been a passenger during her marriage.

Johann von Stiegler does not become a substitute love object for Mary, despite the sexualising, even voyeuristic gaze with which she looks at his hands in the café, and later spies on him through his door; he remains only a form of symbolic transitional object as part of Mary's *Trauerarbeit*. Yet mourning only comes to a decisive end, according to 'Mourning and Melchanolia', when the survivor has detached his or her emotional tie to the lost object and reattached the free libido to a new object, thus accepting consolation in the form of a substitute for what has been lost. The transfer of the libido to a new object and the possibility of relinquishing ties to the dead becomes a preoccupation in Lavin's later widow stories, and is what is at issue in the embedded story of Bartley Crossen's two marriages, recounted to the widowed protagonist by her elderly herdsman, and by Crossen himself, before and during the fumbled sexual assault that forms the crux of 'In the Middle of the Fields'.

Crossen, a neighbouring farmer engaged by the nameless protagonist to mow her neglected pasturage, recalls, apparently absently, how he had once courted a girl in those same fields when he was young. Ned the herdsman later tells the story of Crossen's first marriage to that girl, the vivid, 'wild as a hare' Bridie Logan, which has seemingly been all but forgotten by everyone, including Crossen himself, long since contentedly remarried.[49] A brief, passionate relationship, the first marriage ends tragically when Bridie, newly delivered of their first child, over-exerts herself to accompany her husband to milk, and haemorrhages to death: 'Mad with love, that's what they were, both of them — she only wanting to draw him on, and he only too willing!'[50] A stolid subsequent marriage with 'more to it', in the form of several sons, succeeds the first. The protagonist, tormented by 'dry love and barren longing' for her own dead husband, is desperate to be reassured that Crossen's apparent forgetting of his first wife is genuine, and is assured by Ned that she too will forget: 'Take my word for it. Everything passes in time and is forgotten … When the tree falls, how can the shadow stand?'[51]

However, Crossen returns by night to the protagonist's house and makes a bungled attempt to kiss her, apparently stirred by the loose hair she hasn't had time to pin up, which makes her look 'like a young girl', after she has confided to him her fear of being alone downstairs after dark.[52] His subsequent shame leads him to pour out the circumstances of his second marriage, and how, by his second wife's ministrations to his motherless baby, he was 'knit back into a living man': 'I saw it was better I took her than wasted away after the one that was gone. And wasn't I right?'[53] The story ends with the protagonist, who wants him only to forget his shame and leave, enigmatically crying out to blame 'the other one': '"That girl — your first wife — Bridie! It was her! Blame her! She's the one did it! … You thought you could forget her," she said, "but see what she did to you when she got the chance!"'[54]

The text emerges as an oblique parable about memory, mourning, and the necessity, as Freud sees it, to sever one attachment to make a new one possible, which Lavin frequently depicts as easier for the male psychic economy than the female. Crossen's homespun rhetoric of male helplessness in the face of female wisdom — 'men are fools as women well know, and she knew before me what was right and proper for us both'— covers a naturalising of the ego's repudiation of the lost other, and assimilation of the loss to a consoling substitute.[55] His story illustrates how Freudian mourning involves less a lament for the passing of a unique other, and more a process geared toward restoring a certain economy of the subject, which is 'knit back into a living man' as a result.[56] As if to confirm this, there is even another Bartley Crossen in the shape of his adult son, repeating and reinforcing his father's identity.

The protagonist's outburst, on the other hand, is that of a suffering mourner who has not yet reached this stage. If her apparently irrational blaming of passionate, long-dead Bridie Logan for Crossen's assault is on the one hand an attempt to redirect his self-blame harmlessly onto the dead, it is also an attempt to recall a phantom from the past, to unlay the ghost of the dead spouse, to reawaken her own fresh pain in another who has ceased to mourn. 'In the Middle of the Fields' does not end with the satisfying Freudian telos of 'In a Café', in which the *Trauerarbeit* is concluded, and the protagonist set free. Instead, the reader is left with only the protagonist's accusation of the dead, and Crossen's response, a final, inscrutable 'God rest her soul', which, uncommented upon by the narrative voice, ends the story.

It is also possible, however, that it is not the newness of the grief of the protagonist of 'In the Middle of the Fields', compared to Bartley Crossen's, that is at issue, but her gender. As stated earlier, Lavin's widowers quickly conclude their grief work; 'Heart of Gold', which first appeared in *The New Yorker* on 27 June 1964, offers a broad, comic-Gothic take on widowerhood and remarriage seen through the eyes of the long-discarded youthful sweetheart, reinstated with unseemly haste as second wife for the domestic comfort of the widower.[57] Lavin's widows after 'In a Café' tend more towards the interminable mourning Julia Kristeva associates with women, whom — rejecting Freudian mourning theories' assumption of a traditionally masculine model of bounded subjectivity founded upon rupture — she views as culturally and constitutionally prone to become 'failed mourners'.[58] Lavin's later widows mourn in ways that are less idealistic, and more ambivalent, even aggressive, and manifest a desire for fundamental independence from both the lost other and from social determinations of widowed behaviour. While the Vera Traske of 'The Cuckoo-Spit', first published in *The New Yorker* four months after 'Heart of Gold', and like it, republished in the collection *In the Middle of the Fields* in 1967, comes closer than Lavin's other widows to a replacement of the lost love by another, she refutes totalising ideas of mourning as redemptive and consolatory.[59]

'The Cuckoo-Spit' details the tentative attraction between an older widow, living alone on her husband's dairy farm, and the much younger visiting nephew of a neighbouring farmer. The story chronicles what Nouri Gana calls the 'overwhelming spiral of desire and mourning' which ensures that 'the affective closure of the work of mourning is but a rebirth of eros'.[60] There are resonances with 'In the Middle of the Fields': an isolated farm with neglected grasslands, a lone woman afraid of the dark, and a nocturnal visitor invoking the dead. This story, however, does not relegate the Freudian intertwinedness of eros and thanatos to an embedded story, as Fergus' attraction to Vera clearly derives largely from his perception of the unusual strength of her marriage, which he had witnessed as a boy on his visits to his uncle's farm, and which forms the source of her bereaved torment. The short-lived rapprochement between the two is triangulated with the presence of the dead, memory and the past, as the ardent, inexperienced Fergus comes to envy a dead man his happiness, and realises that meeting his widow has given him, for the first time, a 'clear idea of what I would want from marriage'.[61]

It is less simple for the clear-sighted, disabused Vera, who has come to terms with her own mourning, asserting that 'there is, after all, a kind of peace at last when you face up to life's defeats ... I couldn't bear anything now — even happiness ... there is a strange peace about knowing that the best in life is gone forever.'[62] Discussing the (unspecified) age gap that, for her, renders their relationship 'unnatural', she notes her own attraction to younger people since her bereavement, worrying that her 'heart was like a clock that had stopped at the age [Richard] was when he died', before recognising that she is in fact seeking her own self as it was before her marriage, forced back into individual subjectivity and agency by death: 'I knew I had to get back to being that other person again, just as he, when he was dying, had to get back to being the kind of person he was before he met me.'[63] This reconciliation with reality, or the reality-testing about which Freud writes, is, for Nouri Gana, 'an attempt at exorcising the estrangement effect produced by the loss of the object, [as] the mourner attempts to make reality his *own* again after being *alienated* from it by the loss of his or her loved object'.[64] The refamiliarization with reality involves a refamiliarization with the technique of repression of the knowledge of death and mortality involved in the search for new love objects. However, Vera cannot quite manage the premeditated forgetting of the harsh knowledge of death under the illusion of life, cannot forget that all loves are loves that can be lost — finally, cannot repress her unwilling knowledge of death.

As their relationship unfolds over three night visits and a single encounter in Dublin after which Vera drives away abruptly from Fergus while he does an errand, she recognizes that desire is structured by mourning; that the movement out of mourning is precisely the road leading back into it, as the mourner falls in love again with an object she knows is equally subject to mortality. This inability to distinguish between love and death is crystallized in her sudden joy at seeing Fergus on St Stephen's Green, when she involuntarily thinks of a line from a mortuary card given to her by a nun at the time of her husband's death — 'Oh, the joy to see you come' — whose 'facile promise' had quenched 'her pallid belief in a life beyond the grave'.[65]

'The Cuckoo-Spit' is unsettled by the underlying tensions between Vera's loss and the futility of the available strategies of transcendence with which she is equipped in the form of the blandishments of religion. The relationship is, finally, abortive; Fergus in no sense replaces Richard for Vera, and the final scene, when Fergus again encounters Vera at her door a year later, but cannot accompany her to the cemetery to see about her husband's unstable headstone on the anniversary of his death, is ambivalent in Lavin's characteristically inscrutable mode. If we privilege the incident that gives the story its oblique name — the discovery of a concealed plant louse on a rose Vera picks for Fergus on their second encounter — the suggestions are of an ugly underlying reality to a traditional symbol of love, which is perceived and understood by Vera, but not by the naïve Fergus. Death, here, remains the stronger force, with the slipping memorial stone indicating a certain remaining vigour and agency in the dead in the mind of the mourner, which living substitutes and traditional modes of transcendence cannot approach, far less defuse.

In conclusion, Lavin's characters, like Beckett's, are perpetually in mourning, haunted by the tenacious trace of irretrievable lost ones. If Freudian mourning, and the traditional (male) elegiac writing that depends upon it, rehearses an act of identity that depends essentially upon rupture, Lavin's widow stories after 'In a Café' refuse any such straightforward process of substitution and consolation. Rather, Lavin's mourners are closer to the later topography of the grieving psyche Freud outlined in *The Ego and the Id*, in that they retain a melancholic trace of the lost other, and her work envisages selfhood as a Freudian 'precipitate of abandoned object-cathexes' — in other words, an 'embodied history of lost attachments'.[66] All selves are, by definition, elegiac, defined by lost or impossible attachments. If her widow stories are, finally, grimly affirmative as elegies, it is because Lavin is a writer who examines ceaselessly the nature of lost love, and whose lovers fight against the repressive forces that attempt to deny or diminish it, even when those forces include the urge toward recovery and forgetting. As Freud wrote in a 1929 letter, nine years after the death of his daughter:

> Although we know that after such a loss the acute state of mourning will subside, we also know we shall remain inconsolable and will never find a substitute. No matter what may fill the gap, even if it be filled completely, it nevertheless remains something else. And actually, this is how it should be. It is the only way of perpetuating love which we do not want to relinquish.[67]

Endnotes

1   B. McKeon, 'An Arrow in Flight: The Pleasures of Mary Lavin', *Paris Review Daily*, 12 June 2012. Online: http://www.theparisreview.org/blog/2012/06/12/an-arrow-in-flight-the-pleasures-of-mary-lavin/.

2   L. Marlowe, 'Mary Lavin: An arrow still in flight', *The Irish Times*, 30 April 2012. Online: http://www.irishtimes.com/newspaper/features/2012/0430/1224315363056.html.

3   S. Deane, 'Mary Lavin', in P. Rafroidi and T. Brown (eds), *The Irish Short Story* (Buckinghamshire: Colin Smythe Ltd., 1979), p.238.

4   A. Martin, 'A Skeleton Key to the Stories of Mary Lavin', *Studies* 52, 208 (Winter 1963), p.402; M. Koenig, 'Mary Lavin: The Novels and the Stories', *Irish University Review*, 9, 2, (Autumn 1979), p.252.

5   V.S. Pritchett, 'Introduction', in M. Lavin, *Collected Stories* (Boston: Houghton Mifflin, 1971), p.xii; J. Dunne, 'Review of Mary Lavin, *A Family Likeness and Other Stories*', *Books Ireland*, 102, (1986), p.79.

6   T. Brown, *Ireland: A Social and Cultural History, 1922–1985* (London: Fontana 1985), p.158.

7   D. Lloyd, 'Colonial Trauma/Postcolonial Recovery', *Interventions: International Journal of Postcolonial Studies*, 2, 2, (2000), p.218.

8   Martin, 'A Skeleton Key', p.402.

9   Dating for all stories is for their first publication, and based on Heinz Kosok's dateline in 'Mary Lavin: A Bibliography', *Irish University Review*, 9, 2, (1979), pp.279–312.

10 E. Walsh Peavoy, 'Preamble', in M. Lavin, *In a Café: New Selected Stories* (Dublin: Townhouse, 1995), pp.xiii–xvi; L. Leveson, *The Four Seasons of Mary Lavin* (Dublin: Marino Books, 1998), p.45.

11 A. O. Weekes, 'Mary Lavin: Textual Gardens', in *Irish Women Writers: An Uncharted Tradition* (Lexington, KY: University Press of Kentucky, 1990), p.143. 'Happiness' was initially published in *The New Yorker* in December 1968 and then in Lavin's collection *Happiness and Other Stories* in 1969.

12 E. L. Santner, *Stranded Objects: Mourning, Memory and Film in Postwar Germany* (Ithaca NY and London: Cornell University Press, 1990), p.2; S. Freud, 'Mourning and Melancholia', in J. Strachey (ed.), *The Standard Edition of the Complete Psychological Works of Sigmund Freud, Volume 14* (London: Hogarth Press, 1953–74), pp.244–5.

13 Ibid., p.246

14 S. Freud, *The Ego and the Id*, in Strachey *The Standard Edition, Volume 19*: pp.12–26.

15 Deane, 'Mary Lavin', p.237.

16 Ibid., p.242.

17 'Stranded objects' is Santner's term, who, in turn, attributes it to a colleague who provided it unknowingly. Santner, *Stranded Objects*, p.2.

18 V. Shklovsky, 'Art as Device', in *The Theory of Prose*, trans. B. Sher (Bloomington, IL: Dalkey Archive Press, 1991).

19 M. Lavin, 'The Cuckoo-Spit', in *Collected Stories* (Boston, MA: Houghton Mifflin, 1971), p.374.

20 M. Lavin, 'In the Middle of the Fields', in *Selected Stories* (Harmondsworth: Penguin, 1964), p.181.

21 Ibid., p.172.

22 Lavin, 'The Cuckoo-Spit', p.374.

23 Ibid.

24 J. Heaney, '"No Sanctuary from Hatred": A Re-Appraisal of Mary Lavin's Outsiders', *Irish University Review*, 28, 2, (1998), pp.303, 307.

25 F. O'Connor, *The Lonely Voice: A Study of the Short Story* (London: Macmillan, 1965), p.21.

26 E. Relph, *Place and Placelessness* (London: Pion, 1976), p.1.

27 M. Lavin, 'In a Café', in *The Stories of Mary Lavin, Volume 1* (London: Constable, 1964), p.347.

28 Ibid.

29 Ibid., pp.352–3.

30 Ibid., p.353.

31 M. Lavin, 'Villa Violetta', in *A Memory and Other Stories* (London: Constable, 1972), p.131.

32 Ibid, p.150.

33 M. Lavin, 'What's Wrong with Aubretia?' in *Pick of Today's Short Stories*, 10, (London: Putnam, 1959), pp.131–141 (under the title 'The Villas'); later published in *The Great Wave and Other Stories* (London: Macmillan, 1961).

34 M. Lavin, 'Happiness', in *Selected Stories*, p.204; M. Lavin, 'In the Middle of the Fields', in *Selected Stories*, p.181.

35 Deane, 'Mary Lavin', p.244.

36 J.E. Dunleavy, 'The Making of Mary Lavin's "Happiness"', *Irish University Review*, 9, 2, (Autumn 1979), p.231. Other Lavin stories have considerably more drafts — the catalogue of the Lavin papers at Southern Illinois University Carbondale contains thirty manuscript versions of 'The Cuckoo-Spit'. Online: http://irishliterature.library. emory.edu/content.php?id=MSS044_1001262.

37 L. Robert and S. Stevens, 'An Interview with Mary Lavin', *Studies*, 86, 341, (Spring 1997), p.43.

38 J. Kristeva, 'On the Melancholic Imaginary', trans. L. Burchill, in S. Rimmon-Kenan (ed.) *Discourse on Psychoanalysis and Literature* (London: Methuen, 1987), p.108.

39 P.M. Sacks, *The English Elegy: Studies in the Genre from Spenser to Yeats* (Baltimore, MD: Johns Hopkins Press, 1985), pp.2, 5.

40 Freud, 'Mourning and Melancholia', p.253.

41 Ibid., p.245.

42 Lavin, 'In a Café', p.349.

43 Ibid., p.349.

44 Ibid., p.351.

45 Ibid., p.357.

46 Ibid., p.359.

47 Ibid., p.360.

48 T. Clewell, 'Mourning Beyond Melancholia: Freud's Psychoanalysis of Loss', *Journal of the American Psychoanalytic Association*, 52, 1, (2004), p.44.

49 Lavin, 'In the Middle of the Fields', p.183.

50 Ibid., p.184.

51 Ibid., p.185.

52 Ibid., p.187.

53 Ibid., pp.183, 194.

54 Ibid., p.194.

55 Ibid.

56 Ibid., p.193.

57 M. Lavin, 'Heart of Gold', *The New Yorker*, 40 (27 June 1964), pp.29–38 . Republished in *In the Middle of the Fields and Other Stories* (London: Constable, 1967).

58 J. Kristeva, *Black Sun: Depression and Melancholia*, trans. L. S. Roudiez (New York: Columbia University Press, 1989), p.33 and following.

59 M. Lavin, 'The Cuckoo-Spit', *The New Yorker*, 40 (3 October 1964), pp.58–94. Republished in *In the Middle of the Fields*.

60 N. Gana, *Signifying Loss: Towards a Poetics of Mourning* (Lewisburg, PA: Bucknell University Press, 2011), p.55.

61 Lavin, 'The Cuckoo-Spit', p.381.

62 Ibid., p.377.

63 Ibid., p.393.

64 Gana, *Signifying Loss*, p.24.

65 Lavin, 'The Cuckoo-Spit', p.390.

66 S. Freud, *The Ego and the Id*, in J. Strachey (ed.), *The Standard Edition of the Complete Psychological Works of Sigmund Freud, Volume 19* (London: Hogarth Press, 1953–74), p.29. Clewell, 'Mourning Beyond Melancholia', p.56.

67 E. Freud (ed.), *Letters of Sigmund Freud*, trans T. and J. Stern (New York: Basic Books, 1960), p.386.

Bibliography

Archives

1912 Walpole Census, East Walpole Historical Society Archives, Massachusetts, USA.

Howard Gotlieb Archive, Boston University, MA, USA.

Ellery Sedgwick papers, Massachusetts Historical Society, Boston, MA, USA: Mary Lavin folder.

Mary Lavin Collection, Mugar Memorial Library, Boston, MA, USA.

Mary Lavin Papers, James Joyce Library, Special Collections, University College Dublin, Ireland.

Mary Lavin Papers, 1953–1964, Morris Library, Special Collections Research Center, Southern Illinois University, Carbondale, USA. Online: http://irishliterature.library. emory.edu/content.php?id=MSS044_1001262.

The New Yorker Records, Manuscripts and Archives Division, The New York Public Library, USA. Astor, Lenox, and Tilden Foundations.

Newspapers

The New York Times

The Irish Times

Books and Articles

Abel, E., Hirsch, M., and Langland, E. *The Voyage In: Fictions of Female Development* (Hanover: University Press of New England, 1983).

Anon. 'Recent Fiction', *The Irish Times*, 30 September 1950, p.6.

Anon. (ed.), *Stories from The New Yorker 1950–1960* (New York: Penguin, 1965).

Arensberg, C.M. and Kimball, S.T. *Family and Community in Ireland*, 2nd edition (Cambridge: Harvard University Press, 1968).

Arndt, M., 'Narratives of Internal Exile in Mary Lavin's Short Stories', *International Journal of English Studies*, 2, 2 (2002), pp.109–22.

Barreca, R., *'Untamed and Unabashed': Essays on Women and Humor in British Literature* (Detroit: Wayne State University Press, 1994).

Battersby, E., 'Story Writer Mary Lavin dies at 83', *The Irish Times*, 26 March 1996, p.3.

Beer, G., 'The Body of the People: *Mrs Dalloway* to *The Waves*', in *Virginia Woolf: The Common Ground. Essays by Gillian Beer* (Edinburgh: Edinburgh University Press, 1996), pp.48–73.

Beja, M., *Epiphany in the Modern Novel* (London: Peter Owen, 1971).

Bluemel, K. (ed.), *Intermodernism: Literary Culture in Mid-Twentieth-Century Britain* (Edinburgh: Edinburgh University Press, 2011).

Bourke, A., *Maeve Brennan, Homesick at The New Yorker* (London: Jonathan Cape, 2004).

Bowen, E., *The Collected Stories of Elizabeth Bowen* [1980] (London: Penguin Books, 1983).

Bowen, Z., *Mary Lavin* (London: Associated University Presses, 1975; Lewisburg, PA: Bucknell University Press, 1975).

Brennan, M., 'Author's Note', in *The Long-Winded Lady, Notes from The New Yorker* (Berkeley, CA: Counterpoint, 1997), pp.1–3.

Briggs, S., 'A Man in the House: Mary Lavin and the Narrative of the Spinster', in Marshall, A. and Sammells, N. (eds), *Irish Encounters: Poetry, Politics and Prose since 1880* (Bath: Sulis Press, 1998), pp.90–103.

Briggs, S., 'Mary Lavin: Questions of Identity', *Irish Studies Review*, 15 (1996), pp.10–15.

Brod, H., and Kaufman, M. (eds), *Theorising Masculinities* (London: Sage Publications, 1994).

Brown, T., *Ireland: A Social and Cultural History, 1922–1985* (London: Fontana, 1985).

Brown, T., *Ireland: A Social and Cultural History. 1922–2002* (London: Harper Perennial, 2004).

Burnham, R., 'Mary Lavin's Short Stories in *The Dublin Magazine*', *Cahier du Centre d'Études Irlandaises*, 2 (1977), pp.103–10.

Burns, J., 'Mary Lavin book stalled by daughter', *The Sunday Times*, May 1998.

Butler, J., *Gender Trouble: Feminism and the Subversion of Identity* (New York and London: Routledge, 1990).

Byrne, A., Edmondson, R. and Varley, T. 'Introduction to the Third Edition', in Arensberg, C.M. and Kimball, S.T. *Family and Community in Ireland*, 3rd edition (Ennis: CLASP Press, 2003), pp.1–101.

Cahalan, J.W., *Double Visions: Women and Men in Modern and Contemporary Irish Fiction* (Syracuse: Syracuse University Press, 1999).

Calisher, H., 'Introduction', in Calisher, H. and Ravenell, S. (eds), *The Best American Short Stories 1981* (Boston: Houghton Mifflin, 1981).

Caswell, R., 'Irish Political Reality and Mary Lavin's *Tales from Bective Bridge*', *Éire-Ireland*, 3 (1968), pp.48–60.

Chodorow, N., *The Reproduction of Mothering: Psychoanalysis and the Sociology of Gender* (Berkeley and Los Angeles: The University of California Press, 1978).

Clare, A. *On Men* (London: Chatto and Windus, 2000).

Clarity, J.F., 'Mary Lavin, 83, Wove Tales of Irish Experience', *The New York Times*, 27 March 1996. Online: http://www.nytimes.com/1996/03/27/nyregion/mary-lavin-83-wove-tales-of-irish-experience.html.

Clear, C., *Women of the House: Women's Household Work in Ireland 1926–61* (Portland, OR and Dublin: Irish Academic Press, 2000).

Clewell, T., 'Mourning Beyond Melancholia: Freud's Psychoanalysis of Loss', *Journal of the American Psychoanalytic Association*, 52, 1 (2004), pp.43–67.

Conlon, E., 'Introduction', in Lavin, M., *Tales From Bective Bridge* (London: Faber and Faber, 2012), p.ix.

Conlon, E., 'New Introduction', in Lavin, M., *Tales from Bective Bridge* (Dublin: Town House, 1996).

Connell, R. W., *Masculinities* (Cambridge: Polity Press, 2005).

Corkery, D., *The Threshold of Quiet* (Dublin: Talbot Press; 1917; London: T. Fisher Unwin, 1919).

Crary, J., *Suspensions of Perception: Attention, Spectacle, and Modern Culture* (Cambridge, MA: Massachusetts Institute of Technology, 1999).

Crary, J., *Techniques of the Observer: On Vision and Modernity in the Nineteenth Century* (Cambridge, MA: Massachusetts Institute of Technology, 1992).

Cronin, G., 'The Big House and the Irish Landscape in the Work of Elizabeth Bowen', in Genet, J. (ed.), *The Big House in Ireland: Reality and Representation* (Dingle, Co. Kerry: Brandon Books, 1991), pp.143–62.

Cronin, J., 'Introduction', in Griffin, G., *The Collegians* (1829; Belfast: Appletree Press, 1992), pp.vii–x.

D'hoker, E., 'Beyond the stereotypes: Mary Lavin's Irish Women', *Irish Studies Review*, 16, 4 (2008), pp.415–30.

Deane, S., 'Mary Lavin', in Rafroidi, P. and Brown, T. (eds), *The Irish Short Story* (Atlantic Highlands, NJ: Humanities Press, 1979; Buckinghamshire: Colin Smythe Ltd., 1979; Publications de l'Université de Lille III, 1979), pp.237–48.

Drewery, C., *Modernist Short Fiction by Women: The Liminal in Katherine Mansfield, Dorothy Richardson, May Sinclair and Virginia Woolf* (Farnham, Surrey: Ashgate, 2011).

Dunleavy, J.E., 'Mary Lavin, Elizabeth Bowen, and a New Generation: the Irish Short Story at Midcentury', in Kilroy, J.F. (ed.), *The Irish Short Story* (Boston, MA: Twayne, 1984), pp.145–68.

Dunleavy, J.E., 'The Making of Mary Lavin's "Happiness"', *Irish University Review* 9, 2 (Autumn 1979), pp. 225–232.

Dunne, 'Review of Mary Lavin, *A Family Likeness and Other Stories*', *Books Ireland* 102 (1986), p.79.

Ferguson, S., 'Genre and the Work of Reading in Mansfield's "Prelude" and "At the Bay"', in Iftekharrudin, F. et.al. (eds), *Postmodern Approaches to the Short Story* (Westport: Praeger, 2003), pp.25–38.

Ferguson, S., 'Resisting the pull of plot: Paley's anti-sequence in the "Faith" stories', *Journal of the Short Story in English*, 32 (Spring 1999). Online: http://jsse.revues.org/index180.html.

Ferguson, S., 'Sequences, Anti-Sequences, Cycles, and Composite Novels: The Short Story in Genre Criticism', *Journal of the Short Story in English*, 41 (Autumn 2003). Online: http://jsse.revues.org/index312.html.

Fogarty, A., '"The Horror of the Unlived Life": Mother Daughter Relationships in Contemporary Irish Fiction', in Giorgio, A. (ed), *Writing Mothers and Daughters: Renegotiating the Mother in Western European Narratives by Wome*n (Oxford: Berghahn Books, 2002), pp.85–118.

Foley, M. (ed), *The Best American Short Stories* (Boston: Houghton Mifflin, 1961, 1962, 1965, 1966, 1969, 1974).

Fraiman, S., *Unbecoming Women: British Women Writers and the Novel of Development* (New York: Columbia University Press, 1993).

Freud, E. (ed.), *Letters of Sigmund Freud*, trans. Stern, T and J. (New York: Basic Books, 1960).

Freud, S., 'Mourning and Melancholia', in Strachey, J. (ed.), *The Standard Edition of the Complete Psychological Works of Sigmund Freud, Volume 14* (London: Hogarth Press, 1953–74), pp. 243–58.

Freud, S., *The Ego and the Id*, in Strachey, J. (ed.), *The Standard Edition of the Complete Psychological Works of Sigmund Freud, Volume 19* (London: Hogarth Press, 1953–74), pp.12–26.

Friberg, H., 'Managing Exile: A "Tullamore Discourse" in Mary Lavin's *Mary O'Grady*', *Nordic Irish Studies* 4 (2005), pp. 99–108.

Friday, N., *My Secret Garden: Women's Sexual Fantasies* (New York: Pocket Book, 1974).

Fulmer, J., *Folk Women and Indirection in Morrison, Ní Dhuibhne, Hurston, and Lavin* (Burlington, VT: Ashgate, 2007).

Gana, N., *Signifying Loss: Towards a Poetics of Mourning* (Lewisburg, PA: Bucknell University Press, 2011).

Girard, R., *Deceit, Desire, and the Novel*, trans. Freccero, Y., (Baltimore: Johns Hopkins University Press, 1965).

Gottwald, M., 'Narrative Strategies in the *Selected Stories of Mary Lavin*', in Bramsbäck, B., and Croghan, M. (eds), *Anglo-Irish Literature: Aspects of Language and Culture, Volume 2* (Uppsala: Uppsala University Press, 1988), pp.183–89.

Goulet, A., 'Retinal Fictions: Villiers, Leroux, and Optics at the Fin-de-siècle', *Nineteenth-Century French Studies*, 34, 1&2 (Fall–Winter 2005–2006), pp.107–20.

Gruber, R., *Virginia Woolf: The Will to Create as a Woman* (1935; New York: Carroll and Graf, 2005).

Hale, T., 'Afterword', in Leroux, G., *The Mystery of the Yellow Room* (1907; Sawtry, Cambridgeshire: Dedalus, 2008), pp.232–36.

Hand, D., *A History of the Irish Novel* (Cambridge: Cambridge University Press, 2011).

Hanson, C., *Short Stories and Short Fictions 1880–1980* (London: Macmillan, 1985).

Harmon, M., 'From Conversations with Mary Lavin', *Irish University Review*, 27, 2 (Autumn/Winter 1997), pp.287–92.

Harmon, M., 'Mary Lavin: Moralist of the Heart', in Hayley, B., and Murray, C. (eds), *A Bountiful Friendship: Literature, History and Ideas* (Gerrards Cross: Colin Smythe, 1992), pp.107–23.

Harmon, M., and Brown, B. (ed.), *Selected Essays* (Dublin & Portland, OR: Irish Academic Press, 2006).

Harris, R.M., 'Negotiating Patriarchy: Irish Women and the Landlord', in Cohen, M., and Curtin, N. (eds), *Reclaiming Gender: Transgressive Identities in Modern Ireland* (New York: St. Martin's Press, 1999), pp.207–26.

Harrison, F., 'Introduction', in *The Yellow Book: An Anthology* (1914; Woodbridge, Suffolk: Boydell Press, 1982), pp.7–13.

Head, D., 'James Joyce: The Non-Epiphany Principle', in *The Modernist Short Story: A Study in Theory and Practice* (Cambridge: Cambridge University Press, 2009), pp.37–78.

Heaney, J., '"No Sanctuary from Hatred": A Re-appraisal of Mary Lavin's Outsiders', *Irish University Review* 28, 2 (1998), pp.294–307.

Hunter, A., *The Cambridge Introduction to the Short Story in English* (Cambridge: Cambridge University Press, 2007).

Imhof, R., *A Short History of Irish Literature* (Stuttgart, Ernst Klett, 2002).

Ingman, H., *A History of the Irish Short Story* (Cambridge: Cambridge University Press, 2009).

Jeffers, J., *The Irish Novel at the End of the Twentieth Century: Gender, Bodies, and Power* (New

York and Basingstoke: Palgrave, 2002).

Jewett, S.O., *The Country of the Pointed Firs and Other Stories* (1896, New York; London: W.W., Norton and Company, 1994).

Joyce, J., *Dubliners* (London: Jonathan Cape, 1914; London: Paladin, 1988).

Kandinsky, W., *Concerning the Spiritual in Art* (1911), trans. Sadler M.T.H., Ebook from Project Gutenberg, March 2004. Online: http://www.gutenberg.org/cache/epub/5321/pg5321.html.

Kaufman, M., 'Men, Feminism, and Men's Contradictory Experiences of Power', in Brod, H. and Kaufman, M. (eds), *Theorising Masculinities*, pp.142–65.

Kelly, A.A., *Mary Lavin, Quiet Rebel: A Study of Her Short Stories* (Dublin: Wolfhound Press, 1980).

Kennedy, M., 'The Saturday Interview: Maev Kennedy talked to Mary Lavin', *The Irish Times*, 13 March 1976.

Kiberd, D., *Inventing Ireland: The Literature of the Modern Nation* (Cambridge: Harvard University Press, 1995; London: Jonathan Cape, 1995).

Kimmel, M., 'Masculinity as Homophobia: Fear, Shame and Silence in the Construction of Gender Identity', in Brod, H., and Kaufman, M. (eds), *Theorising Masculinities* (London: Sage Publications, 1994), pp.119–41.

Kilroy, J. (ed.), *The Irish Short Story. A Critical History* (Boston: Twayne, 1984)

Koenig, M., 'Mary Lavin: The Novels and the Stories', *Irish University Review*, 9, 2 (Autumn 1979), pp.244–61.

Kosok, H., 'Mary Lavin: A Bibliography', *Irish University Review* 9, 2 (Autumn 1979), pp.279–312.

Kreilkamp, V., 'Losing It All: The Unmanned Irish Landlord', in Cohen, M., and Curtin, N. (eds), *Reclaiming Gender: Transgressive Identities in Modern Ireland* (New York: St. Martin's Press, 1999), pp.107–22.

Kreilkamp, V., *The Anglo-Irish Novel and the Big House* (Syracuse, NY: Syracuse University Press, 1998).

Kristeva, J., *Powers of Horror: An Essay on Abjection*, trans. Roudiez, L.S., (New York: Columbia University Press, 1982).

Kristeva, J., 'On the Melancholic Imaginary' trans. Burchill, L., in Rimmon-Kenan, S. (ed.), *Discourse on Psychoanalysis and Literature* (London: Methuen, 1987), pp.104–23.

Kristeva, J., *Strangers to Ourselves*, trans. Roudiez, L.S., (New York: Columbia University Press, 1991).

Kristeva, J., *Black Sun: Depression and Melancholia*, trans Roudiez, L.S., (New York: Columbia University Press, 1989).

Laing, K., 'Virginia Woolf in Ireland: A Short Voyage Out', *The South Carolina Review*, 34, 1

(2001), pp.180–7.

Laurence, P., Ondek, *The Reading of Silence: Virginia Woolf in the English Tradition* (Stanford: Stanford University Press, 1991).

Lavin, M., 'Miss Holland', *The Dublin Magazine*, 14 (April–June 1939), pp.30–62.

Lavin, M., *Tales from Bective Bridge* (London: Michael Joseph, 1943, 1945; Dublin: Poolbeg Press, 1978; Dublin: Town House, 1996; London: Faber, 2012).

Lavin, M., *The Long Ago and Other Stories* (London: Michael Joseph, 1944).

Lavin, M., 'Fogger Halt', in Woodrow, W. (ed.), *English Story* (London: Collins, 1944), pp.81–106.

Lavin, M., *The House in Clewe Street* (London: Michael Joseph, 1945; London: Penguin, 1949; London: Faber and Faber, 2009).

Lavin, M., *The Becker Wives and Other Stories* (London: Michael Joseph, 1946).

Lavin, M., *Mary O'Grady* (London: Michael Joseph, 1950; London: Virago, 1986).

Lavin, M., *A Single Lady and Other Stories* (London: Michael Joseph, 1951).

Lavin, M., *The Patriot Son and Other Stories* (London: Michael Joseph, 1956).

Lavin, M., *Selected Stories* (New York: Macmillan, 1959).

Lavin, M., 'Preface', in *Selected Stories* (New York: Macmillan, 1959; Harmondsworth: Penguin, 1964), pp.v–viii.

Lavin, M., *The Great Wave and Other Stories* (London: MacMillan, 1961).

Lavin, M., *The Stories of Mary Lavin, Volume 1* (London: Constable, 1964).

Lavin, M., *In the Middle of the Fields and Other Stories* (London: Constable, 1967; New York: Macmillan, 1969).

Lavin, M., 'Writer at Work: an Interview with Mary Lavin', *St Stephens*, 12, 22 (1967).

Lavin, M., *Happiness and Other Stories* (London: Constable, 1969; Dublin: New Island Books, 2011).

Lavin, M., *Collected Stories* (Boston: Houghton Mifflin, 1971).

Lavin, M., *A Memory and Other Stories* (London: Constable, 1972).

Lavin, M., *The Stories of Mary Lavin, Volume 2* (London: Constable, 1974).

Lavin, M., *The Shrine and Other Stories* (London: Constable, 1977).

M. Lavin, 'Afterword', in Murphy, C., 'Mary Lavin: An Interview' *Irish University Review* 9, 2 (Autumn 1979), pp.222-4.

Lavin, M., *A Family Likeness and Other Stories* (London: Constable, 1985).

Lavin, M., *The Stories of Mary Lavin, Volume 3* (London: Constable, 1985).

Lavin, M., *In a Café*, Walsh Peavoy, E. (ed.) (Dublin: Town House, 1995)

Lavin, M., *In a Café. Selected Stories*, Walsh Peavoy, E. (ed.) (Harmondsworth: Penguin, 1999).

Lepaludier, L., 'Theatricality in the Short Story: Staging the Word?', *Journal of the Short Story in English*, 51 (Autumn 2008), pp.17–28.

Levenson, L., *The Four Seasons of Mary Lavin* (Dublin: Marino Books, 1998).

Litz, A.W., 'Introduction', in Ellmann, R., Litz, A.W., and Whittier-Ferguson, J. (eds), *Poems and Shorter Writings: Including Epiphanies, Giacomo Joyce and 'A Portrait of the Artist'* (London: Faber, 1991).

Lloyd, D., 'Colonial Trauma/Postcolonial Recovery', *Interventions: International Journal of Postcolonial Studies*, 2, 2 (2000), pp. 218–28.

Magennis, C., and Mullen, R. (eds), *Irish Masculinities: Reflections on Literature and Culture* (Dublin: Irish Academic Press, 2011).

Mann, S., *The Short Story Cycle: A Genre Companion and Reference Guide* (New York: Greenwood, 1989).

Mansfield, K., *The Collected Stories of Katherine Mansfield* (London: Penguin, 1981).

Marlowe, L., 'Mary Lavin: An arrow still in flight', *The Irish Times* 30 April 2012. Online: http://www.irishtimes.com/newspaper/features/2012/0430/1224315363056.html.

Martin, A., 'A Skeleton Key to the Stories of Mary Lavin', *Studies* 52, 208 (Winter 1963), pp.393–406.

Martin, A., 'Afterword', in Lavin, M., *Mary O'Grady* (1950; London: Virago Press, 1986).

Maxwell, W., 'The Art of Fiction No. 71', interviewed by John Seabrook, *The Paris Review* 85 (Fall 1982). Online: http://www.theparisreview.org/interviews/3138/the-art-of-fiction-no-71-william-maxwell.

May, C.E., *The Short Story: The Reality of Artifice* (New York: Routledge, 2002).

McCormack, O., 'Exploring Masculinities – The Sequel', PhD Thesis, University of Limerick, 2010

McKeon, B., 'An Arrow Still An Arrow in Flight: The Pleasures of Mary Lavin', *The Paris Review*, 12 June 2012. Online: http://www.theparisreview.org/blog/2012/06/12/an-arrow-in-flight-the-pleasures-of-mary-lavin/.

Meaney, G., *Gender, Ireland, and Cultural Change: Race, Sex, and Nation* (New York: Routledge, 2010).

Meszaros, P., 'Woman as Artist: The Fiction of Mary Lavin', *Critique: Studies in Modern Fiction*, 21, 1 (Fall 1982), pp.39–54.

Murphy, C., 'Mary Lavin: An Interview', *Irish University Review*, 9, 2 (Autumn 1979), pp.218-28.

Murray, T.J., 'Mary Lavin's World: Lovers and Strangers', *Éire-Ireland* 7 (Summer 1972), pp.122–31.

Neary, M., 'Flora's Answer to the Irish Question: A Study of Mary Lavin's *The Becker Wives*', *Twentieth Century Literature*, 42, 4 (1996), pp.516–26.

Nicolson, N. (ed.), *The Question of Things Happening: The Letters of Virginia Woolf, Volume 2: 1912–1922* (London: Hogarth Press, 1979).

Norris, D., 'Imaginative Responses versus Authority Structures: a Theme of the Anglo-Irish Short Story', in Rafroidi, P., and Brown, T. (eds), *The Irish Short Story* (Atlantic Highlands, NJ: Humanities Press, 1979; Buckinghamshire, UK: Colin Smyth, 1979; Publications de l'Université de Lille III, 1979), pp.38–59.

O'Brien Johnson, T., and Cairns, D. (eds), *Gender in Irish Writing* (Buckingham: Open University Press, 1991).

O'Brien, K., 'Short Stories: In and Out of Place', *The Irish Times*, 5 January 1946, p.4.

O'Connor, F., *The Lonely Voice: A Study of the Short Story* (London: Macmillan, 1965; Cork: Cork City Council, 2003).

O'Donovan Sheehy, H., 'Memories', in Lennon, H. (ed.), *Frank O'Connor* (Dublin: Four Courts, 2007), pp.156–65.

O'Faoláin, S., 'Fifty Years of Irish Writing', *Studies*, 51, 201, (Spring 1962), pp.93–105.

O'Faoláin, S., *The Short Story* (Cork: Mercier Press, 1972).

O'Faoláin, S., 'Midsummer Night Madness', in *Midsummer Night Madness and Other Stories* (1932; London: Penguin Books, 1982).

Ondek Laurence, P., *The Reading of Silence: Virginia Woolf in the English Tradition* (Stanford: Stanford University Press, 1991).

Orne Jewett, S., *The Country of the Pointed Firs and Other Stories* (1896; New York; London: W.W., Norton and Company, 1994).

O'Toole, F., 'The Family as Independent Republic', *The Irish Times*, 13 October 1990: Weekend, p.2.

Owens, R.C., *Smashing Times: A History of the Irish Women's Suffrage Movement 1889–1922* (Dublin: Attic Press, 1984).

Pelan, R., 'Edna O'Brien's World of Nora Barnacle', *Canadian Journal of Irish Studies*, 22, 2 (1996), pp.49–62.

Peterson, R.F., *Mary Lavin* (Boston: Twayne Publishers, 1978).

Poe, E.A., 'The Murders in the Rue Morgue' (1841), in *The Fall of the House of Usher and Other Writings* (London: Penguin, 2003), pp.141–76.

Pritchett, V.S., 'Introduction', in Lavin, M., *Collected Stories* (Boston: Houghton Mifflin, 1971), pp.ix–xvi.

Quinn, J., (ed). 'Mary Lavin', in *Portrait of the Artist as a Young Girl* (London: Methuen, 1987), pp.79–91.

Rafroidi, P., 'A Question of Inheritance: The Anglo-Irish Tradition', in Rafroidi, P., and

Harmon, M. (eds), *The Irish Novel in Our Time* (Publications de l'Université de Lille III, 1975–76), pp.11–29.

Relph, E., *Place and Placelessness* (London: Pion, 1976).

Reynier, C., *Virginia Woolf's Ethics of the Short Story* (London: Palgrave Macmillan, 2009).

Robert, L., and Stevens, S., 'An Interview with Mary Lavin', *Studies*, 86, 341, (Spring 1997), pp. 43–50.

Rooks-Hughes, L., 'The Family and the Female Body in the Novels of Edna O'Brien and Julia O'Faolain', *Canadian Journal of Irish Studies*, 22, 2 (1996), pp.83–97.

Ryan, J., 'Inadmissable Departures: Why did the Emigrant Experience Feature so Infrequently in the Fiction of the Mid-twentieth Century?' in Keogh, D., O'Shea, F., and Quinlan, C. (eds), *The Lost Decade in the 1950s* (Cork: Mercier Press, 2004), pp.221–32.

Ryan, L., '"A Decent Girl Well Worth Helping": Women, Migration and Unwanted Pregnancy' in Harte, L., and Whelan, Y. (eds), *Ireland Beyond Boundaries Mapping Irish Studies in the Twenty-first Century* (London; Dublin: Pluto Press, 2007), pp.135–53.

Sacks, P.M., *The English Elegy: Studies in the Genre from Spenser to Yeats* (Baltimore, MD: Johns Hopkins Press, 1985).

Santner, E.L., *Stranded Objects: Mourning, Memory and Film in Postwar Germany* (Ithaca NY and London: Cornell University Press, 1990).

Sealy Lynch, R., '"The Fabulous Female Form": The Deadly Erotics of the Male Gaze in Mary Lavin's *The House in Clewe Street*', *Twentieth Century Literature* 43, 3 (Autumn 1997), pp.326–38.

Segal, L., *Slow Motion: Changing Masculinities, Changing Men,* 3rd edition (New York: Palgrave/Macmillan, 2007).

Seidler, V.J., *Unreasonable Men: Masculinity and Social Theory* (New York and London: Routledge, 1994).

Shklovsky, V., *The Theory of Prose*, trans. Sher, B., (Bloomington, IL: Dalkey Archive Press, 1991).

Singleton, B., *Masculinities and the Contemporary Irish Theatre* (New York: Palgrave/Macmillan, 2011).

Smyth, G., *The Novel and the Nation: Studies in the New Irish Fiction* (London: Pluto, 1997).

Stallybrass, P., and White, A., *The Politics and Poetics of Transgression* (Ithaca, NY: Cornell University Press, 1986).

Stevens, J.A., *Plot Patterns and Plotting Techniques in Mary Lavin's Fiction*, MA Thesis, University College Galway, 1989.

Tallone, G., 'Elsewhere is a Negative Mirror: The "Sally Gap" Stories of Éilís Ní Dhuibhne and Mary Lavin', *Hungarian Journal of English and American Studies*, 10, 1–2 (2004), pp.203–15.

Thompson, R.J., *Everlasting Voices: Aspects of the Modern Irish Short Story* (Troy, NY: Whitston, 1989).

Thurber, J., *The Years with Ross* (Boston: Little, Brown and Co., 1959).

Vertreace, M.M., 'The Goddess Resurrected in Mary Lavin's Short Fiction', in Pearlman, M. (ed.), *The Anna Book. Searching for Anna in Literary History* (Westport: Greenwood Press, 1992), pp.159–66.

Walpole Historical Society, *Images of America: Walpole* (Portsmouth NH: Arcadia, 1998, 2004).

Walsh, C., 'Bective: once you belong you belong', *The Irish Times*, 20 June 1978.

Walsh, D., *Beneath Cannock's Clock: The Last Man Hanged in Ireland* (Cork: Mercier Press, 2009).

Walshe, E., *Sex, Nation and Dissent in Irish Writing* (Cork: Cork University Press, 1997).

Walsh-Peavoy, E., 'Preamble', in M., Lavin, *In a Cafe´: Selected Stories* (London: Penguin, 1995), p. xiii–xvi.

Waters, J., 'Bending facts to prop up myths about male violence', *The Irish Times*, 7 January 2002.

Weekes, A.O., *Irish Women Writers: An Uncharted Tradition* (Lexington KY: University Press of Kentucky, 1990).

White, E.B., 'The Art of the Essay No. 1', *The Paris Review* 48 (Fall 1969). Online: http://www.theparisreview.org/interviews/4155/the-art-of-the-essay-no-1-e-b-white.

Whitehead, S., and Barrett, F. (eds), *The Masculinities Reader* (Cambridge: Polity Press, 2001).

Williams, R., 'Realism and the Contemporary Novel', in Lodge, D. (ed.), *20th Century Literary Criticism: A Reader* (London; New York: Longman, 1972), pp.581-91.

Wills, C., 'Women Writers and the Death of Rural Ireland: Realism and Nostalgia in the 1940s', Éire-Ireland 41 (Spring/Summer 2006), pp.192–212.

Wills, C., *That Neutral Island: A Cultural History of Ireland during the Second World War* (London: Faber and Faber, 2007).

Winston, G.C., 'Mary Lavin', in Malcolm, C.A., and Malcolm, D. (eds), *Dictionary of Literary Biography. Vol. 319: British and Irish Short Fiction Writers, 1945–2000* (Farmington Hills, MI: Gale: 2005), pp.151–64.

Woolf, V., *A Room of One's Own. Three Guineas*, Shiach, M. (ed.) (Oxford: World's Classics, 1992).

Woolf, V., *The Essays of Virginia Woolf, Volume 4: 1925–1928*, McNeillie, A. (ed.) (London: Hogarth Press, 1994).

Woolf, V., *A Haunted House: The Complete Shorter Fiction*, Dick, S. (ed.) (London: Vintage, 2003).

Wray, T., 'The Quest for Flora: Who is She? Establishing One Woman's Place in Mary Lavin's "The Becker Wives"', in Jenčová, K., et al. (eds), *The Politics of Irish Writing* (Prague: Centre for Irish Studies, Charles University, 2010), pp.118–28.

Wright, J.W. (ed.), *A Companion to Irish Literature, Volume 1 & Volume 2* (Malden, MA: Wiley-Blackwell, 2010).

Yagoda, B., *About Town: The New Yorker and the World It Made* (New York: Scribner, 2000).

Yudice, G., 'What's a Straight White Man To Do?' in Berger, M., Wallis, B., and Watson, S. (eds), *Deconstructing Masculinity* (New York: Routledge, 1995), pp.267–83.

Zagarell, S., 'Narrative of Community. The Identification of a Genre', *Signs*, 13, 3 (1988), pp.498–527.

Index